ART NOUVEAU ORNAMENTATION

CHRISTIAN STOLL STUDIOS

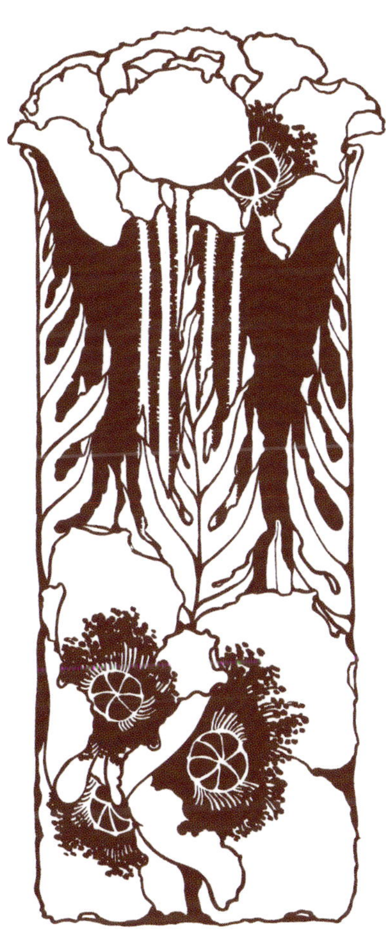

DOVER PUBLICATIONS, INC.
MINEOLA, NEW YORK

Bibliographical Note

Art Nouveau Ornamentation, first published by Dover Publications, Inc., in 2019, is an original compilation of plates published by Christian Stoll Studios, Leipzig, between 1900 and 1910.

The full-color plates, created by Richard Kühnel and Hugo Sachs, were originally published in *Plauen im Vogtland* in 1905. The largest selection of monochrome plates was created by Josef Pilters, and others were created by G. Devresse, G. Görschen, Fritz Herz, Hugo Sachs, and Rudolf Zenker. The monochrome plates were originally published in *Blumen-Ornamentik von Josef Pilters*, *Moderne Blumen-Ornamentik*, *Moderne Motive für die Kleinmusterung der Gewebe*, *Sammel-Mappe für Flächenuerzierung*, *Neue Verzierungen für die Flach von G. Görschen*, *Decoration Florale par G. Devresse*, and *Ornamentik Der Gegenwart*.

Library of Congress Cataloging-in-Publication Data

Names: Stoll, Christian, author.
Title: Art nouveau ornamentation / Christian Stoll Studios.
Description: Mineola, New York : Dover Publications, Inc., [2019] | "Art Nouveau Ornamentation, first published by Dover Publications, Inc., in 2019, is an original compilation of plates published by Christian Stoll Studios, Leipzig, between 1900 and 1910." | Summary: "This splendid source of authentic Art Nouveau designs presents more than 90 breathtaking plates, ranging from single to full color, selected from rare originals of a renowned German studio's stock portfolios"—Provided by publisher.
Identifiers: LCCN 2019025940 | ISBN 9780486836041 (trade paperback)
Subjects: LCSH: Decoration and ornament—Art nouveau—Themes, motives. | Pattern books.
Classification: LCC NK1380 .S795 2019 | DDC 709.03/49—dc23
LC record available at https://lccn.loc.gov/2019025940

Manufactured in the United States by LSC Communications
83604501
www.doverpublications.com

2 4 6 8 10 9 7 5 3 1

2019

CONTENTS

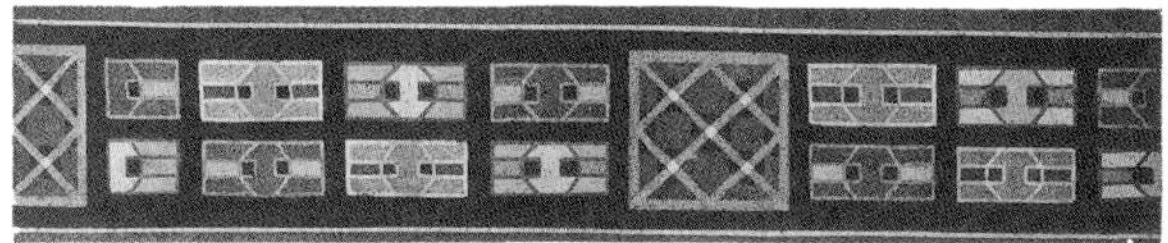

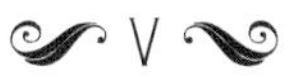

NOTE

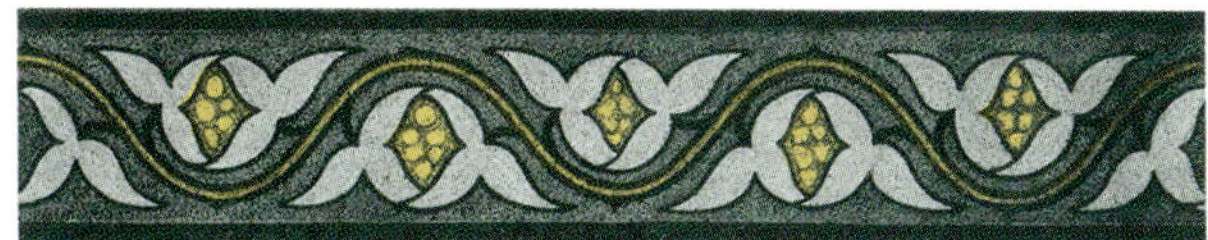

Christian Stoll Studios was a publisher that created dozens of design portfolios, working with a number of artists in the German city of Leipzig. The studio was active from about 1900 until World War I. These portfolios served as stock art and inspiration for other designers the world over.

The plates in this volume appeared in books published by Christian Stoll Studios between 1900 and 1910. Richard Kühnel and Hugo Sachs created all the full-color plates. The largest selection of monochrome plates was created by Josef Pilters, and others were created by G. Devresse, G. Görschen, Fritz Herz, Hugo Sachs, and Rudolf Zenker.

FULL-COLOR PLATES

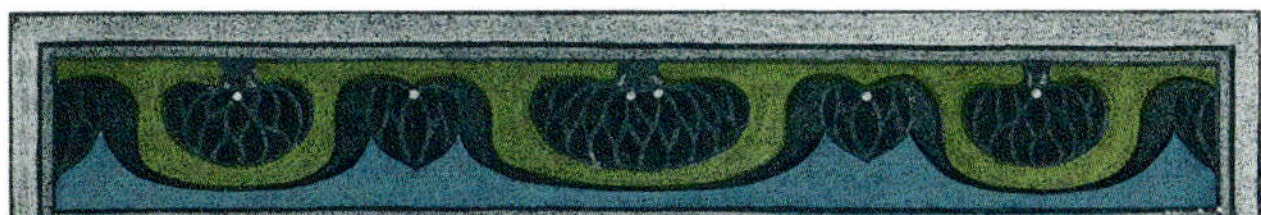

The three-color plates in this collection were originally reproduced by a process known as collotype. This print process is screenless. Collotype is closely related to stone lithography prints and is capable of retaining great detail. In commercial, large-scale printing, collotype was replaced by the less expensive process of offset lithography.

The patterns and designs in this collection range from straightforward illustrations of the floral form to nearly abstract interpretations with only small indicators of their organic roots, foreshadowing the art deco movement and its abandonment of natural motifs.

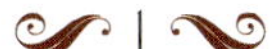

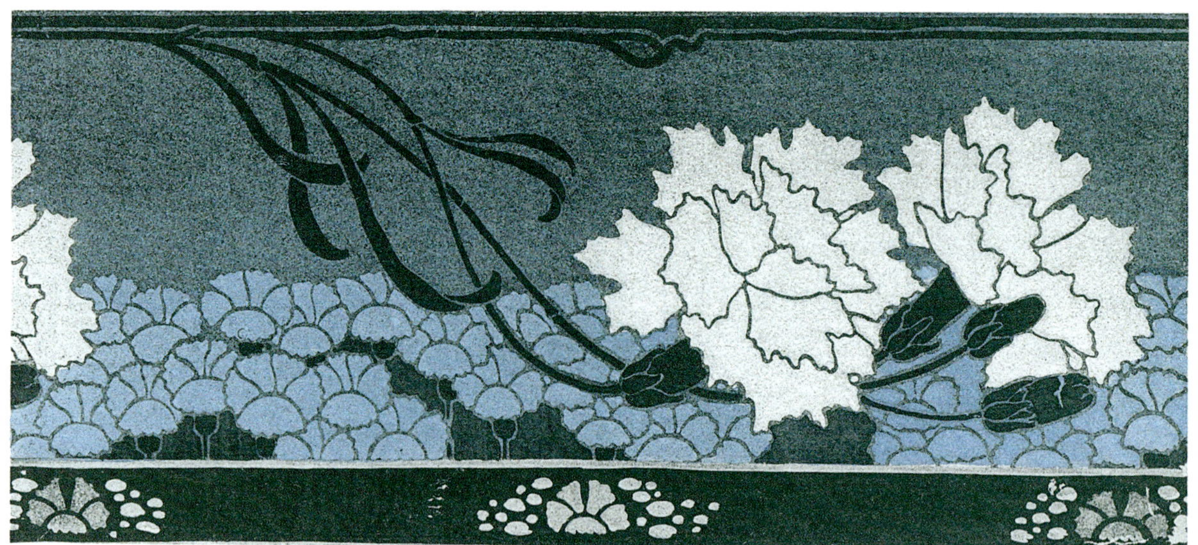

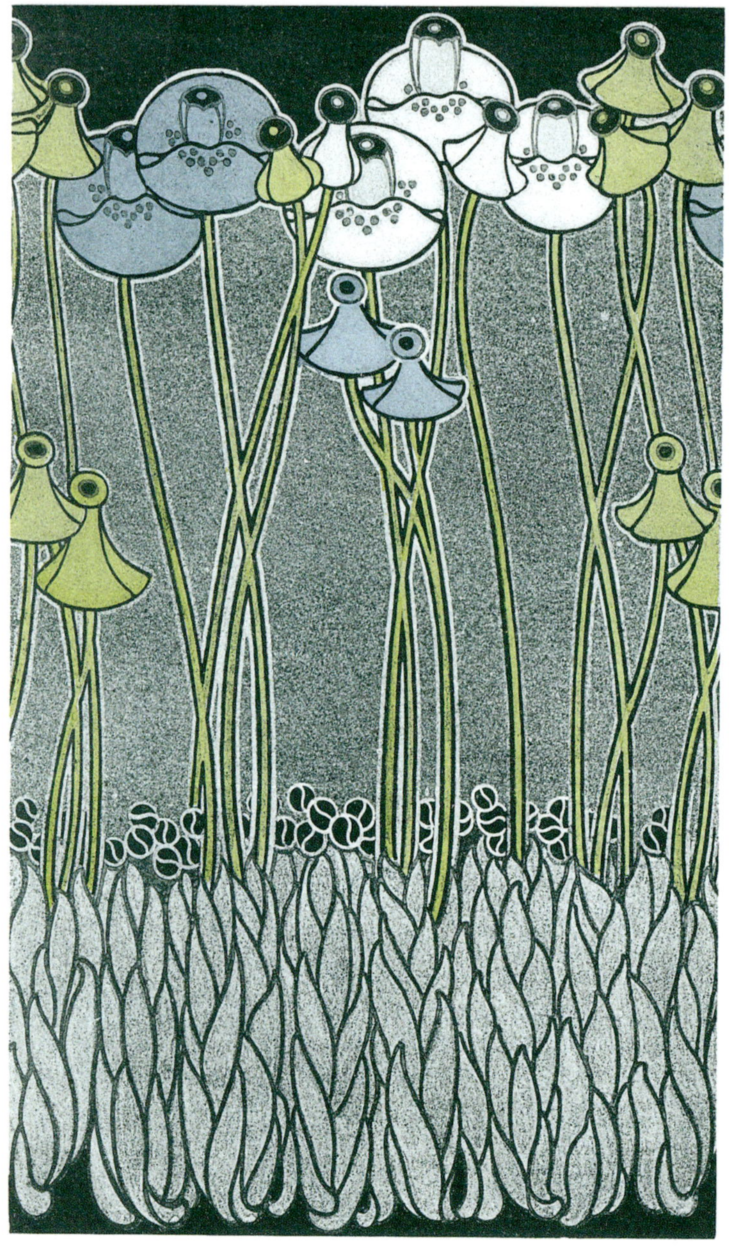

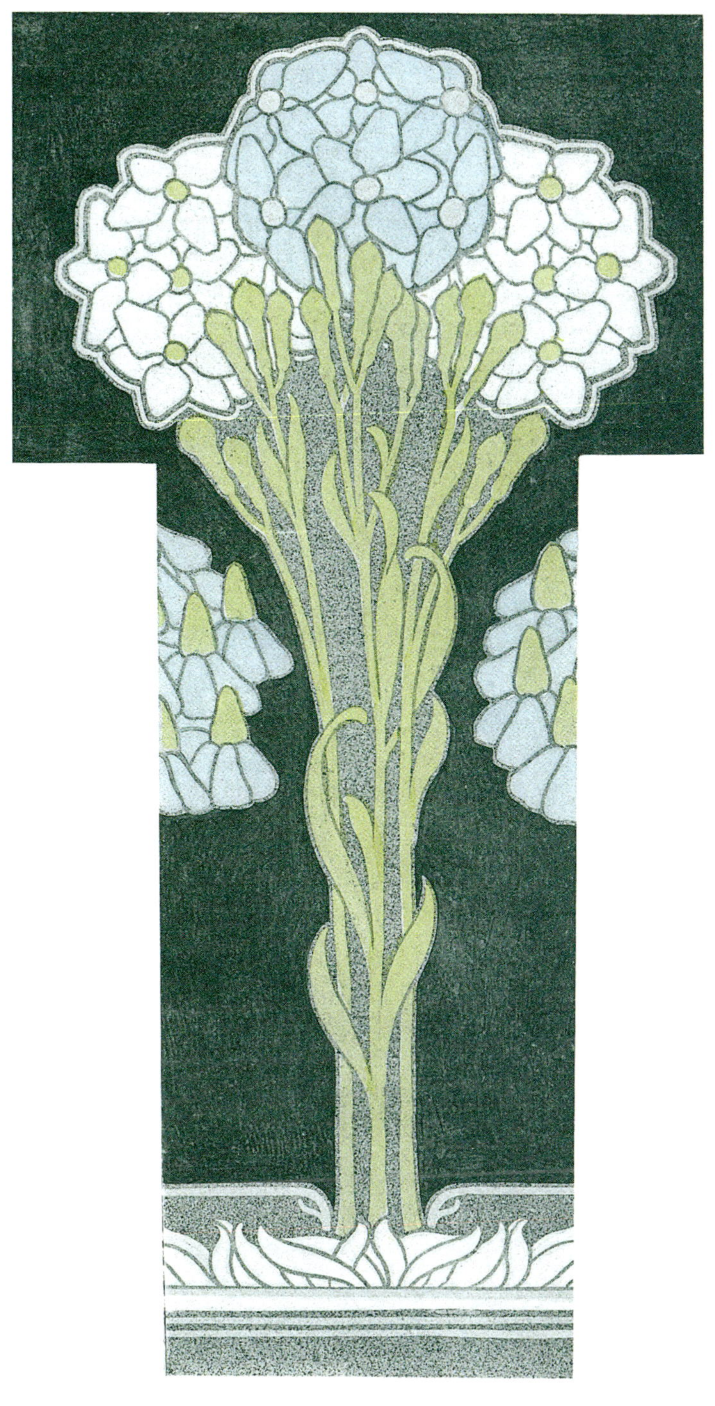

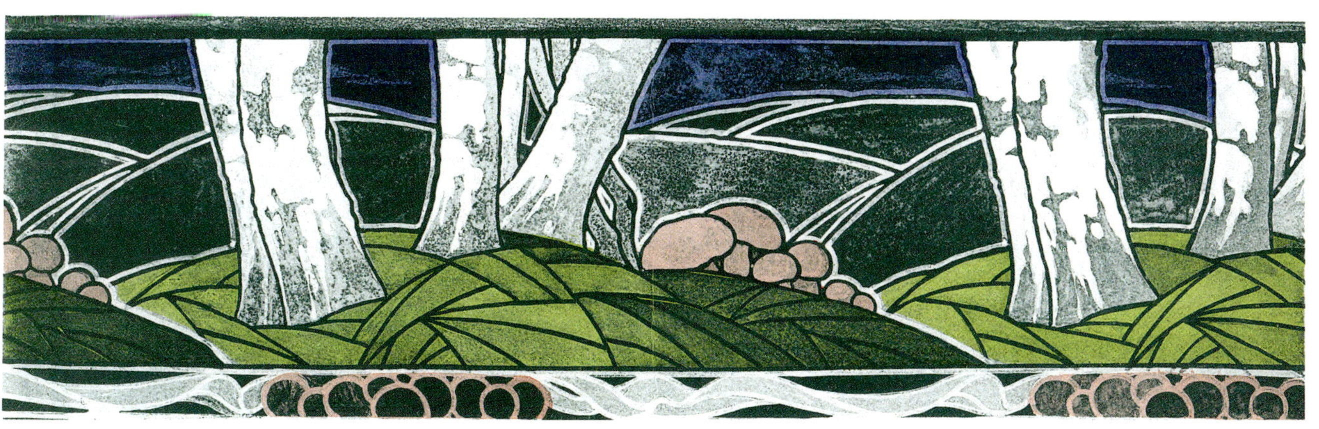

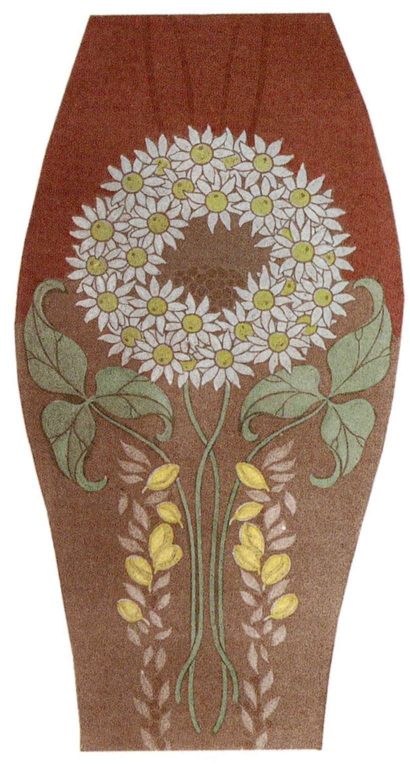
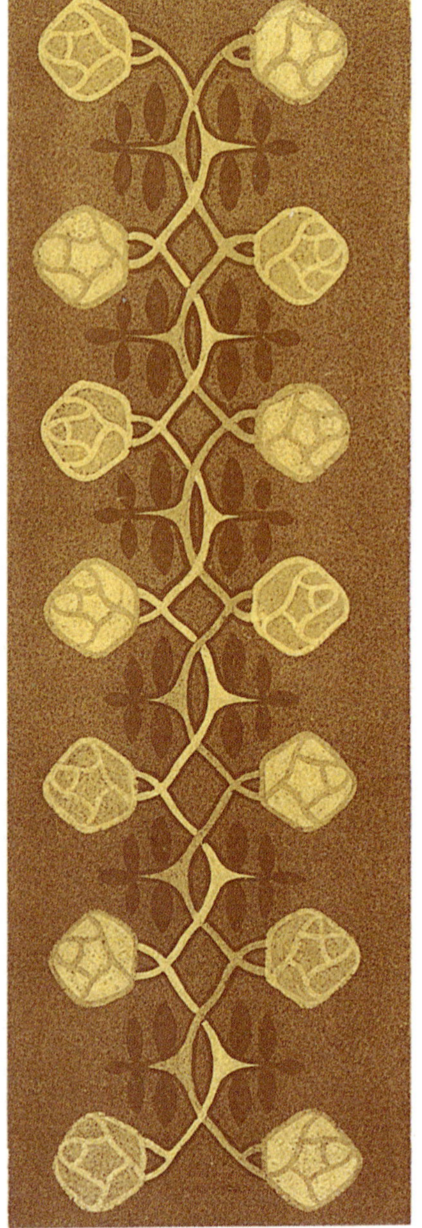
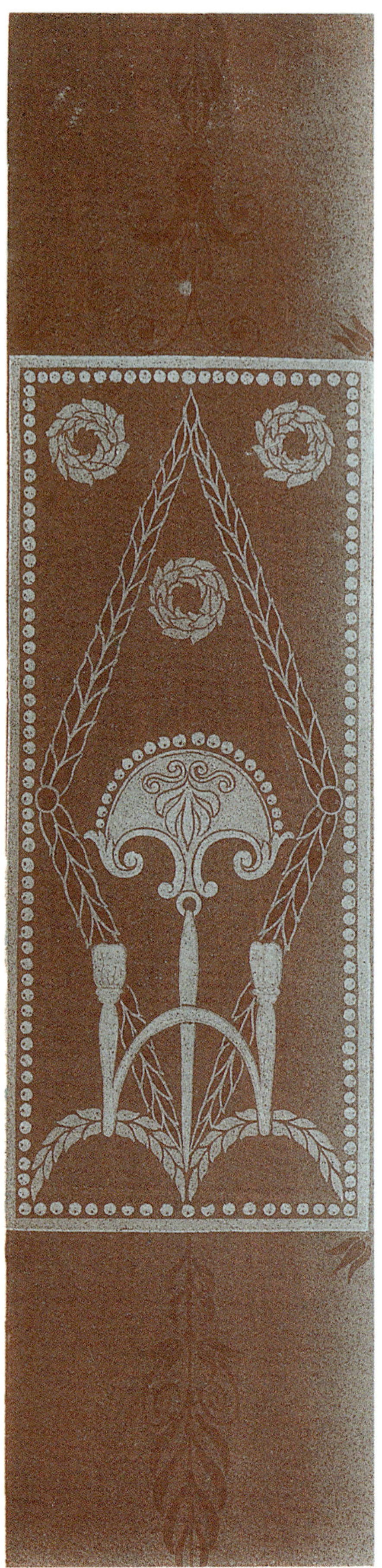
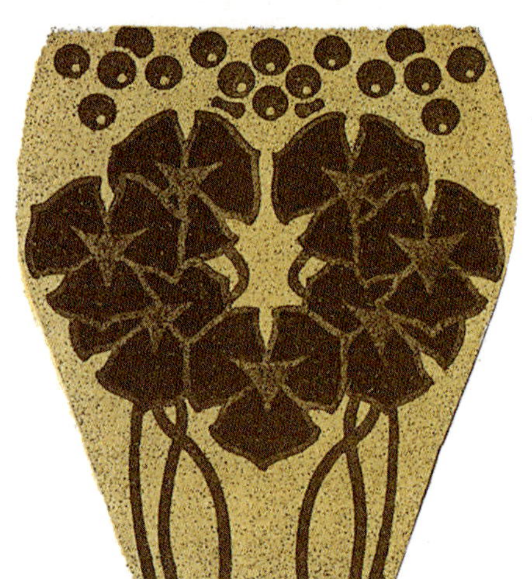
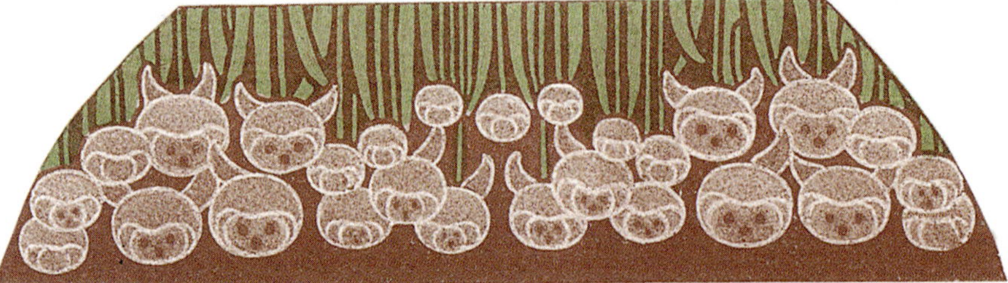
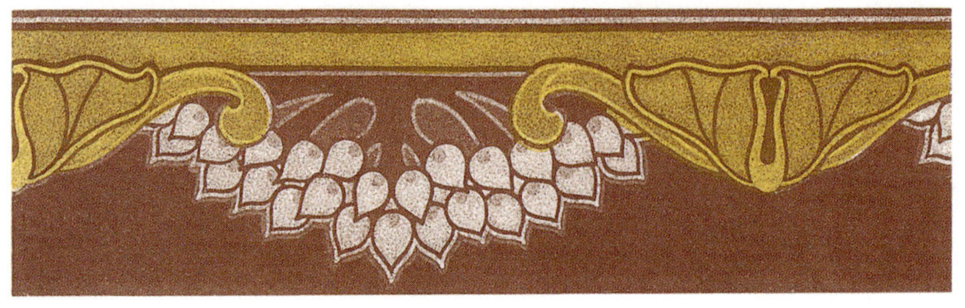

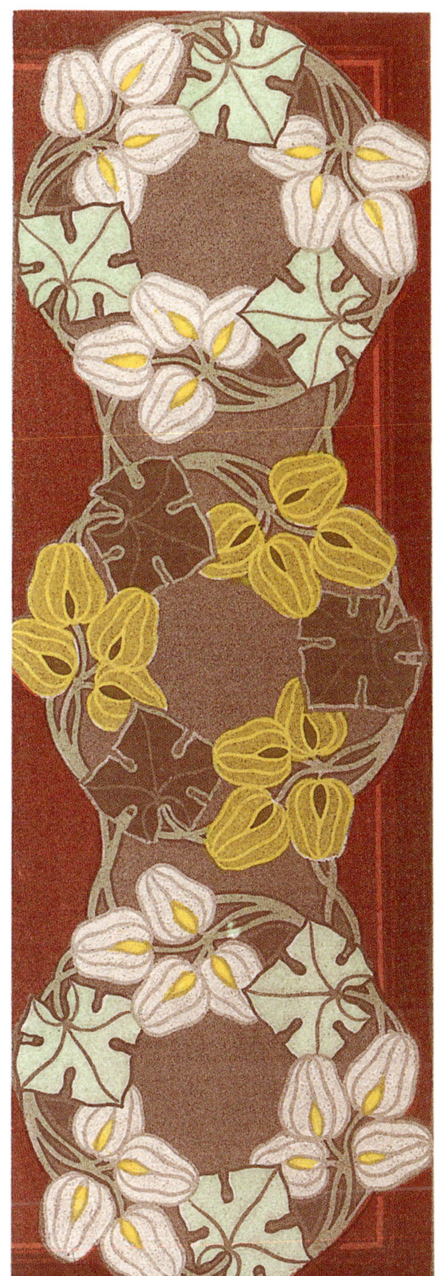
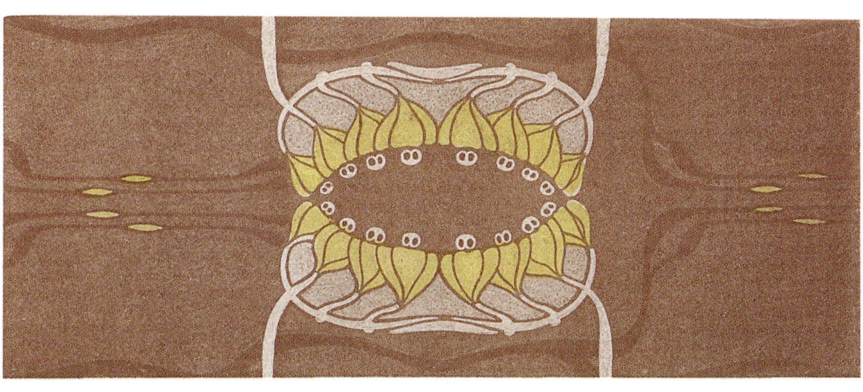
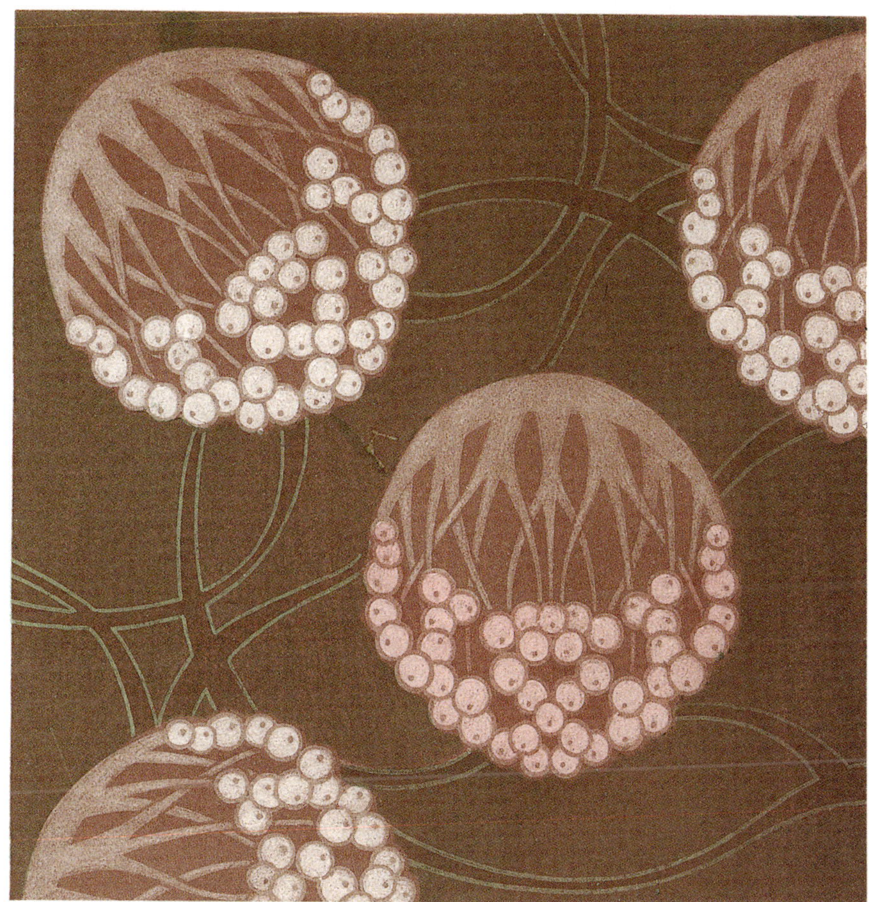
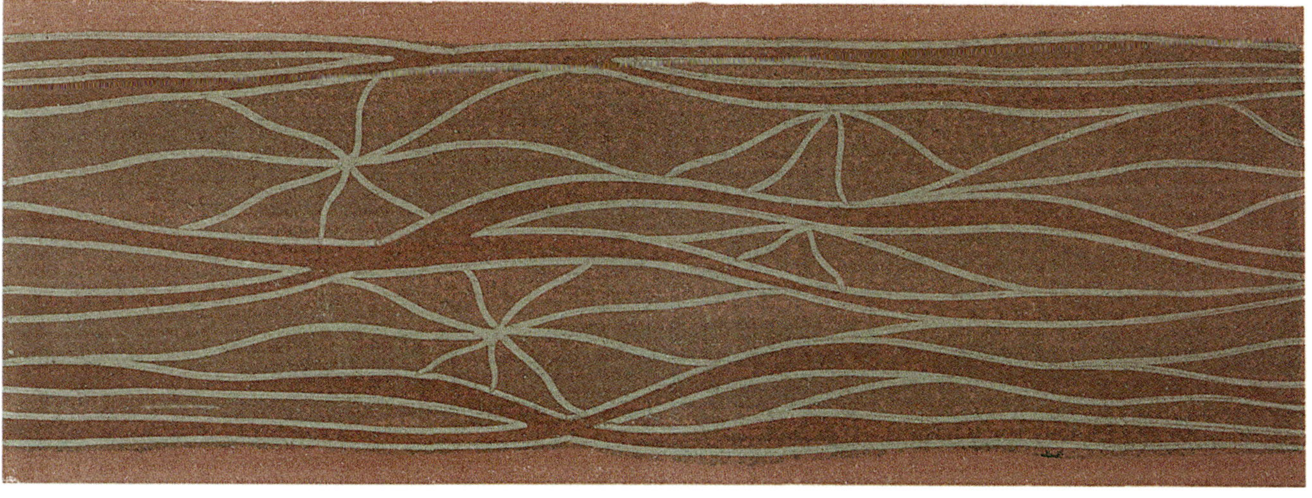

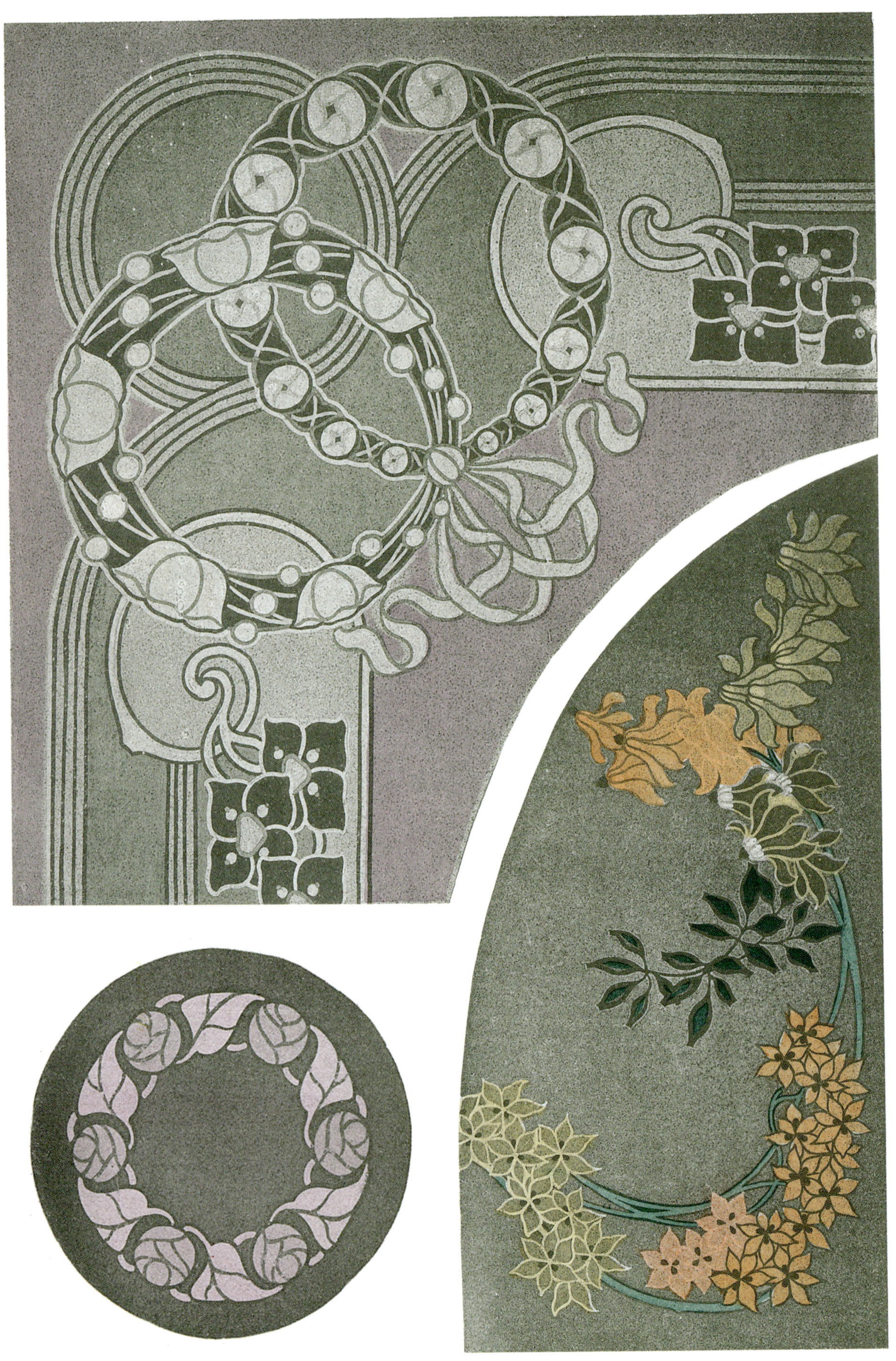

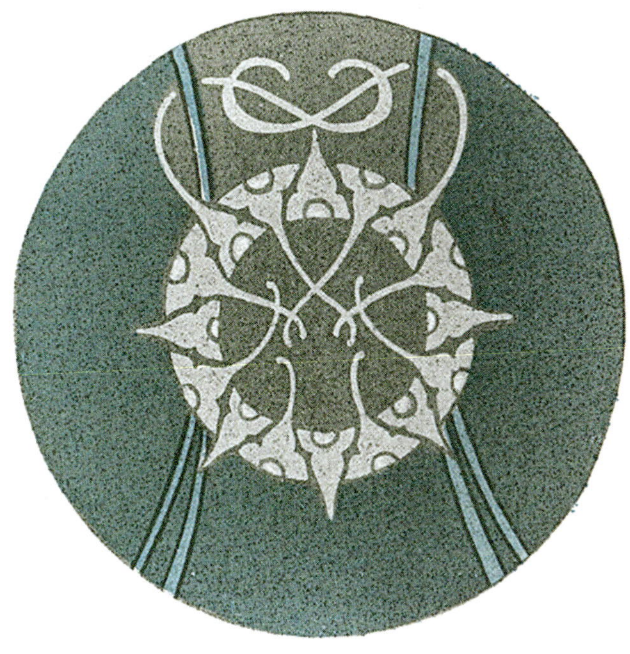

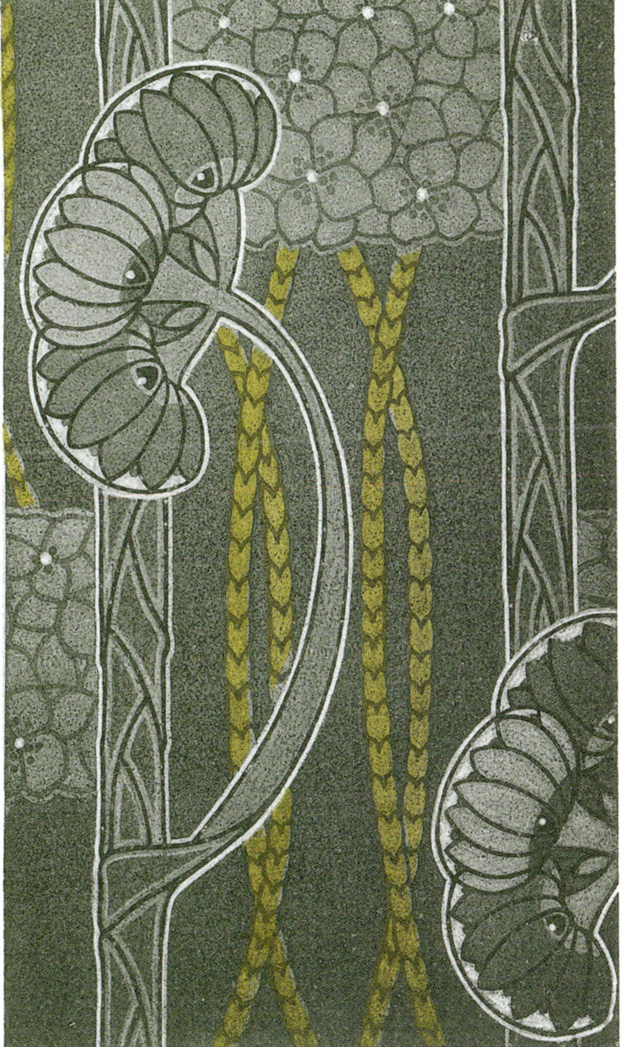

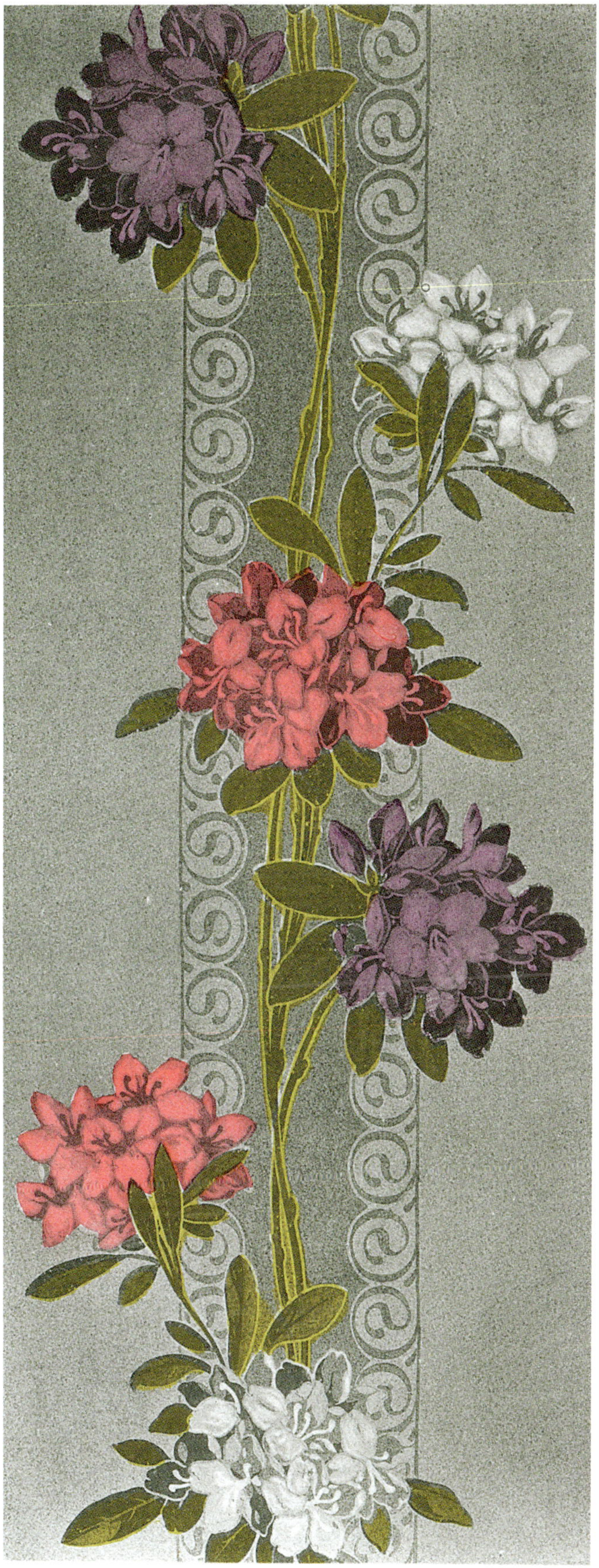

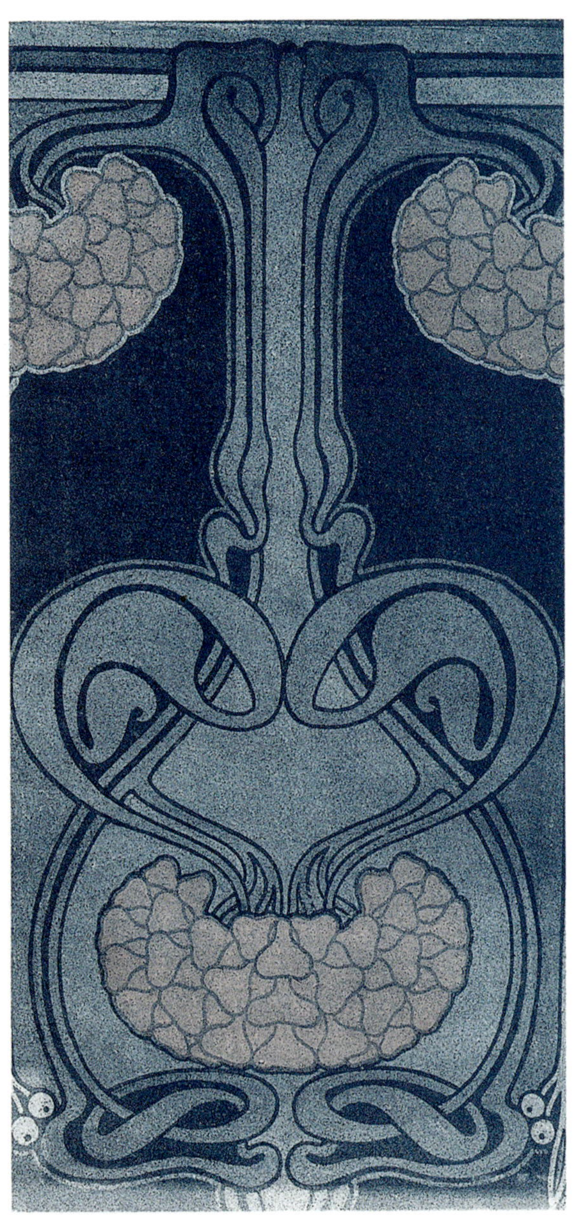
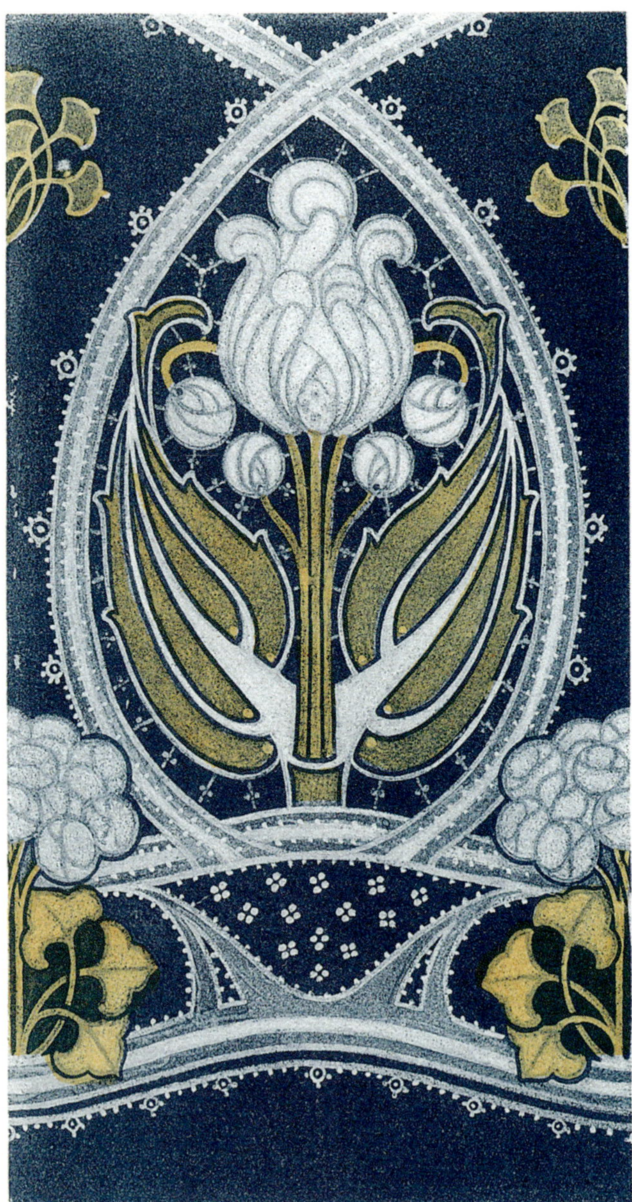
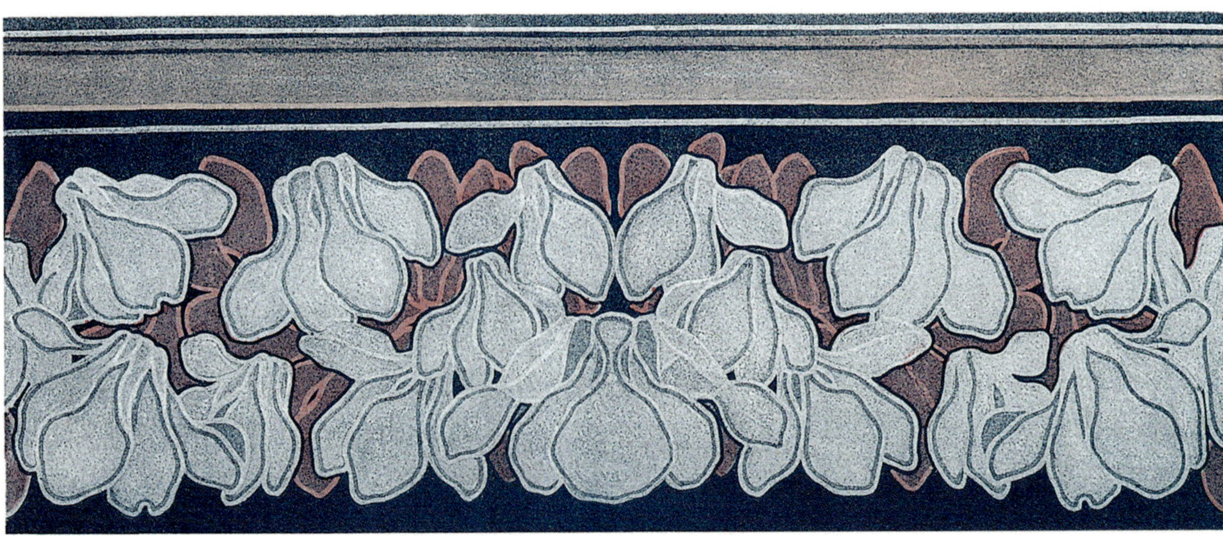

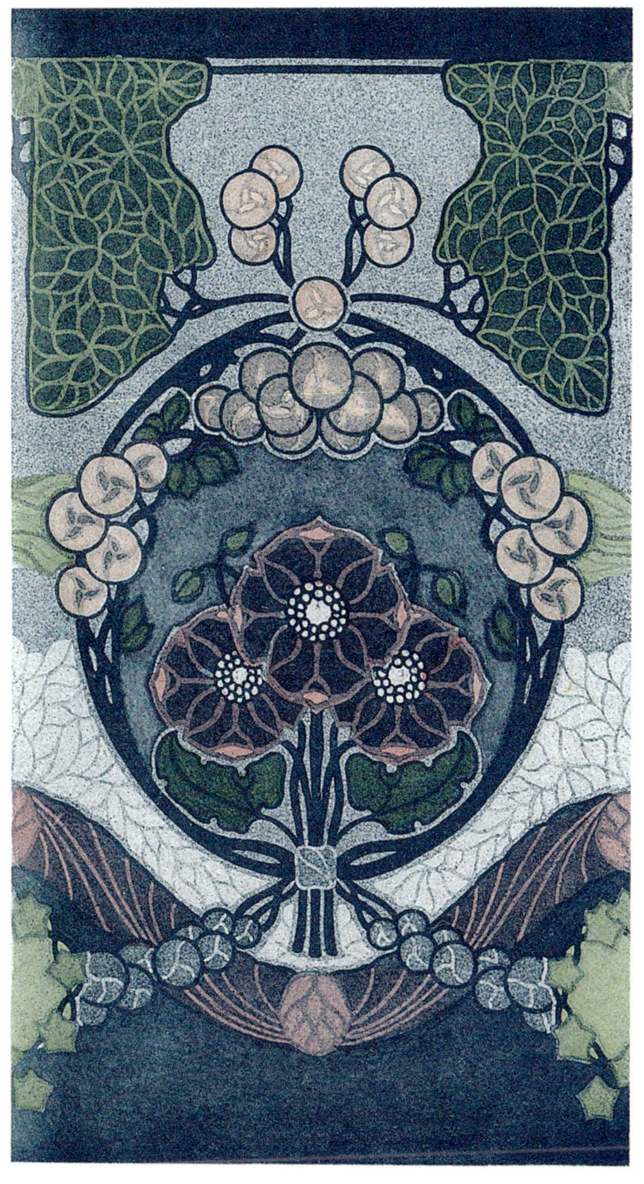
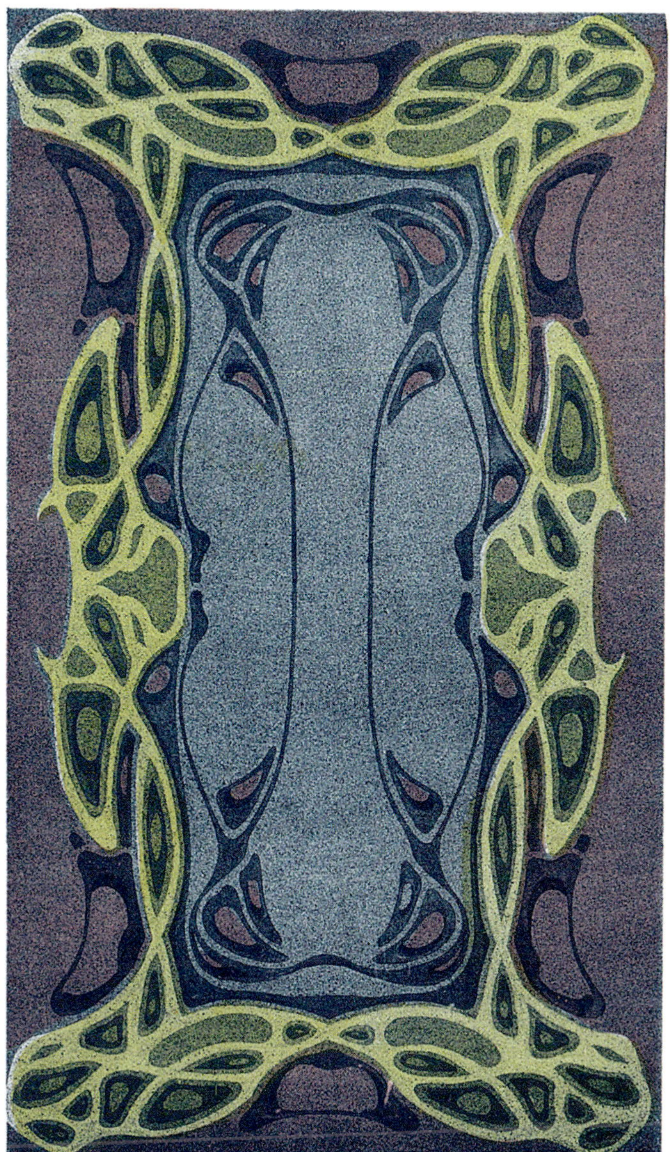
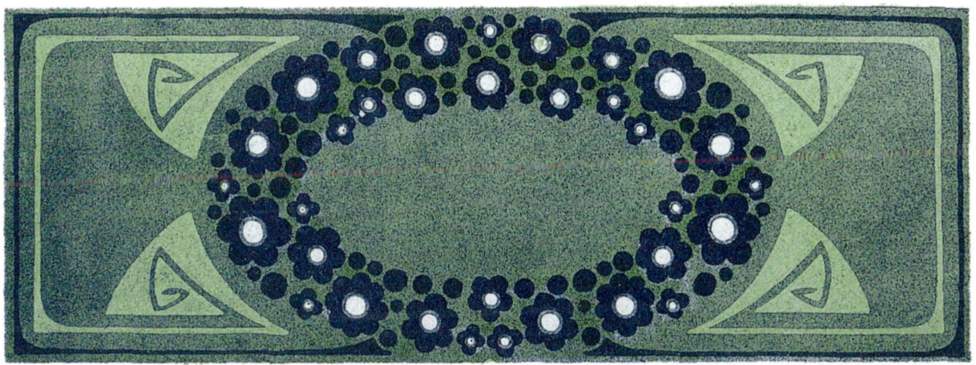
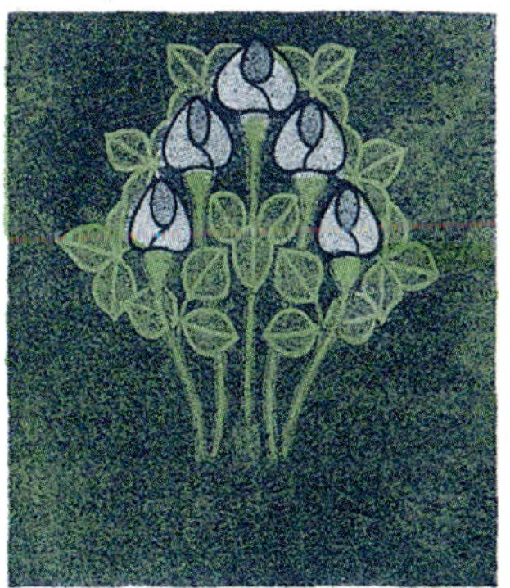
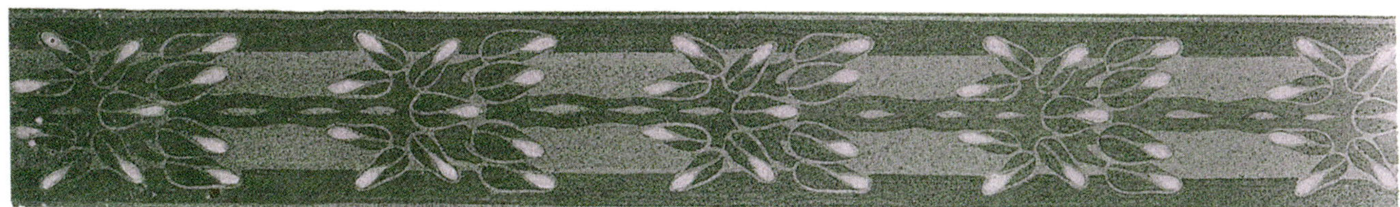

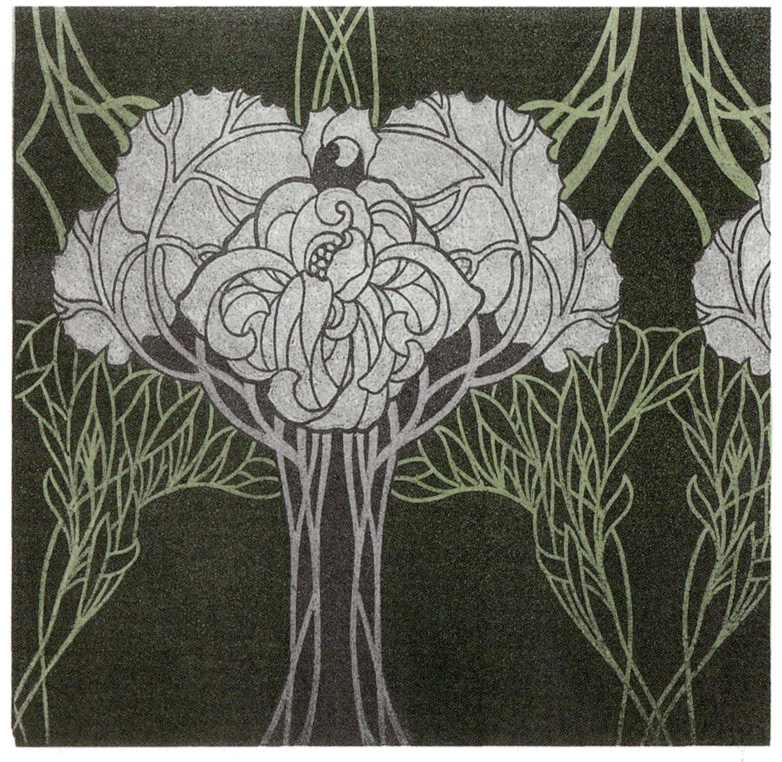
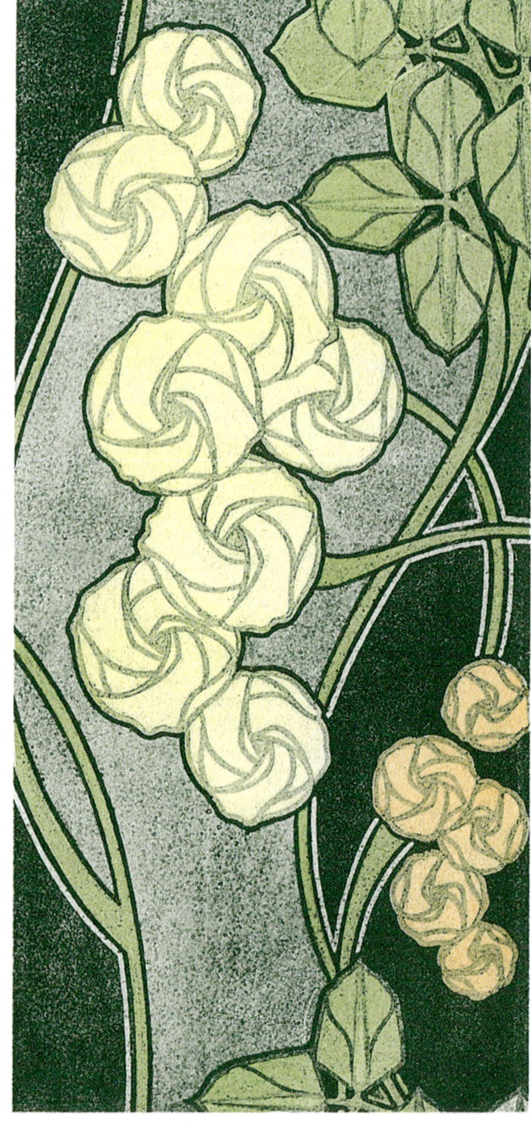
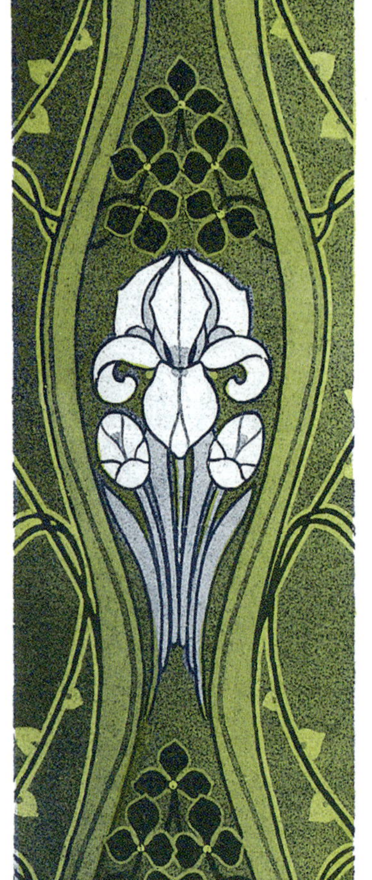
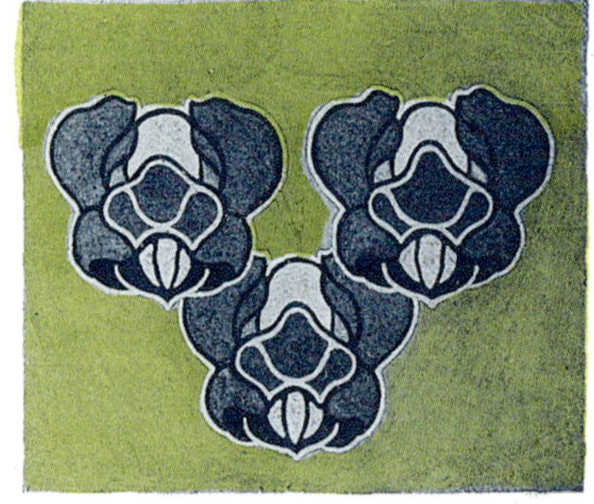
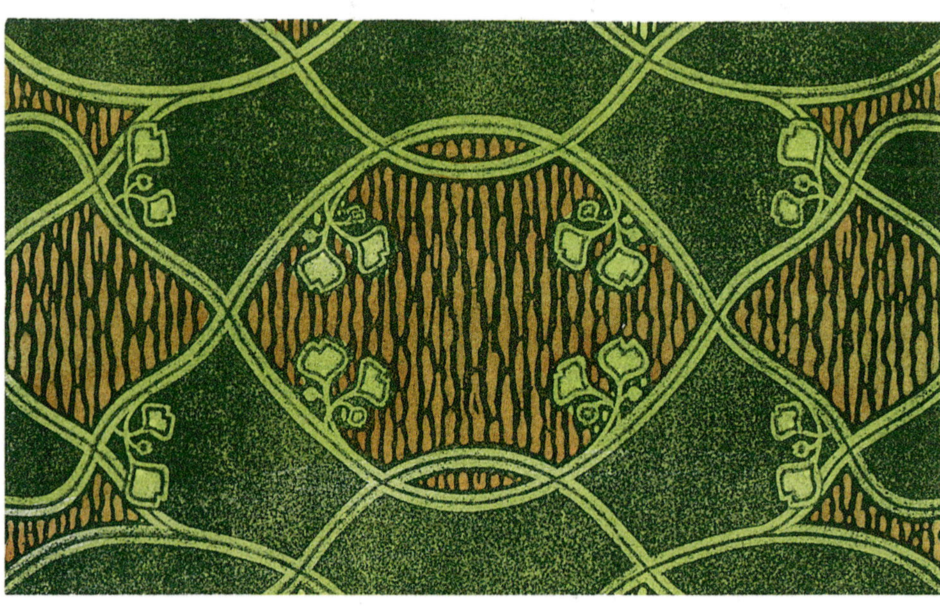

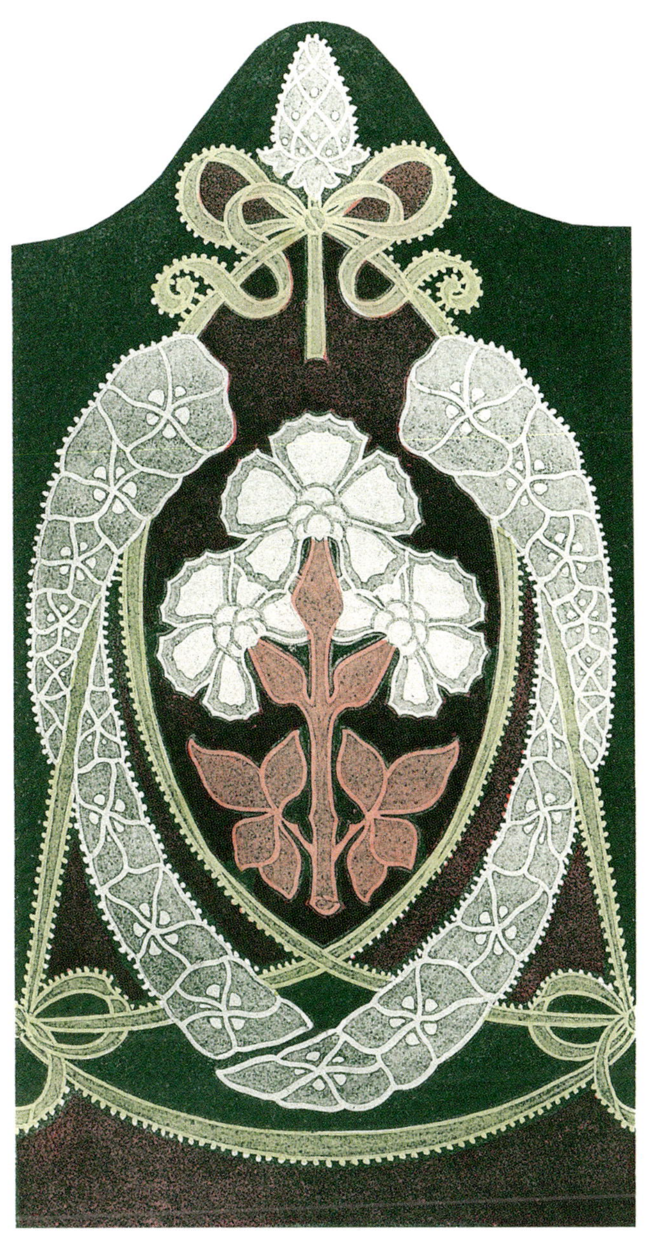
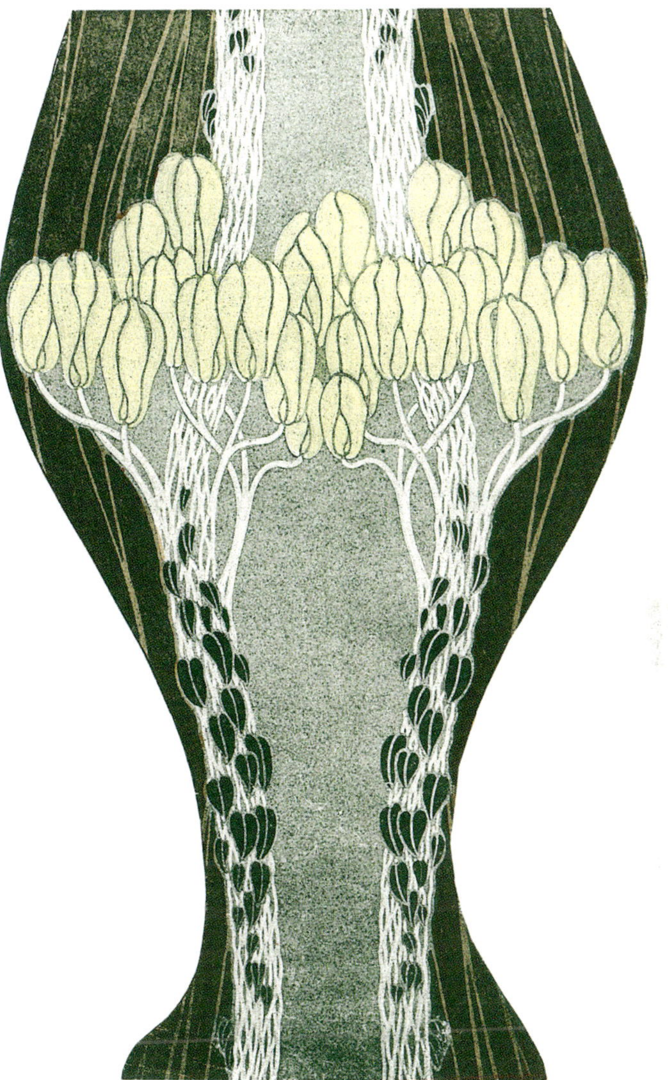
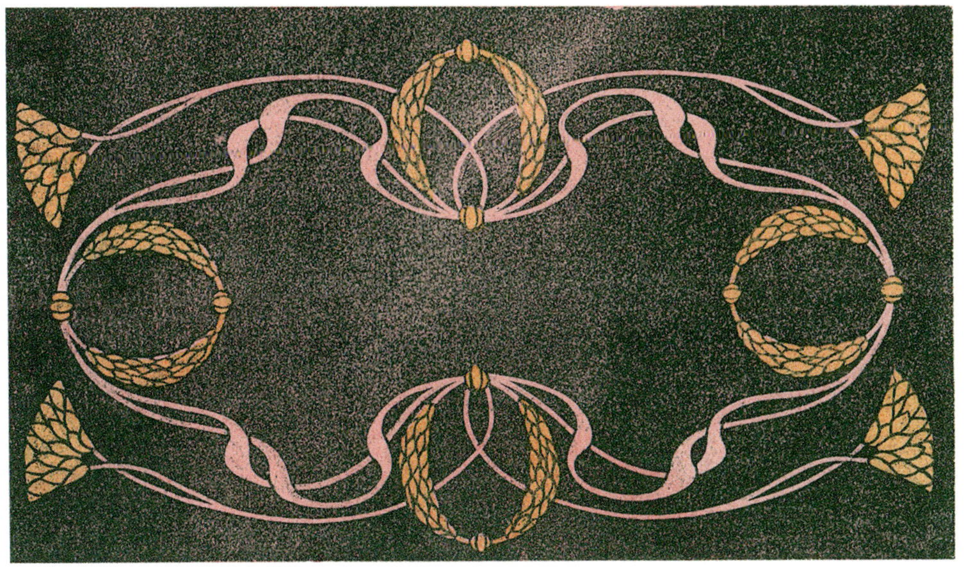

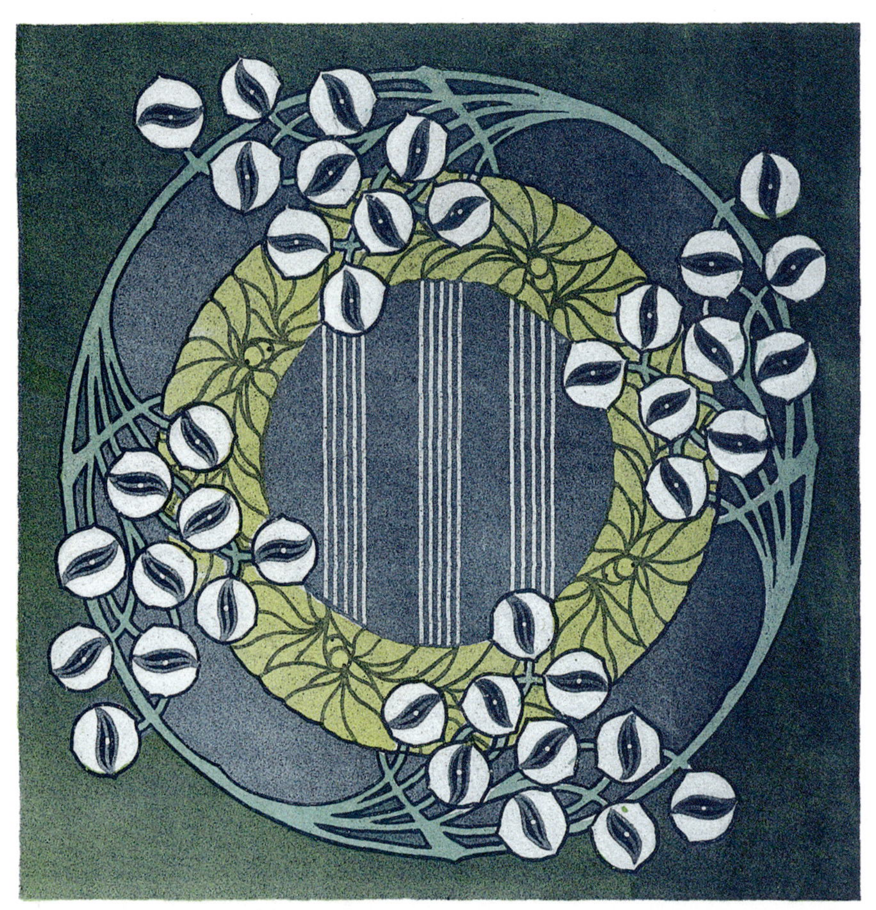

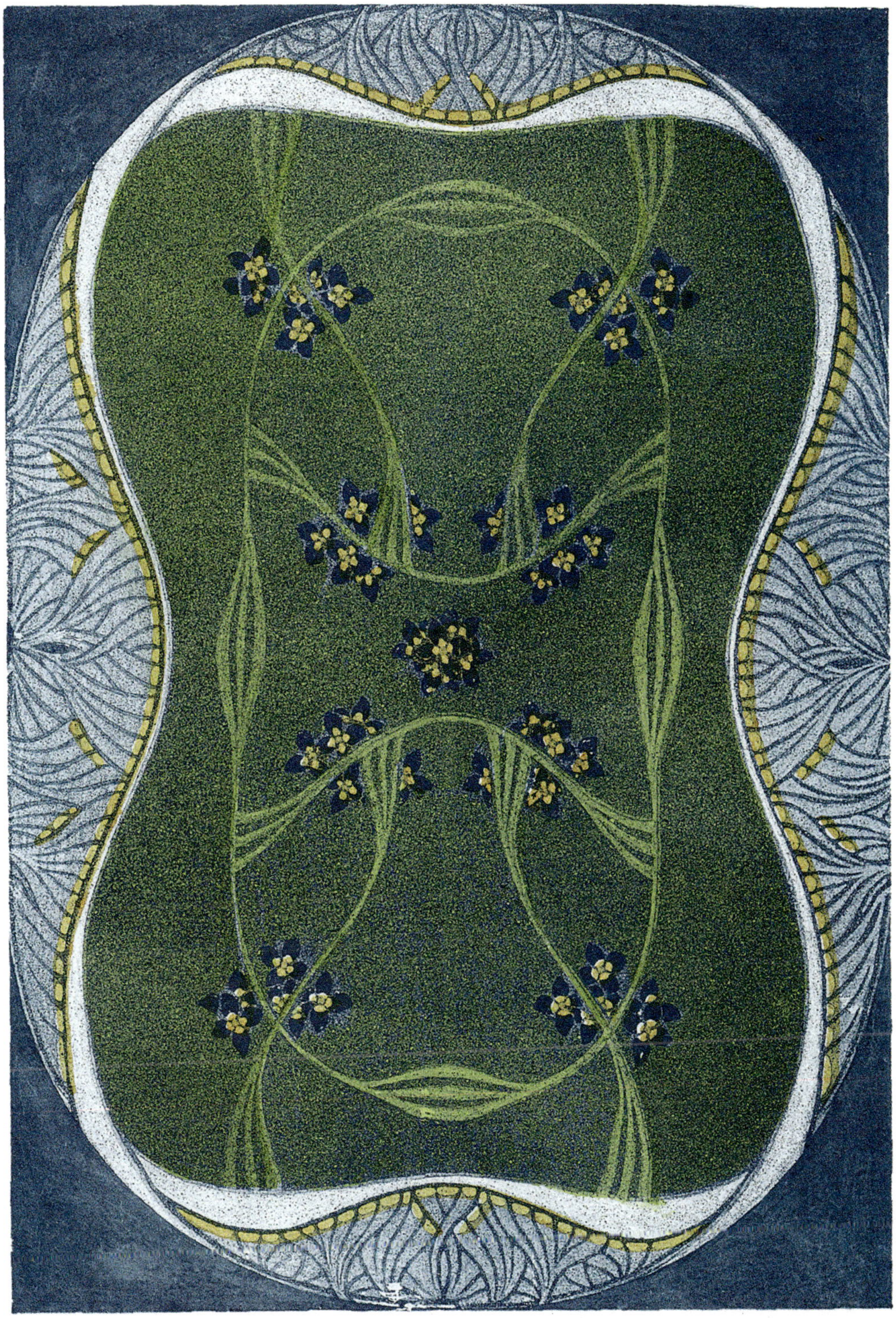

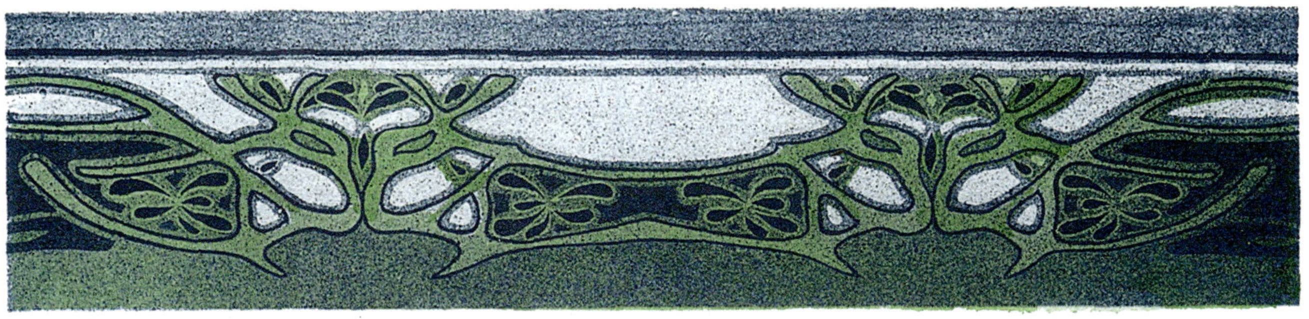

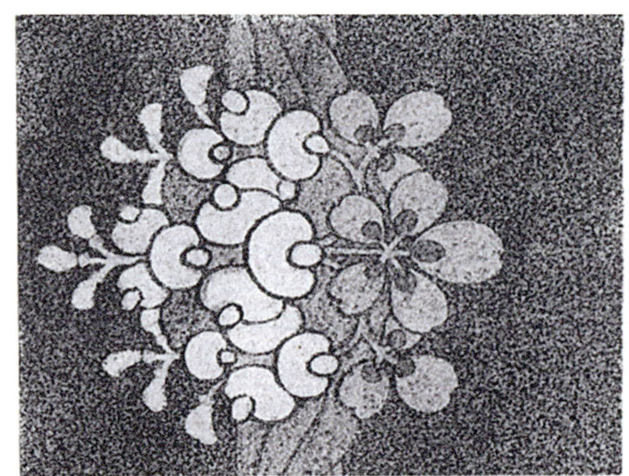
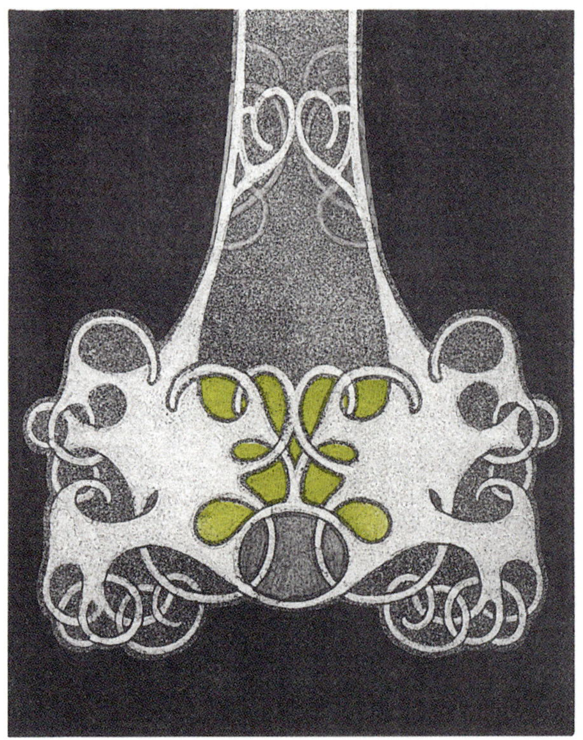
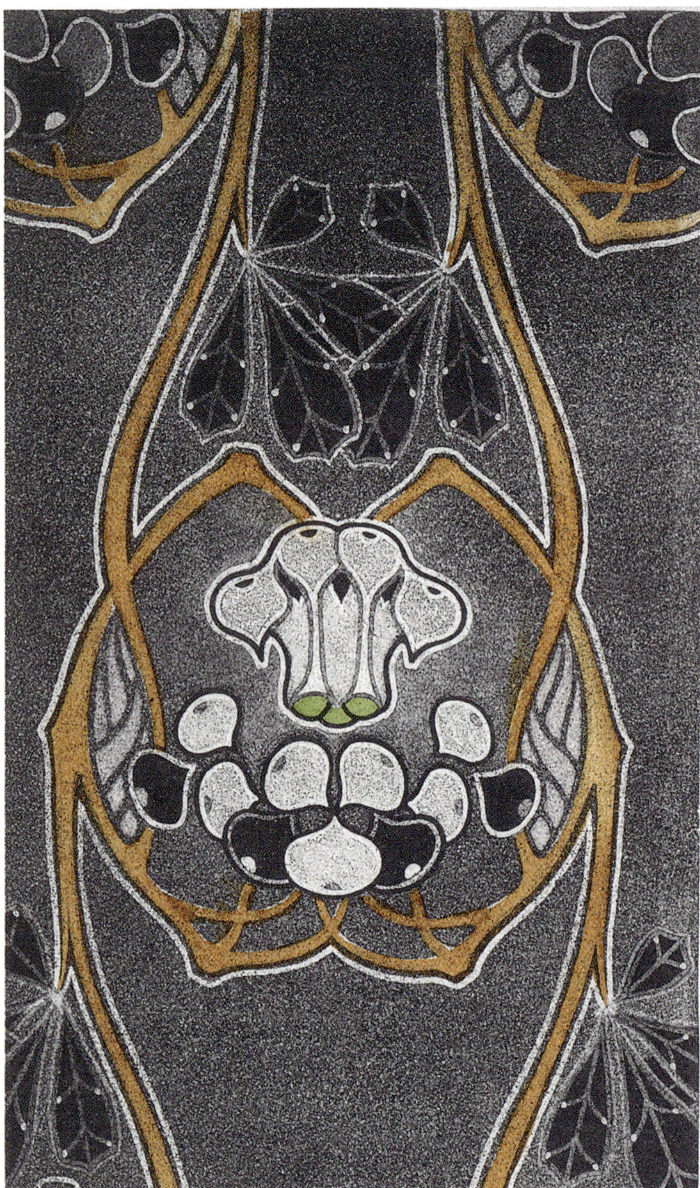
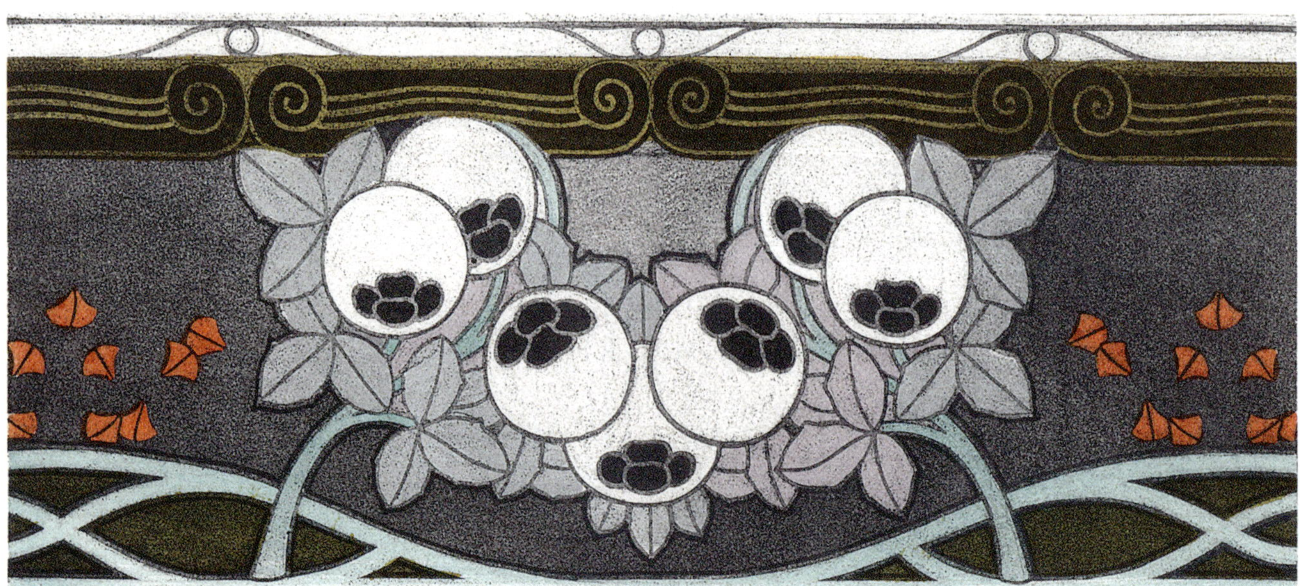

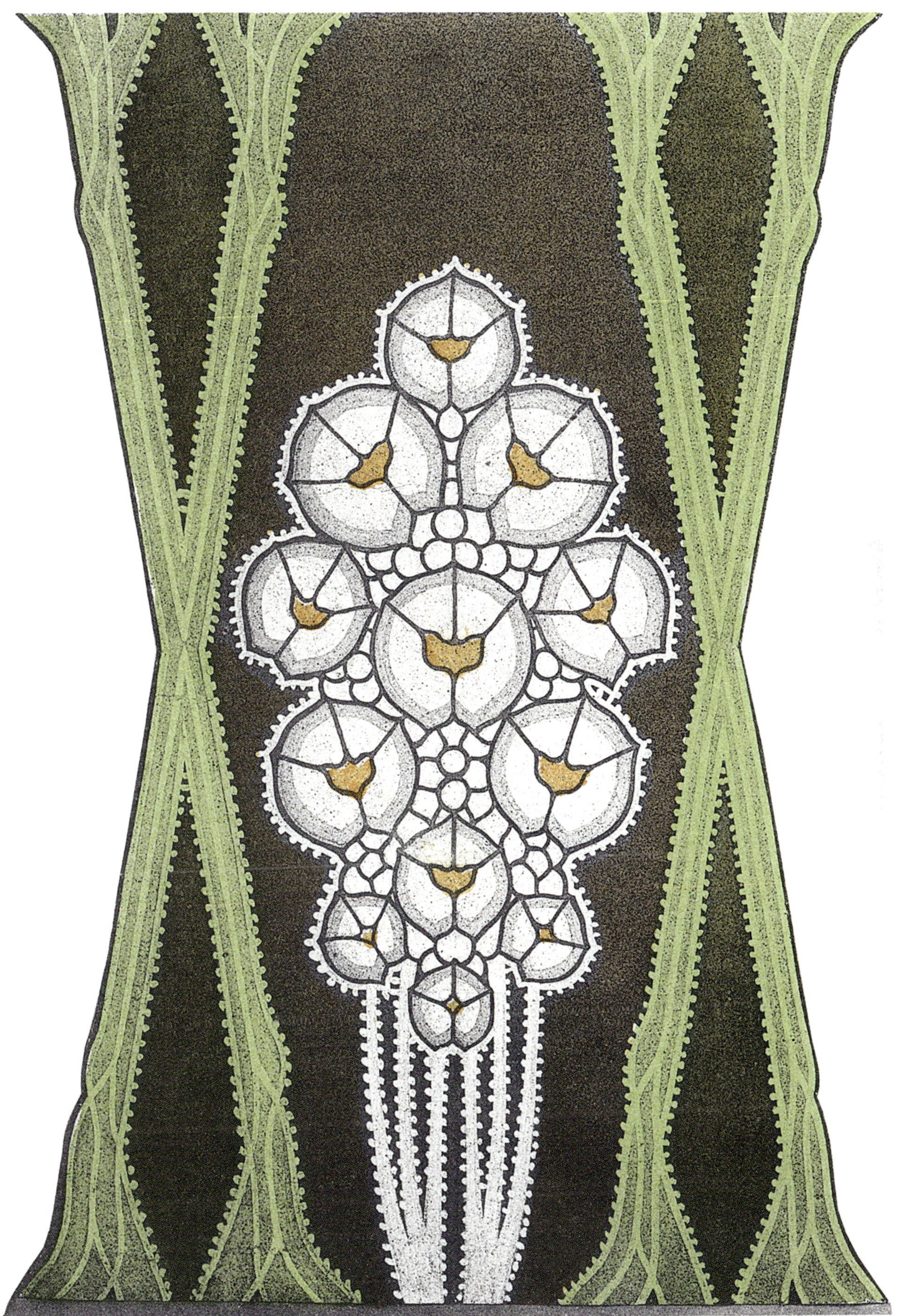

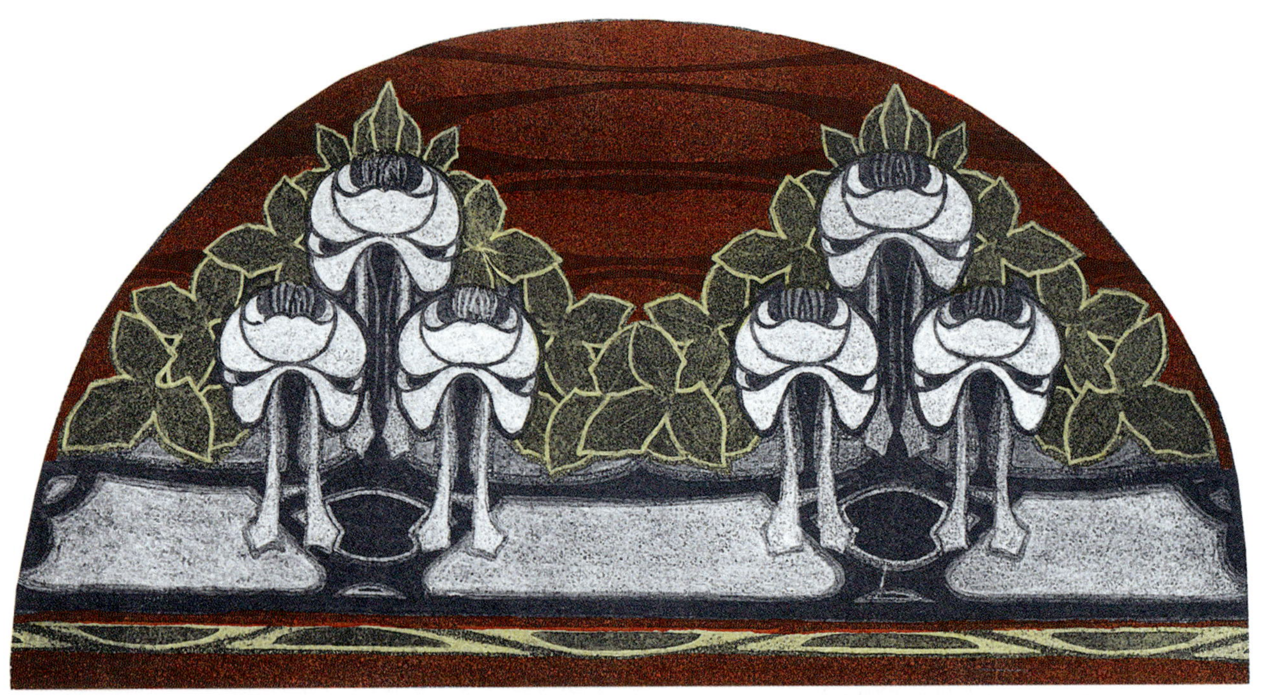

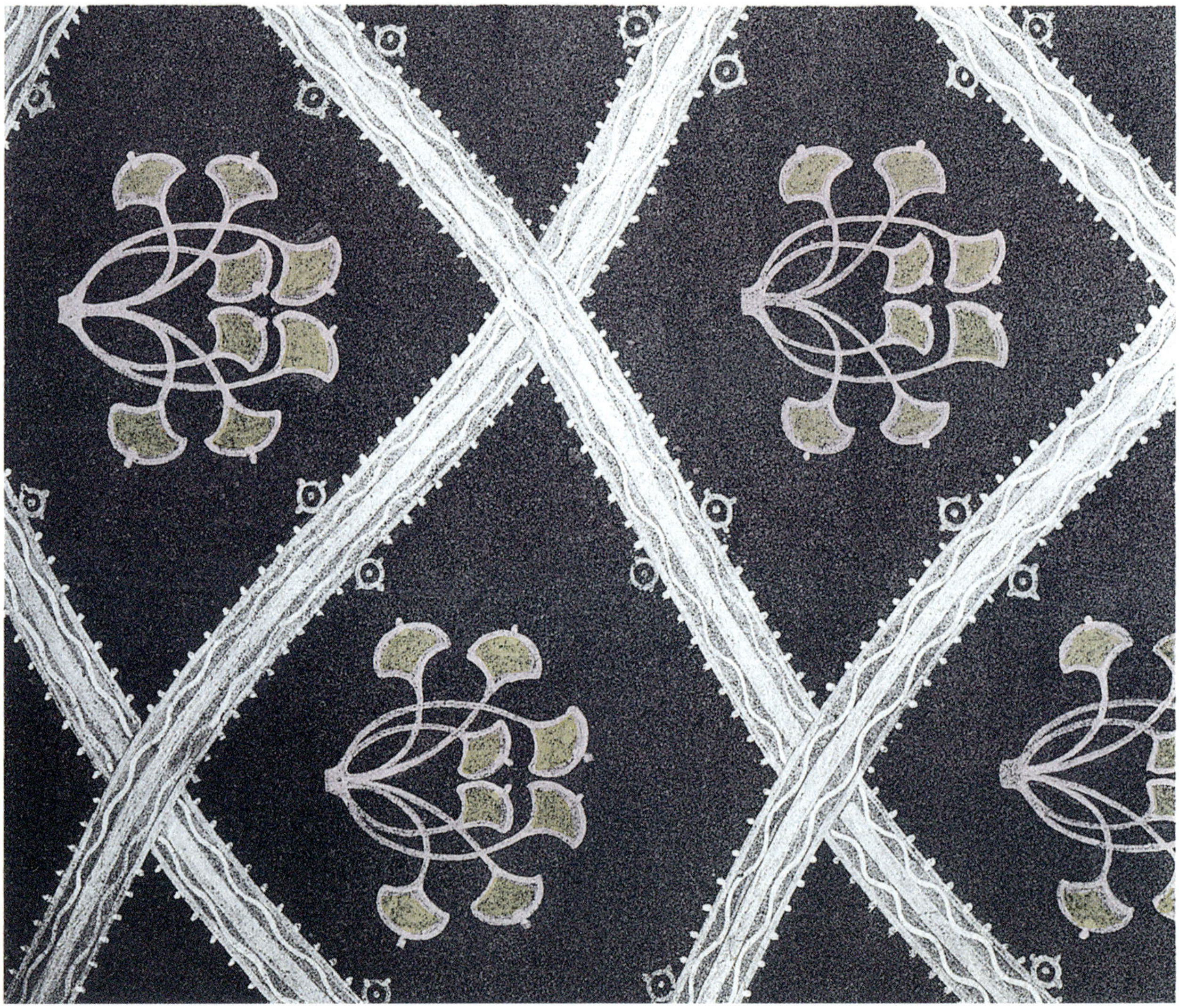

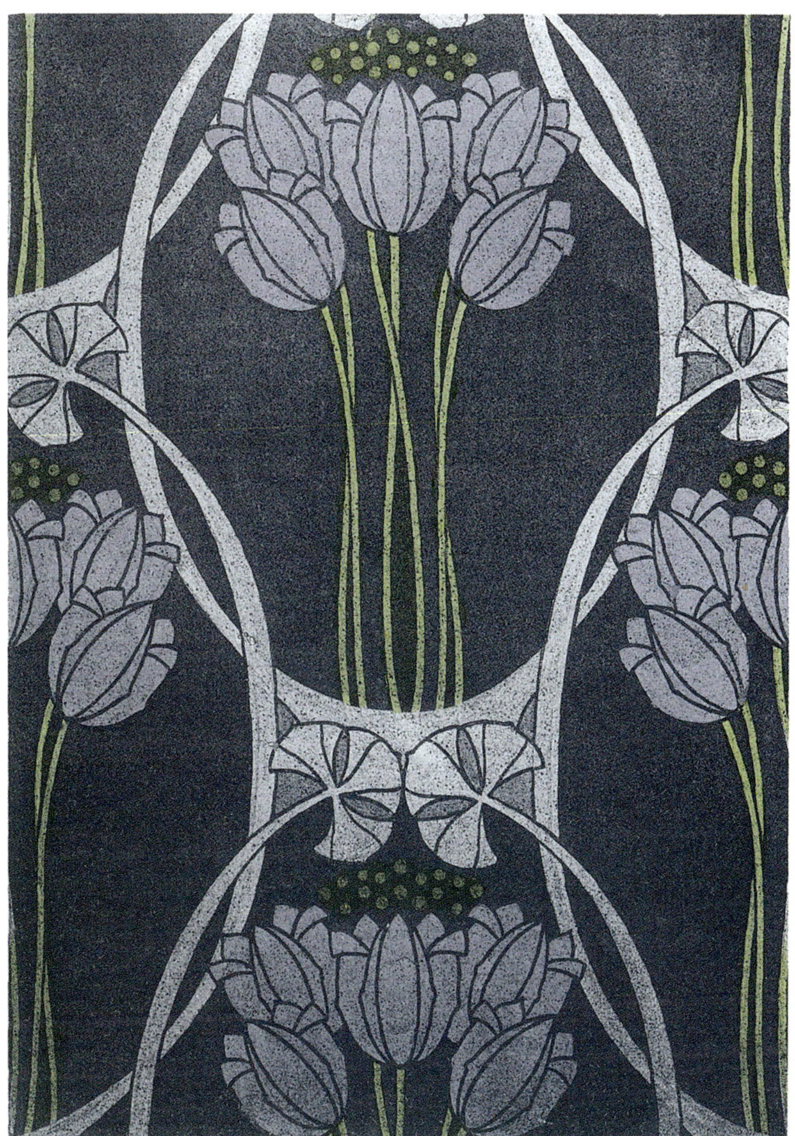

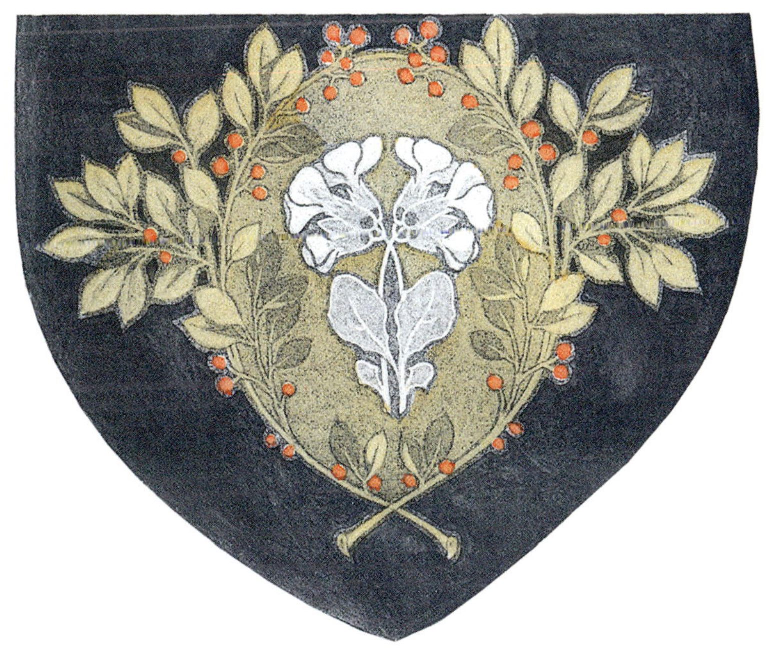

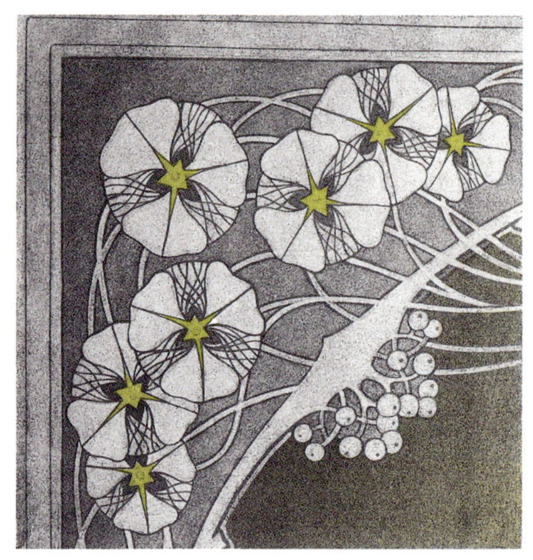
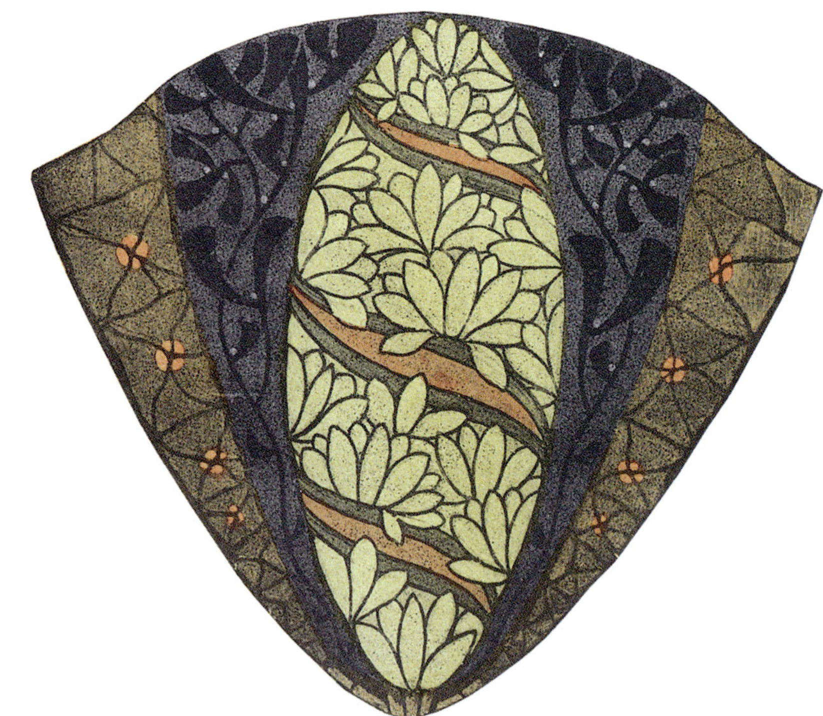
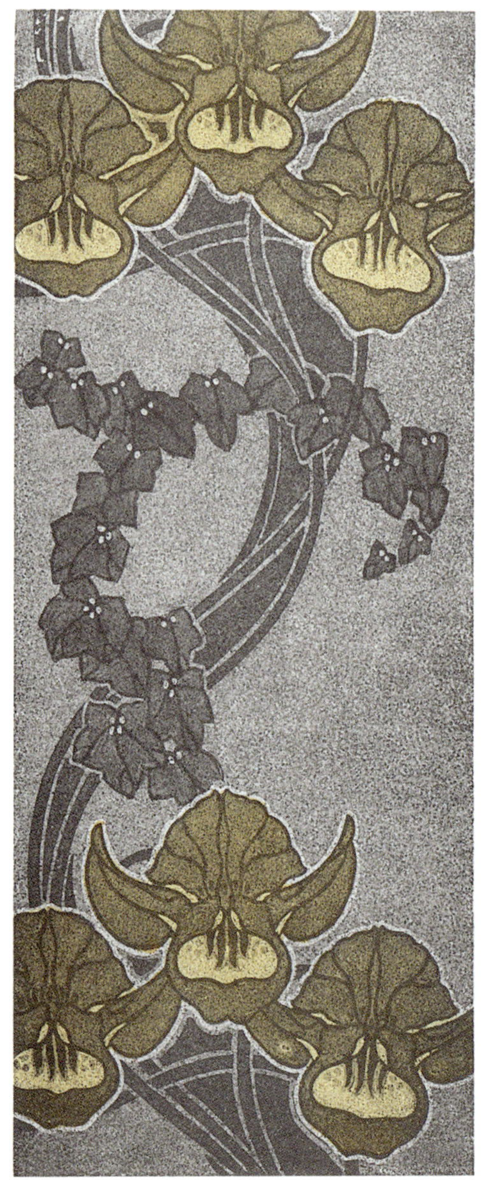
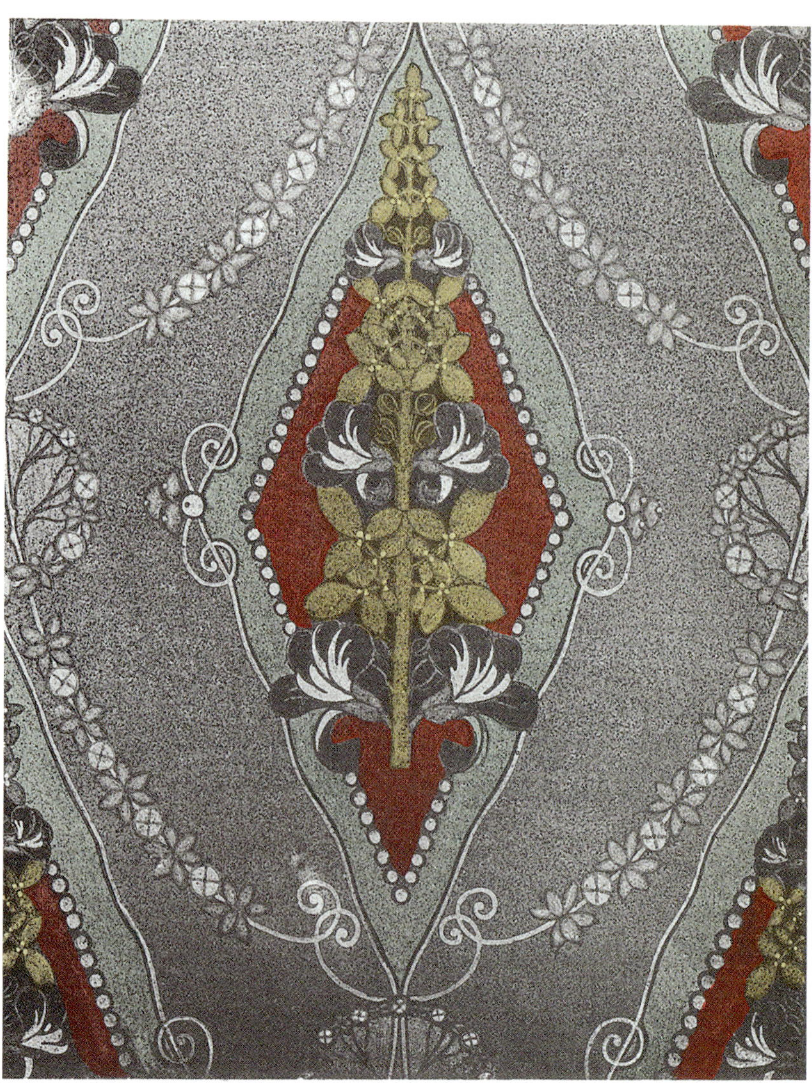

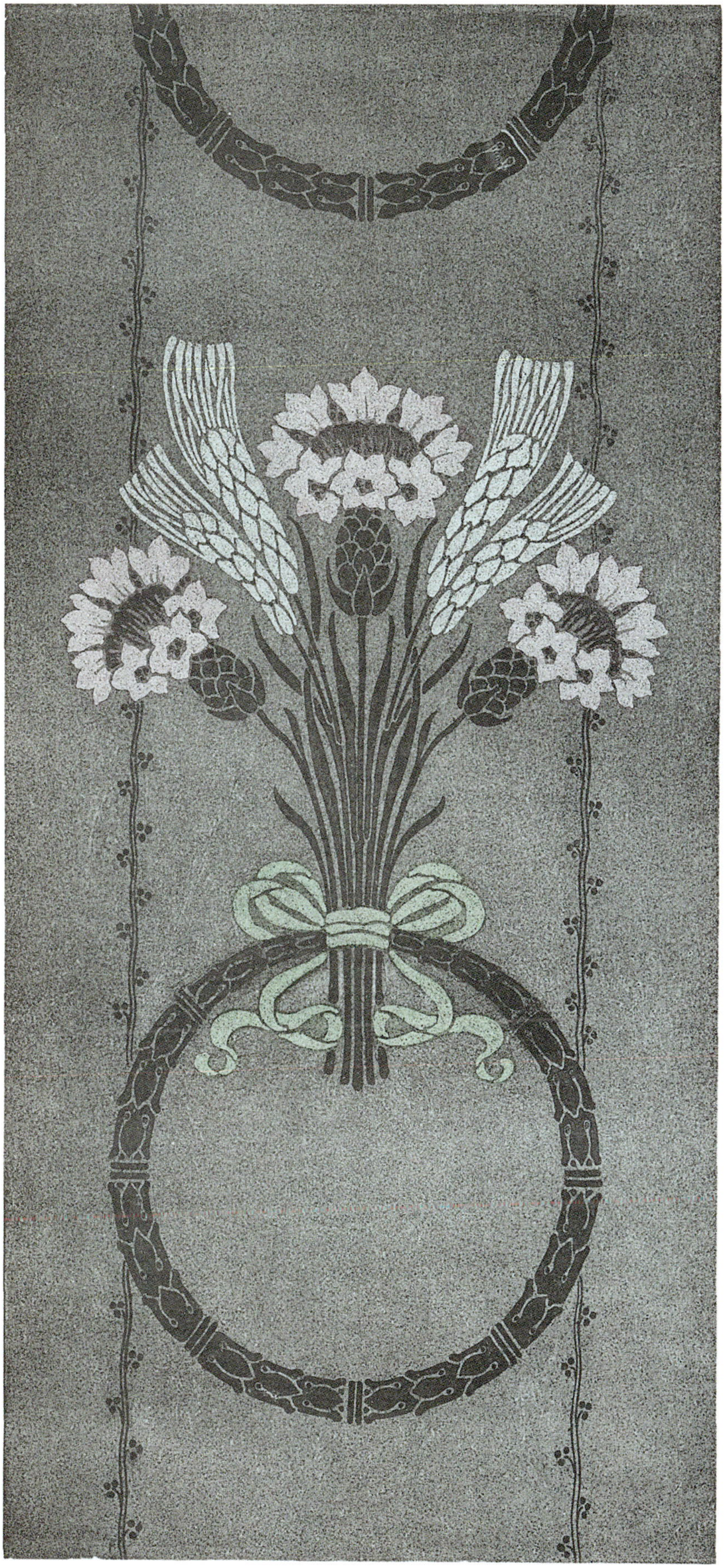

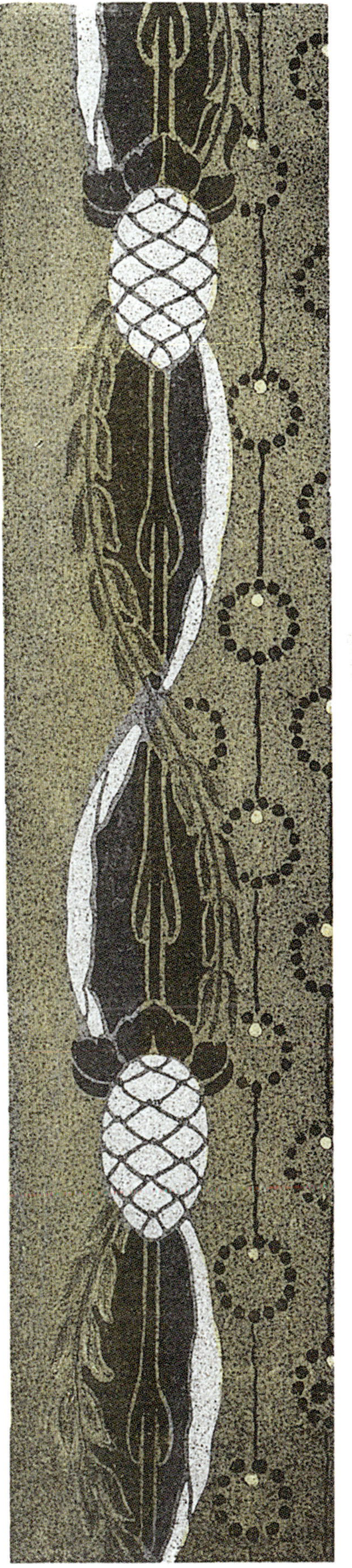

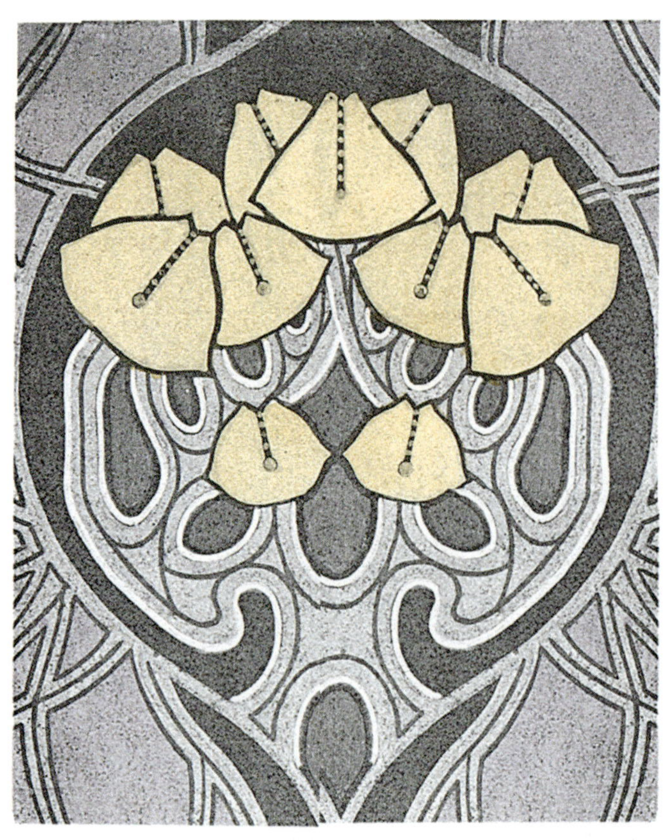

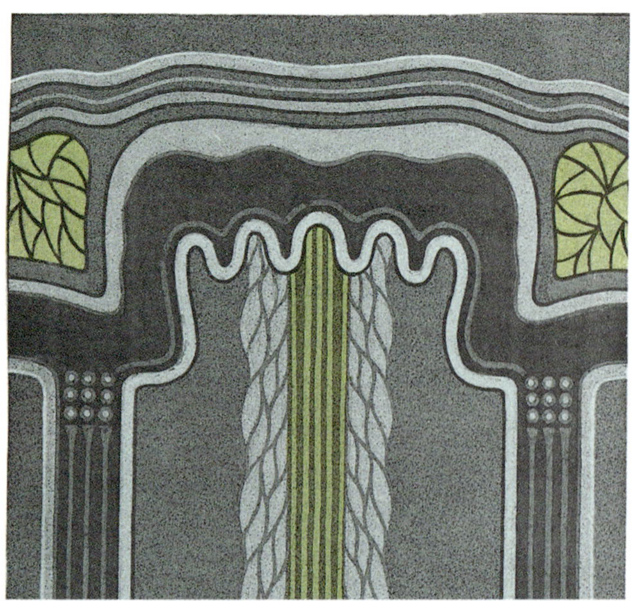

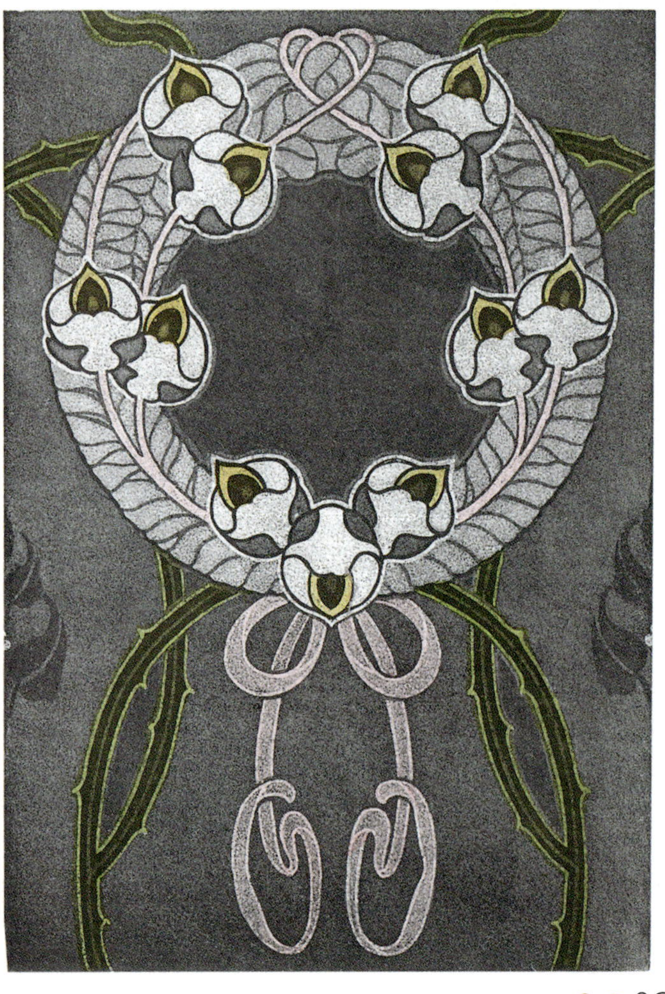

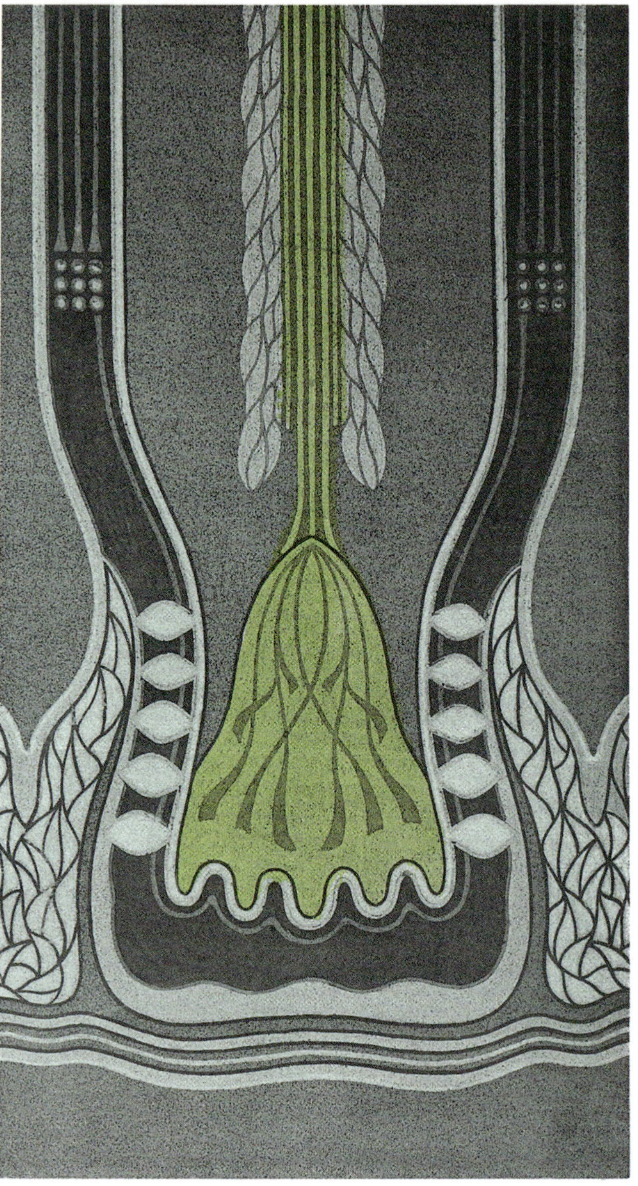

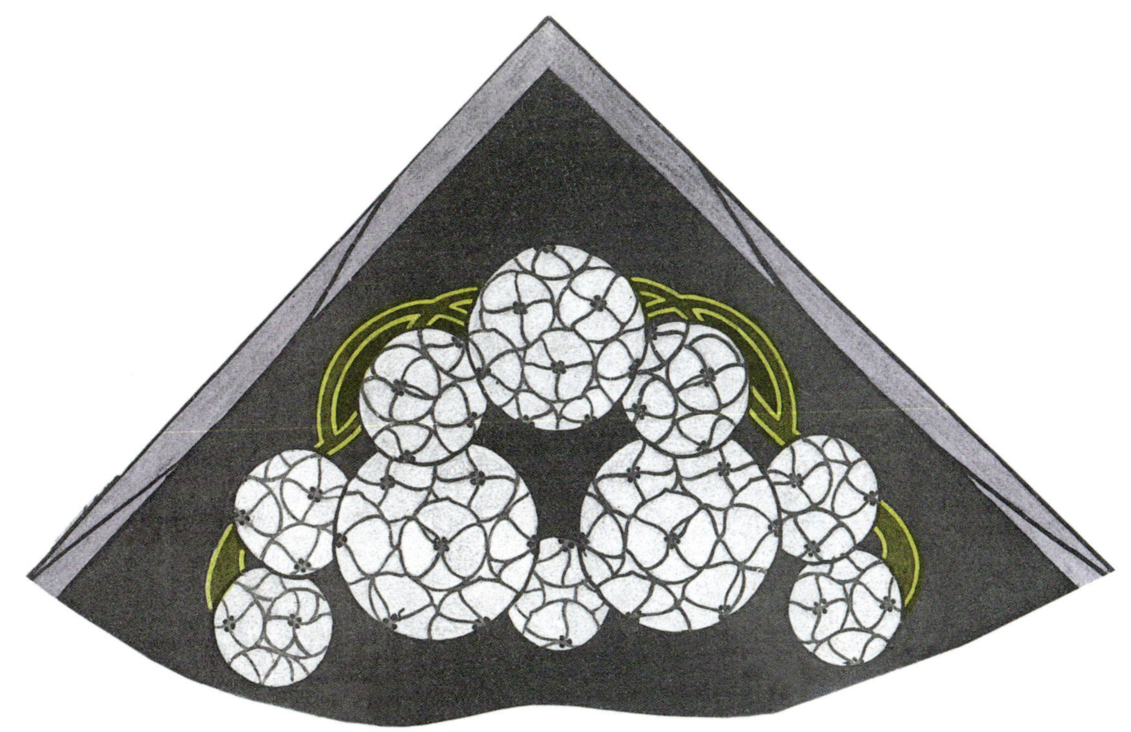

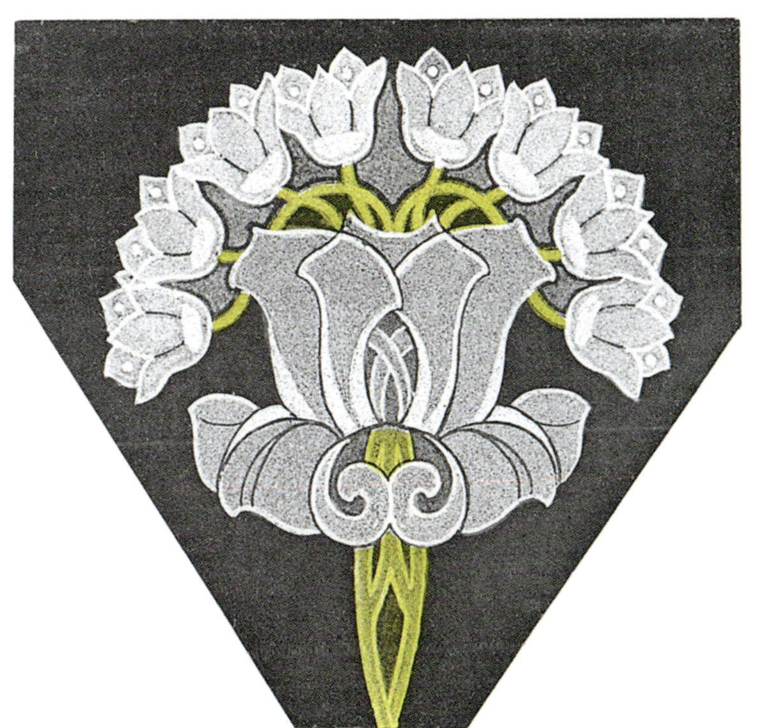

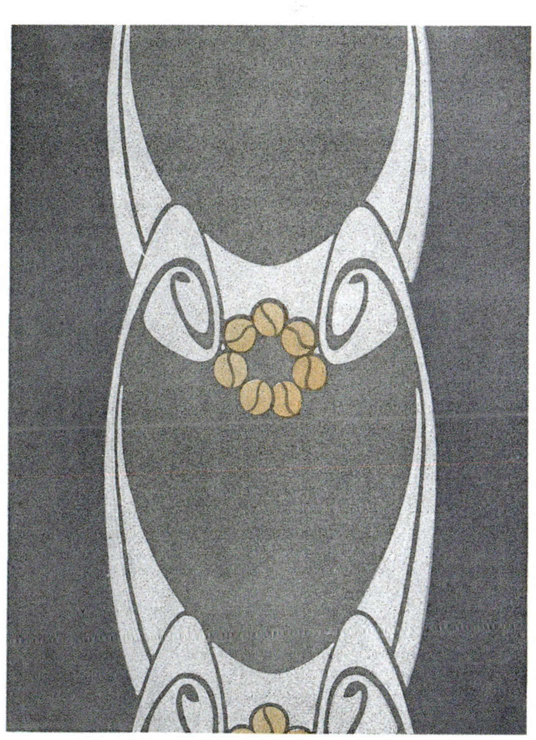

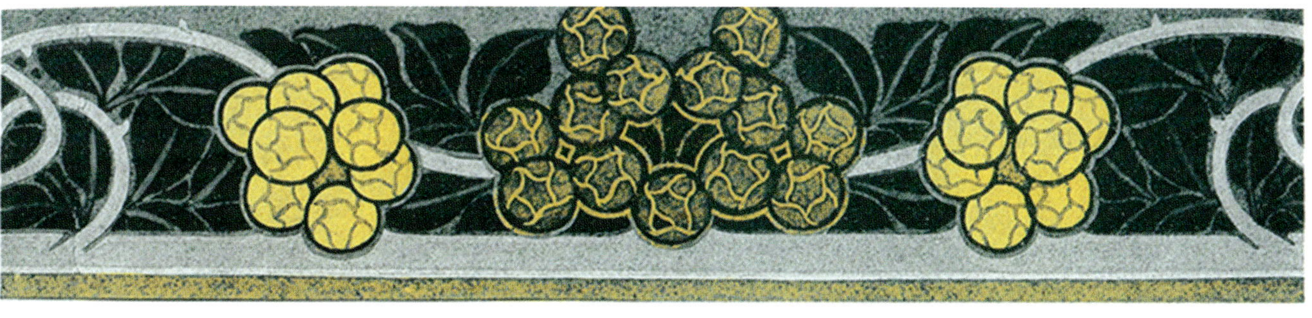

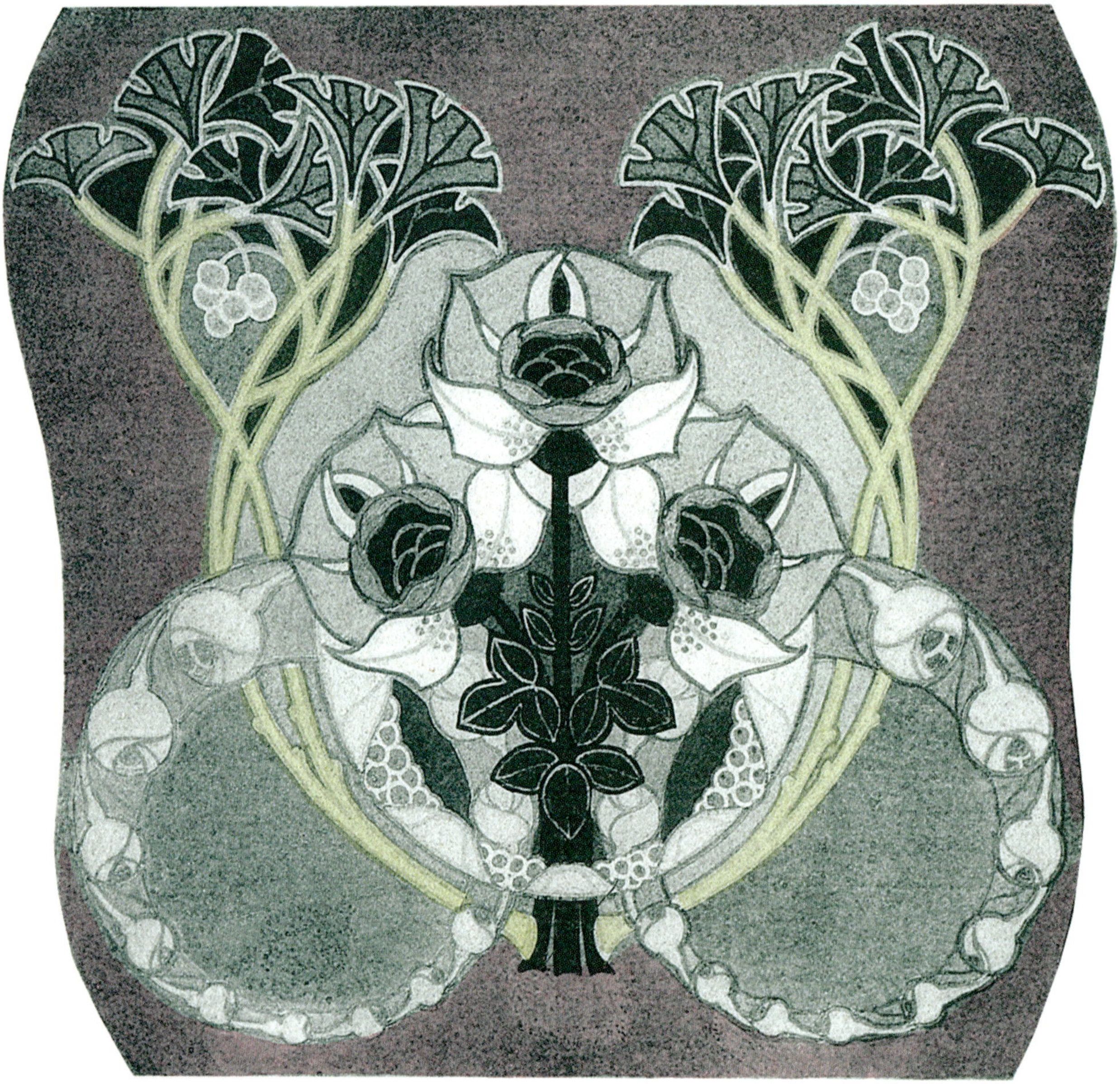

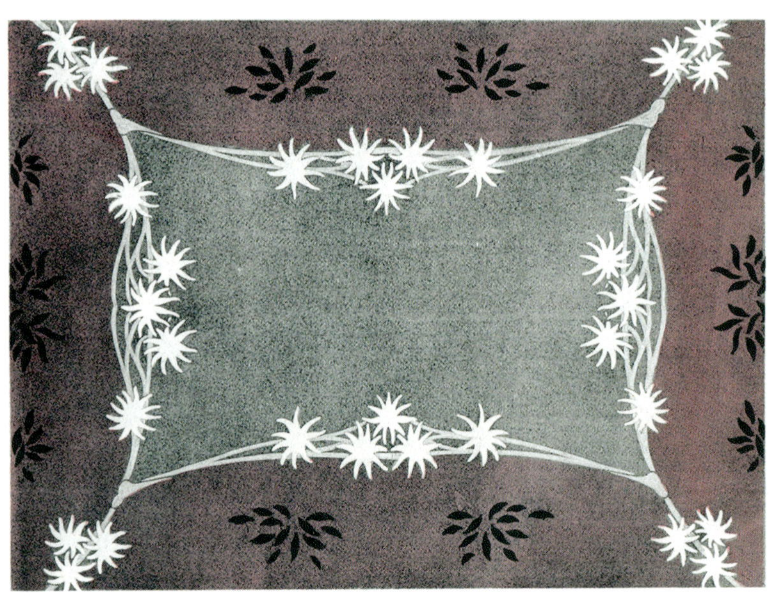

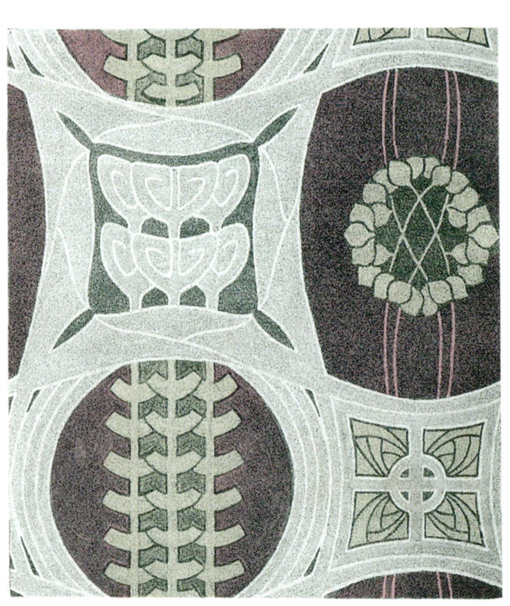

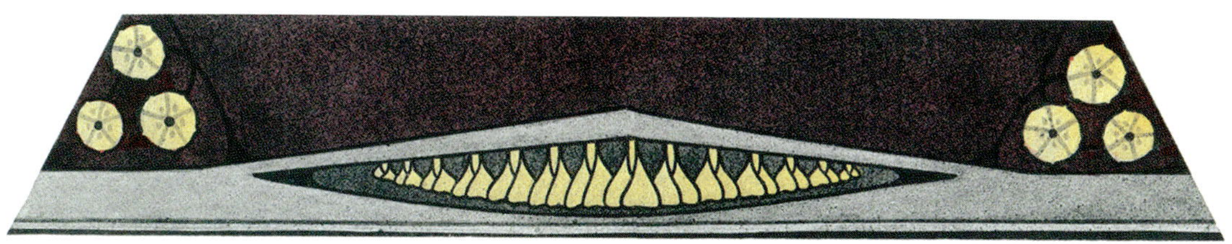

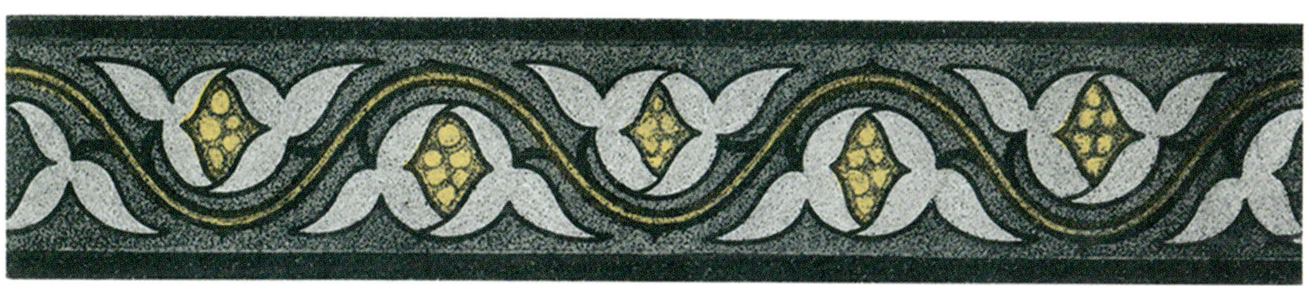

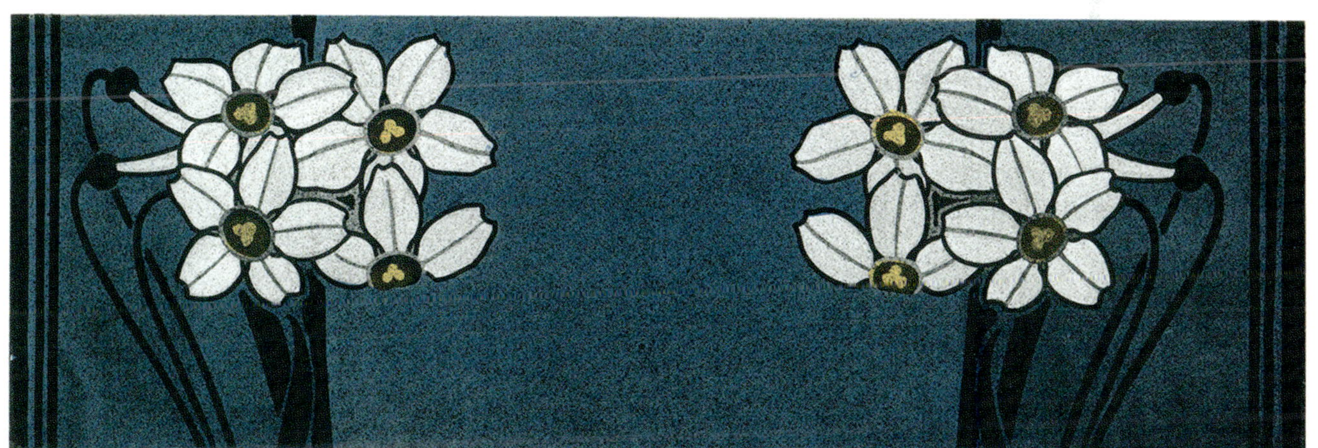

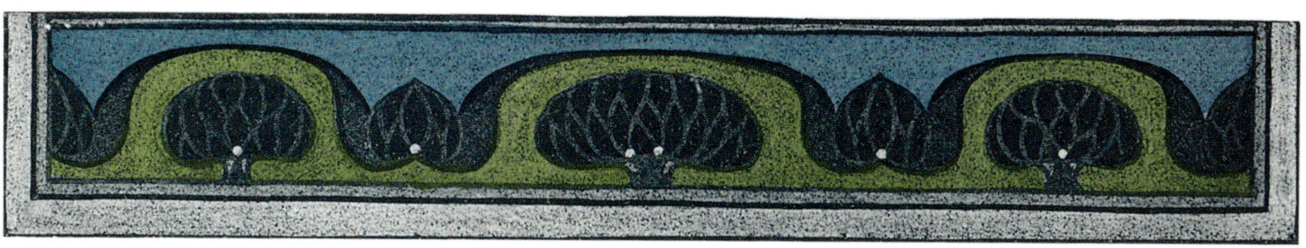

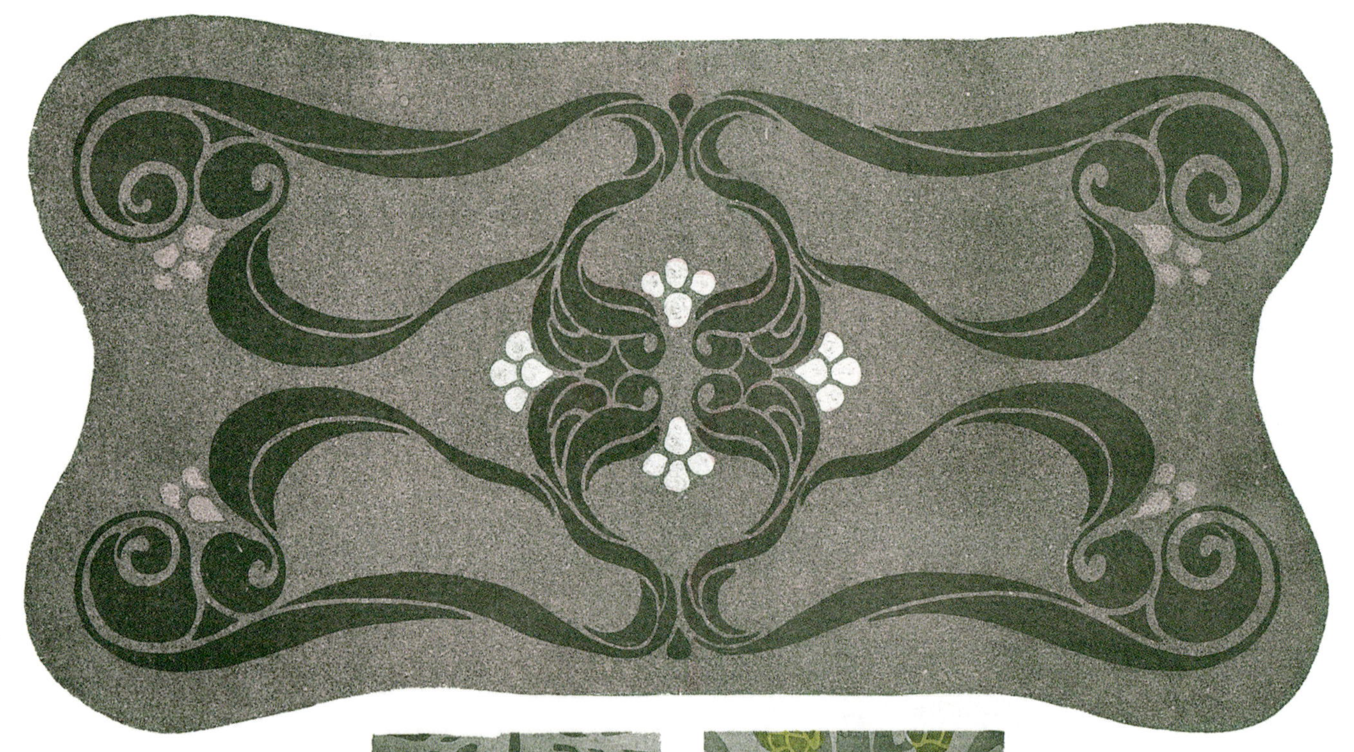

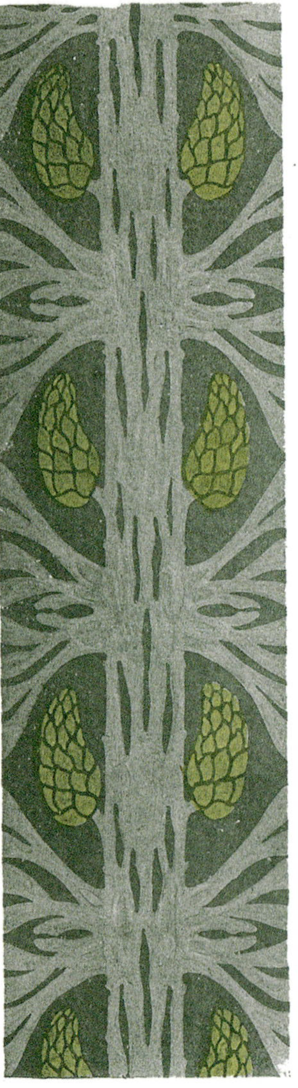

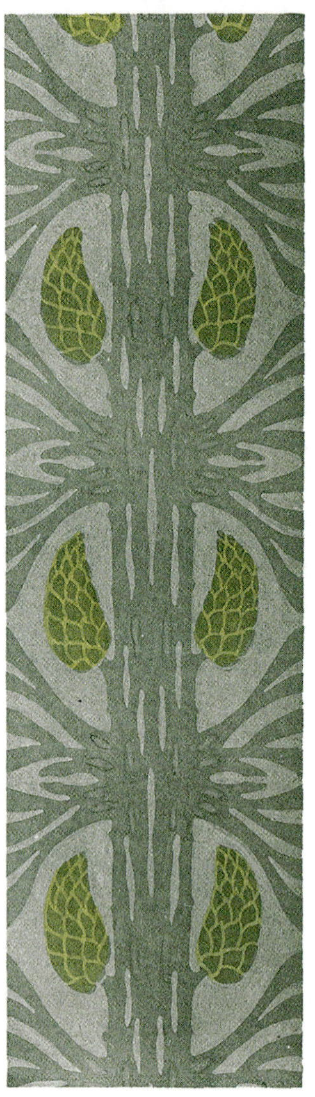

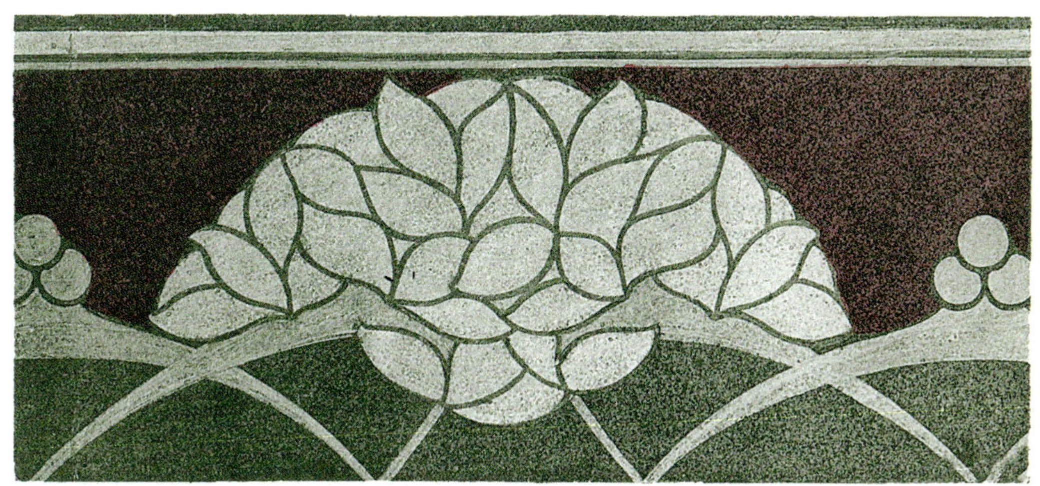

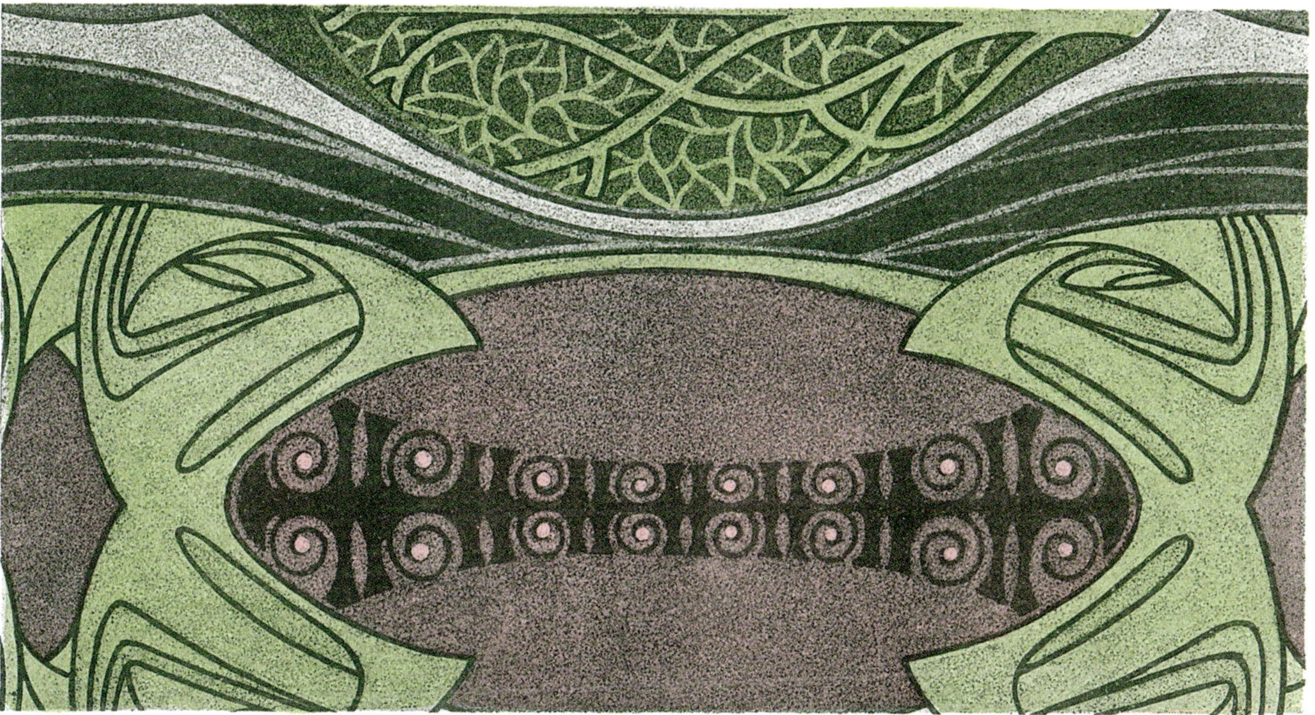

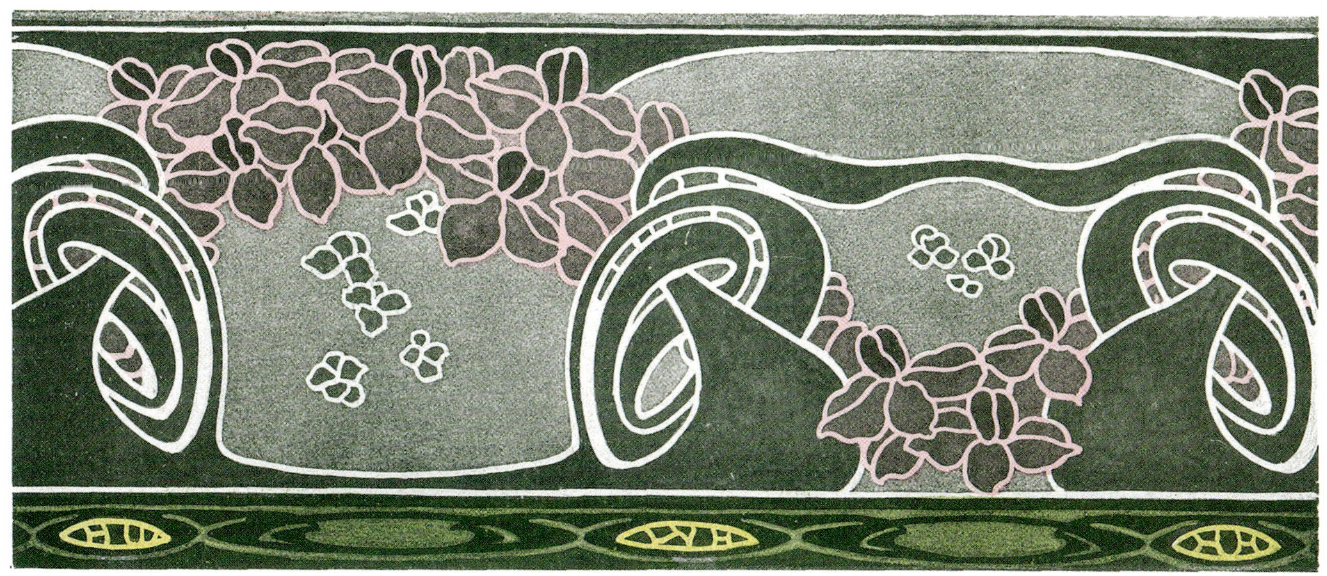

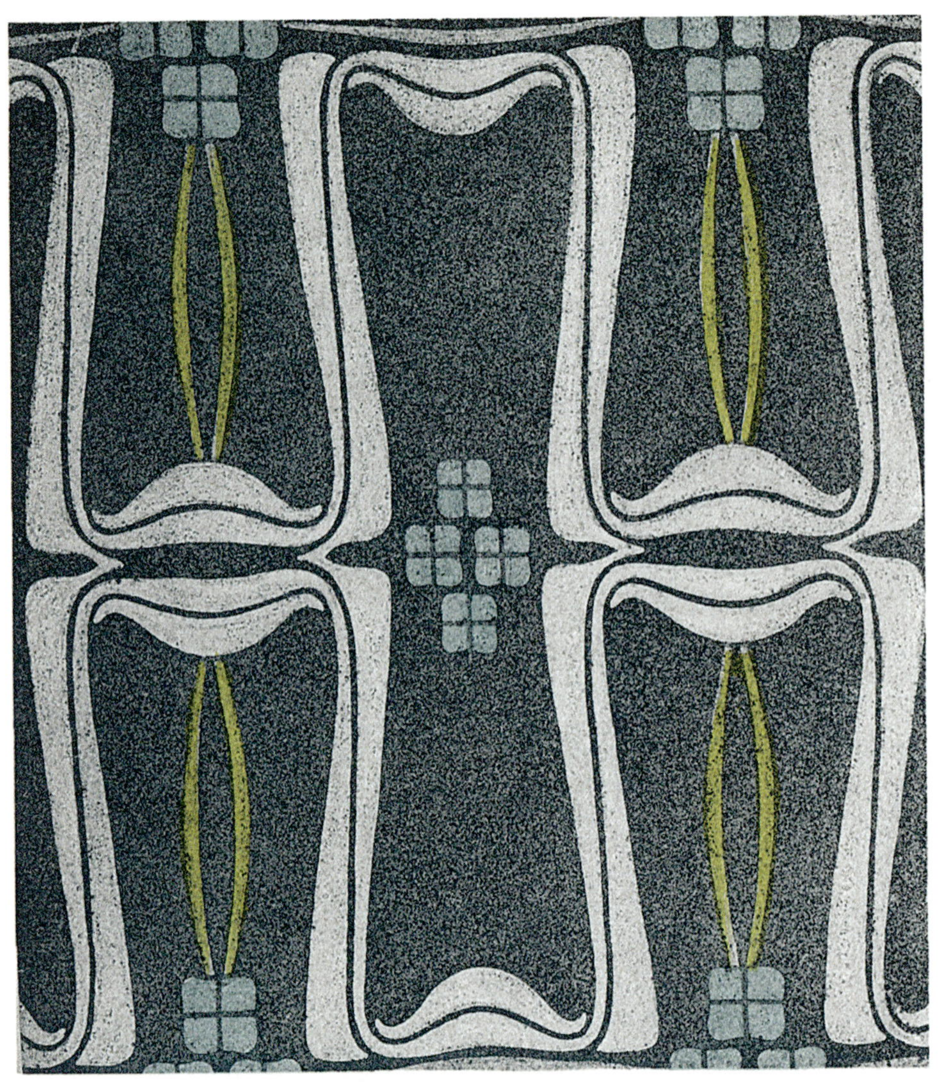

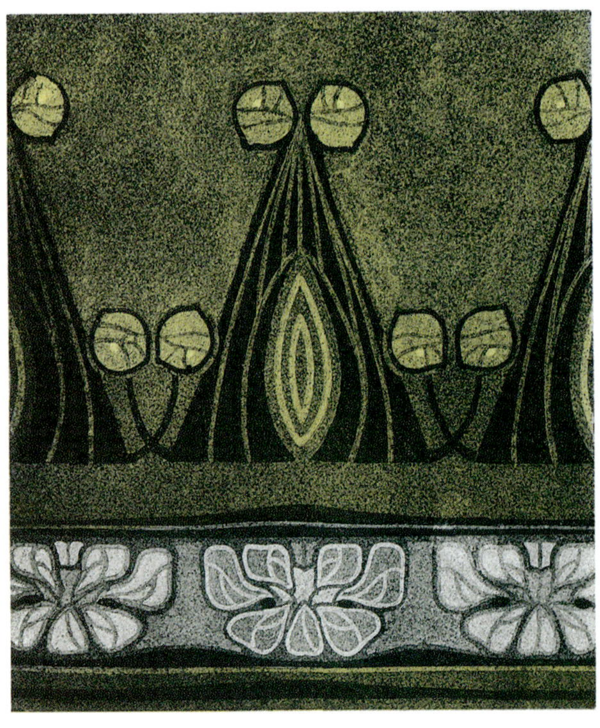

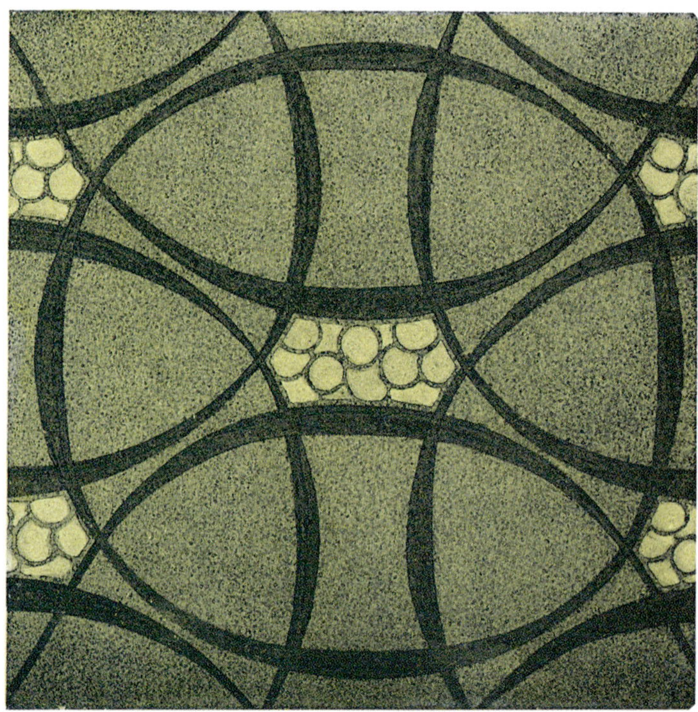

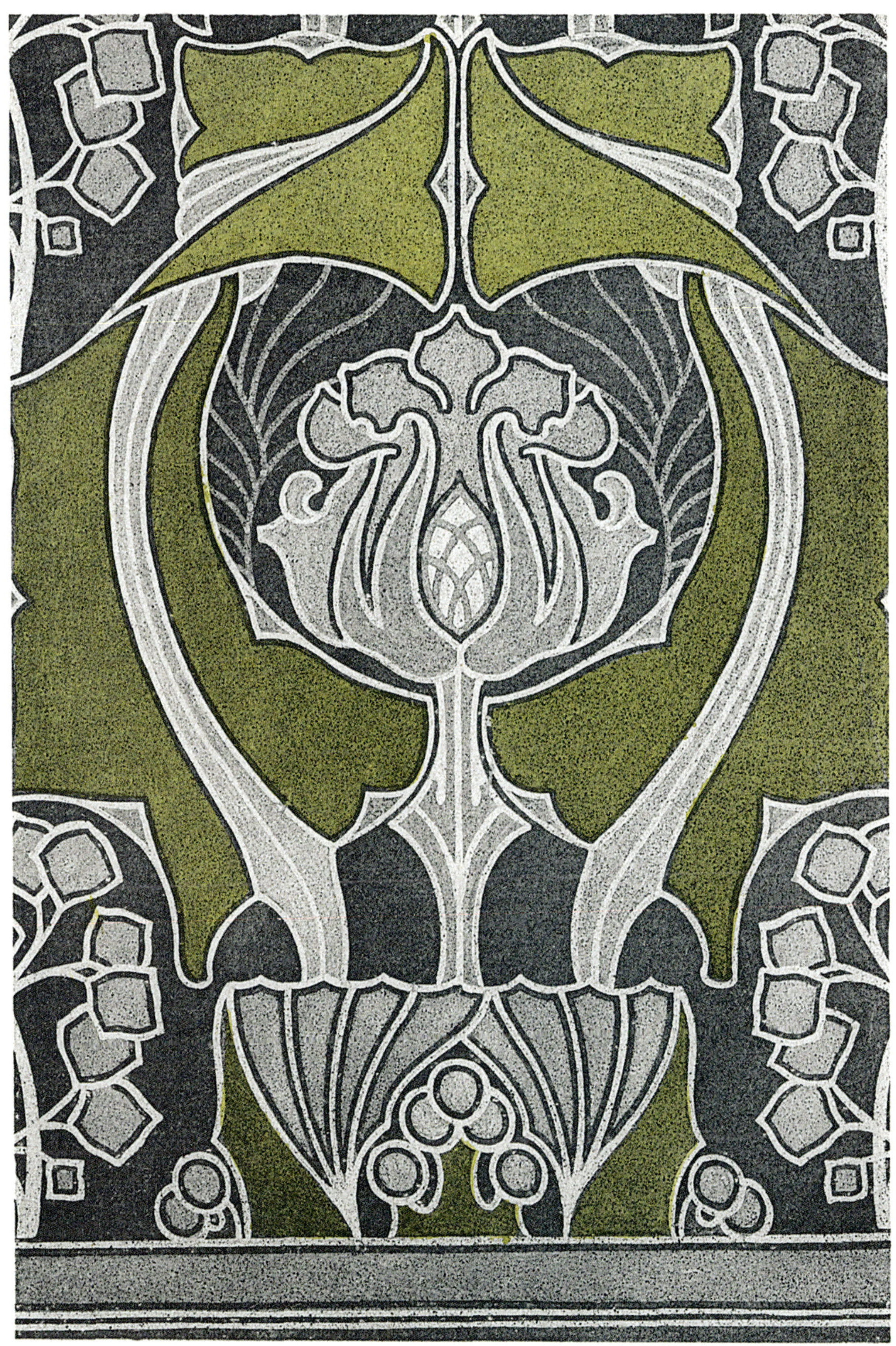

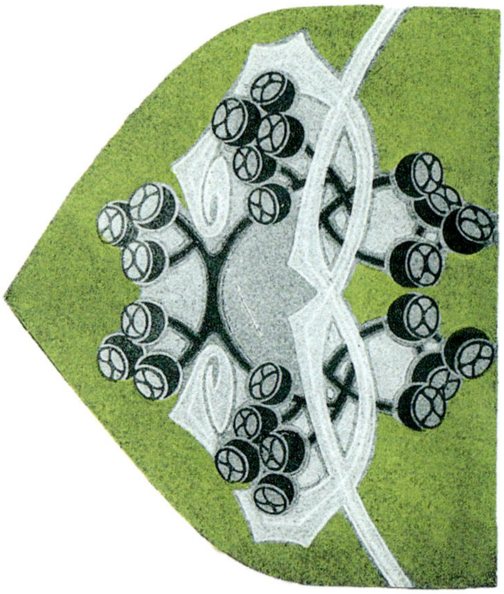

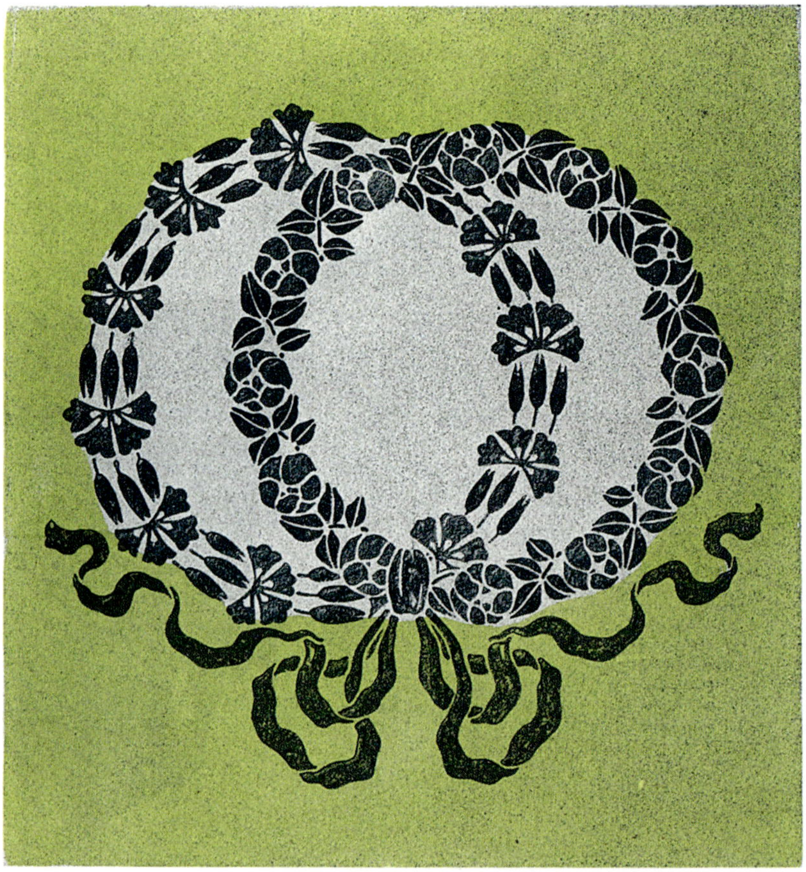

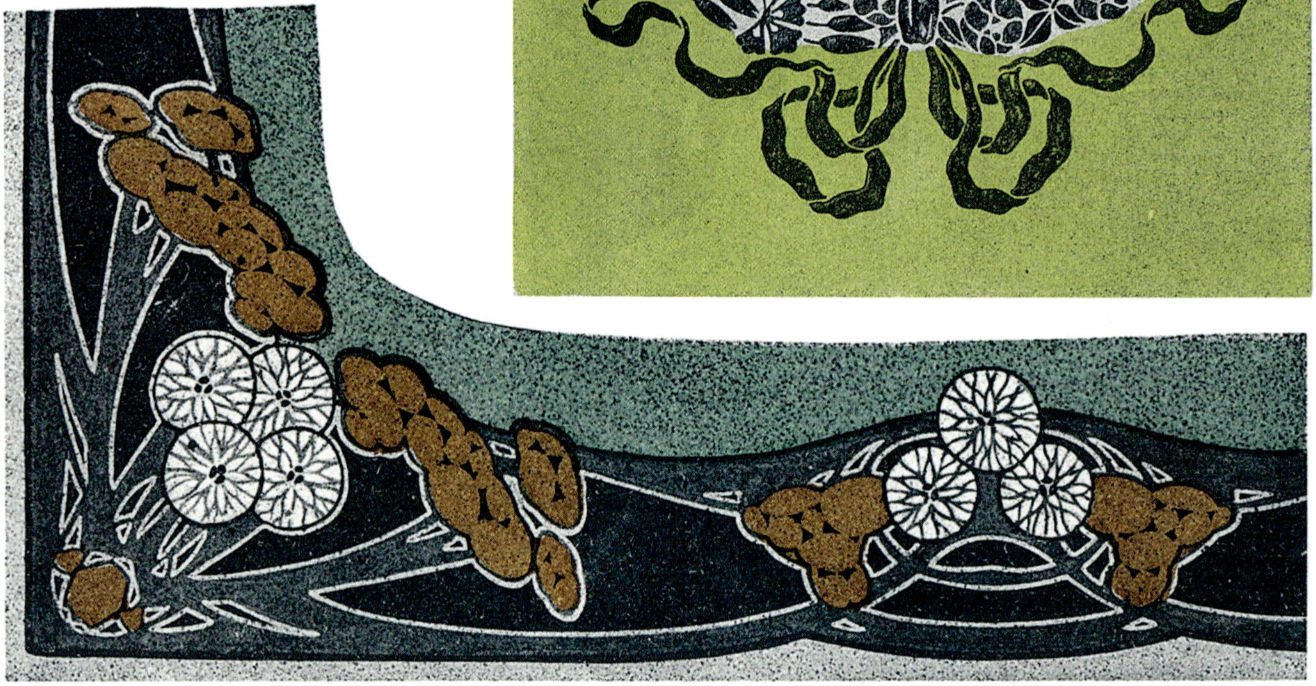

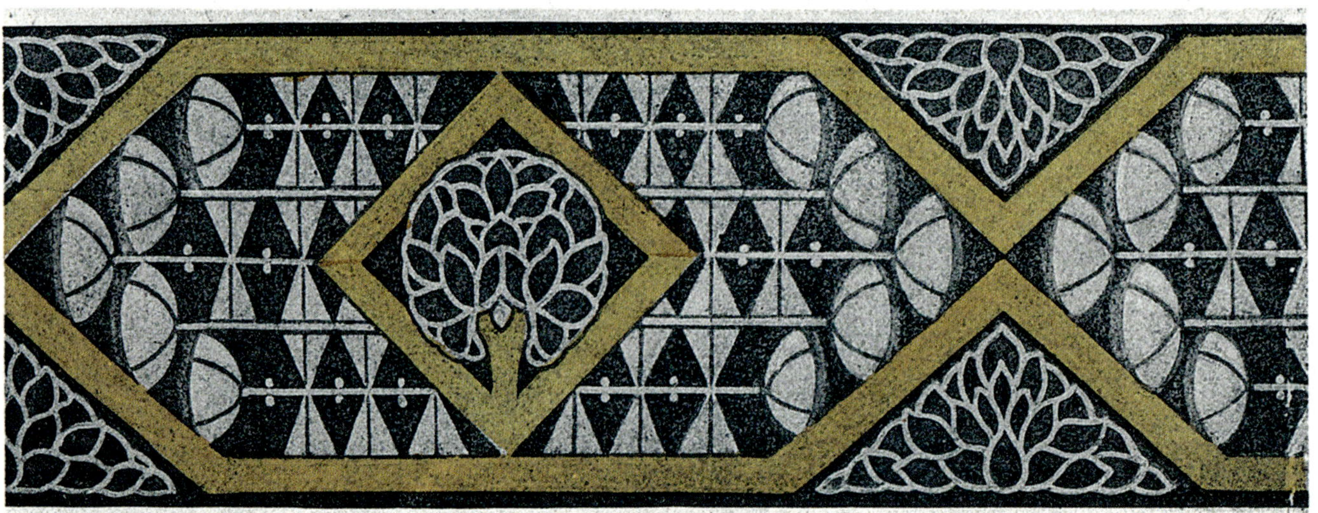

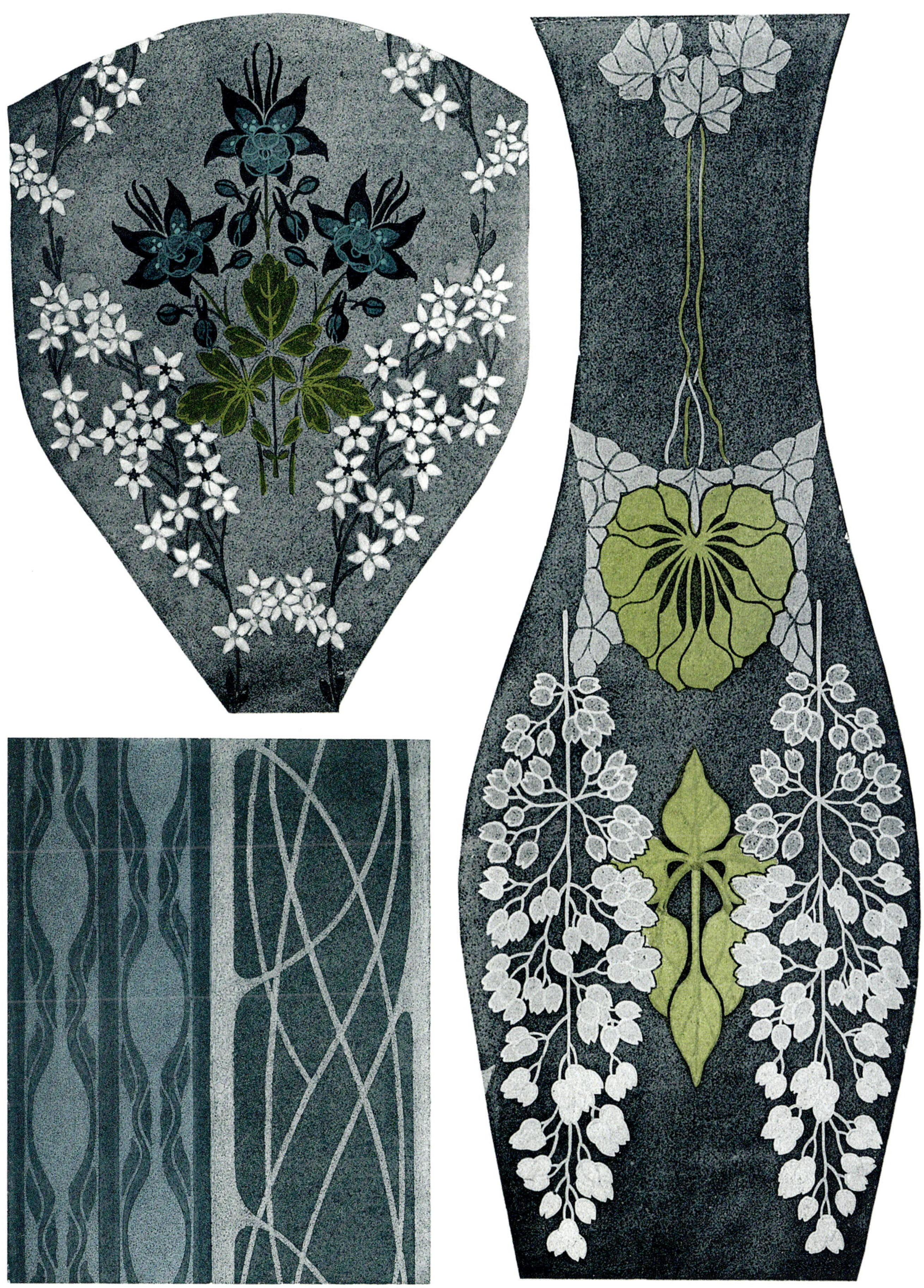

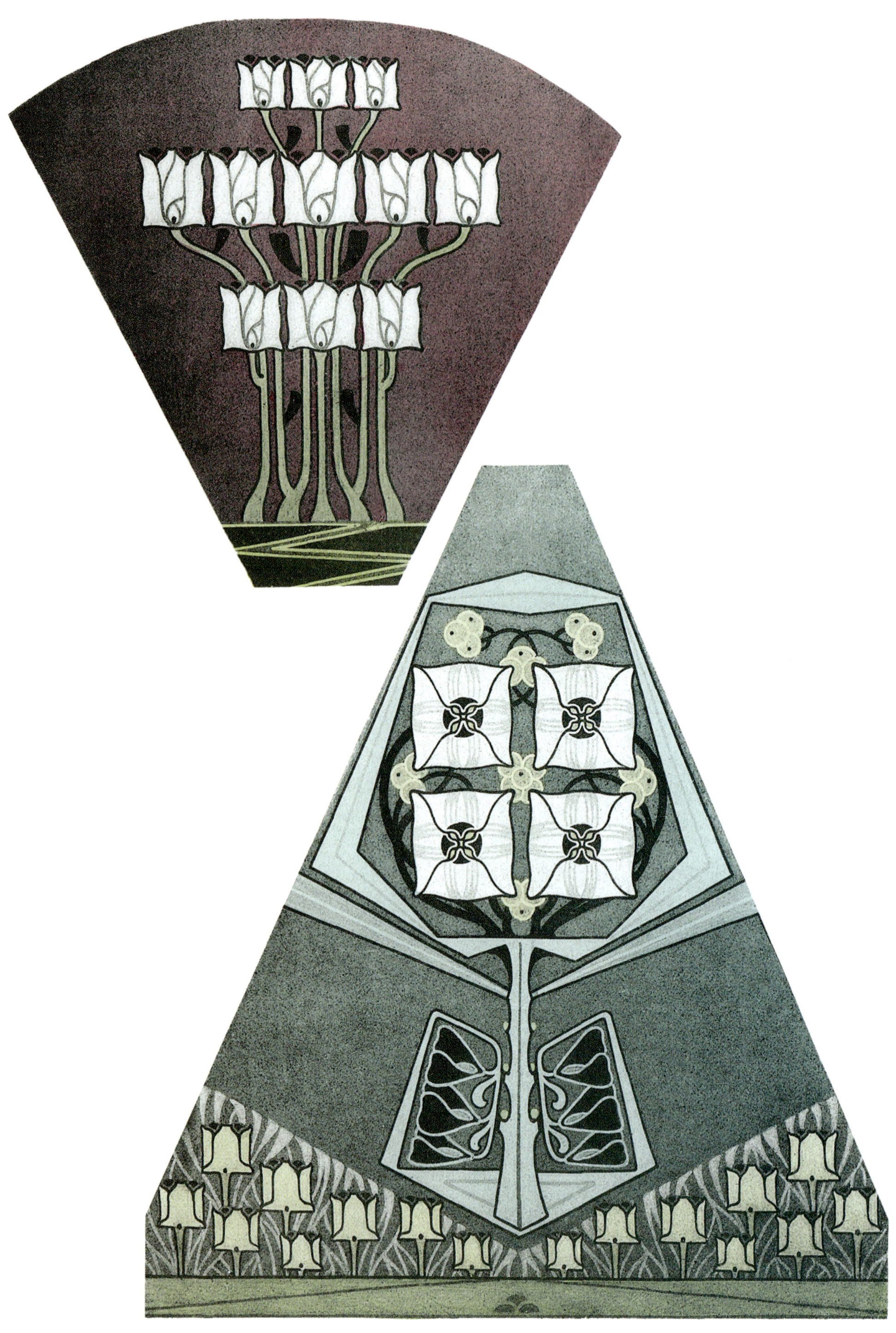

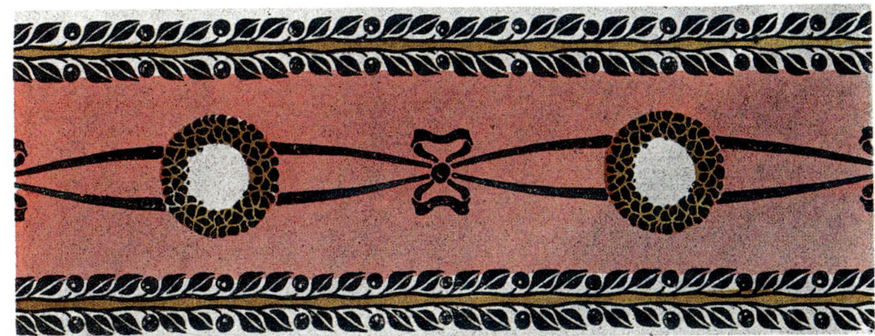
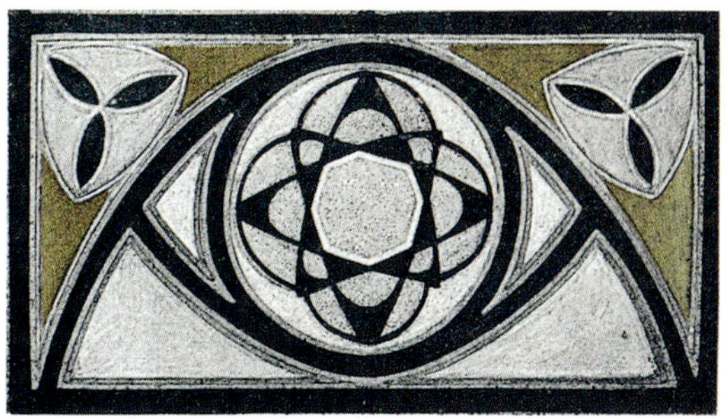

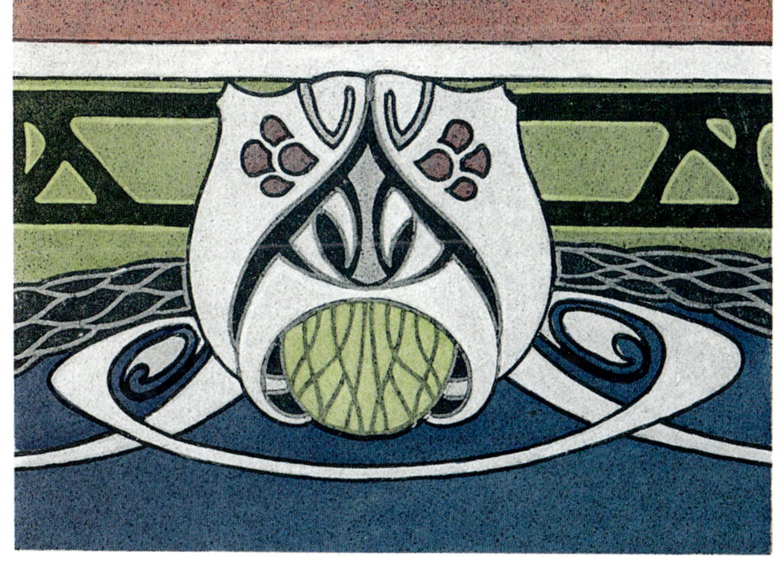
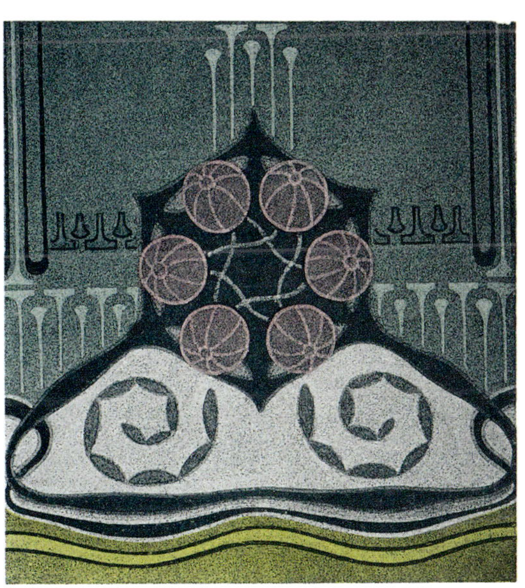

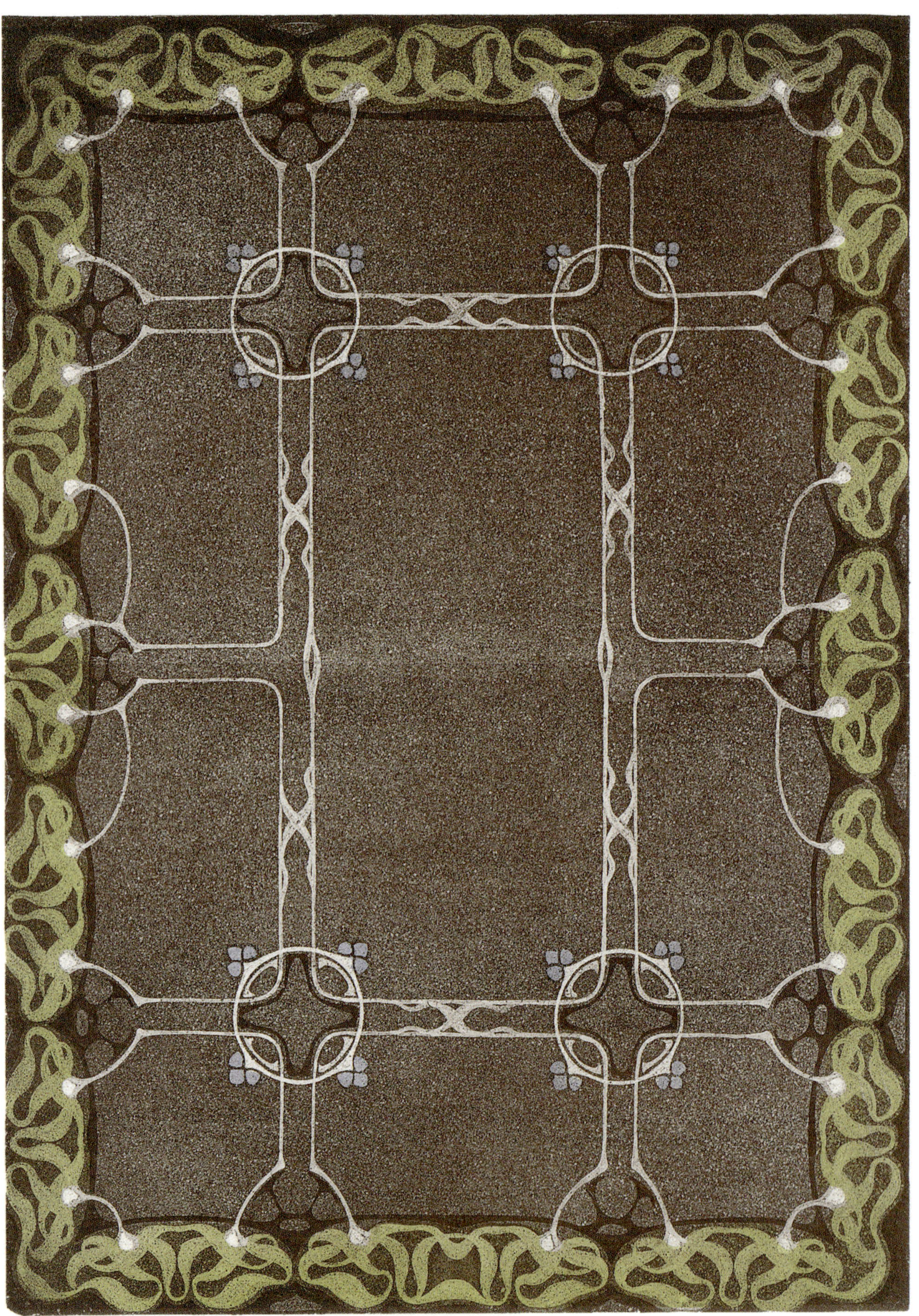

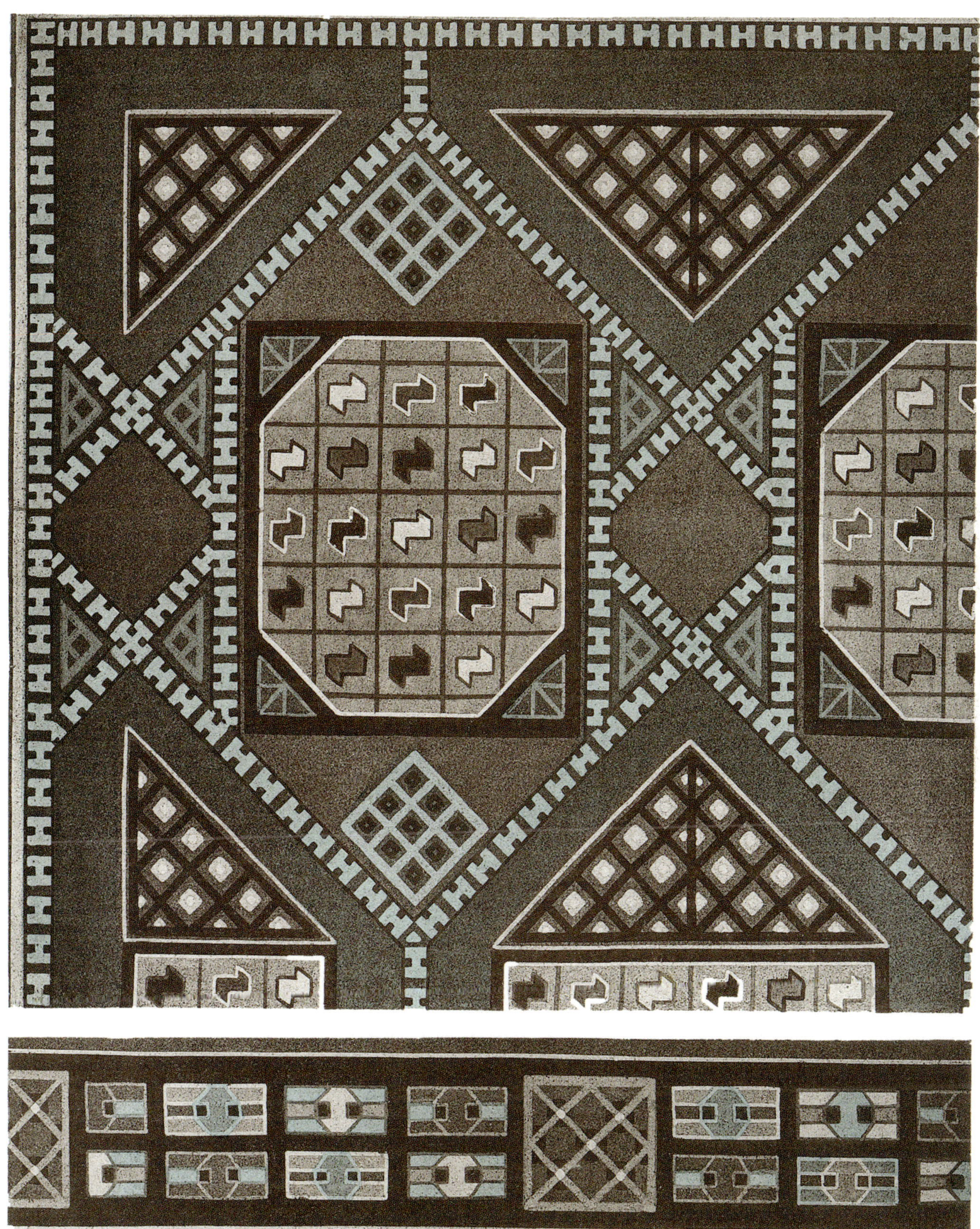

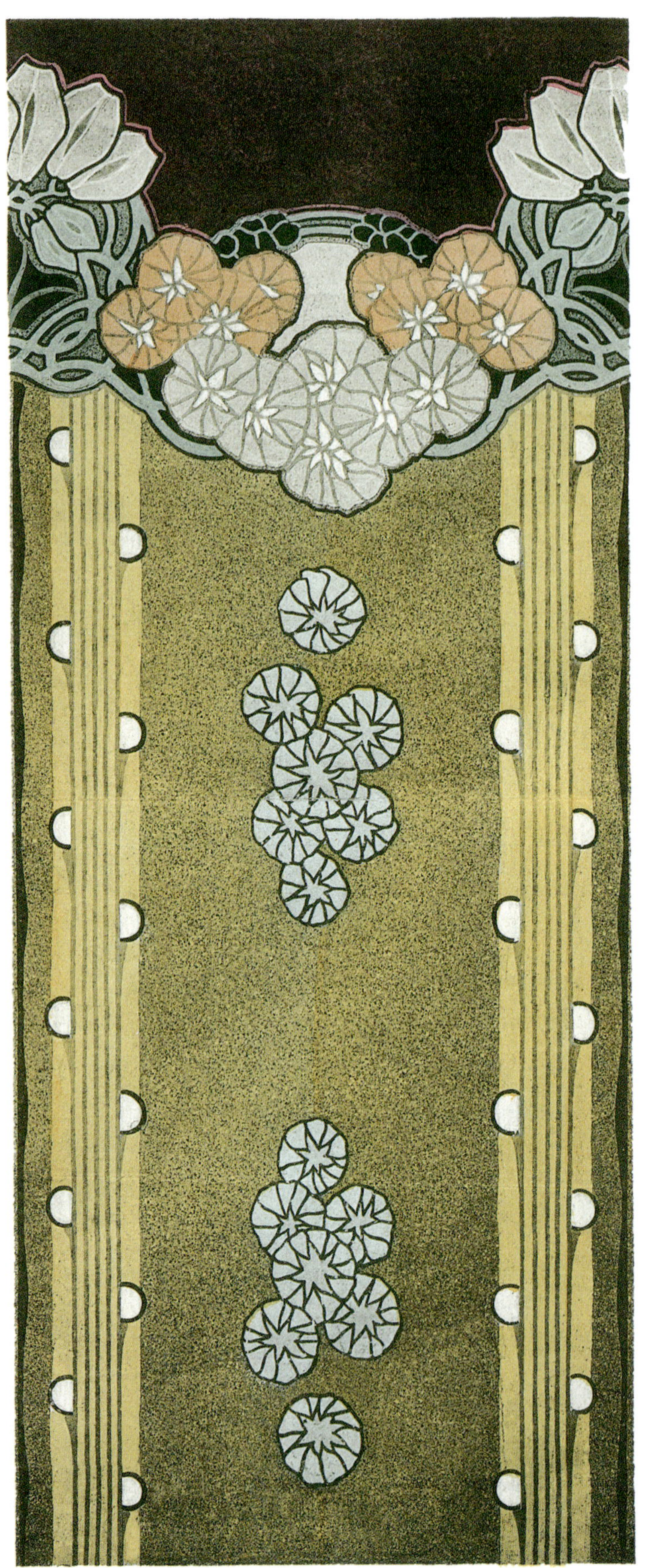

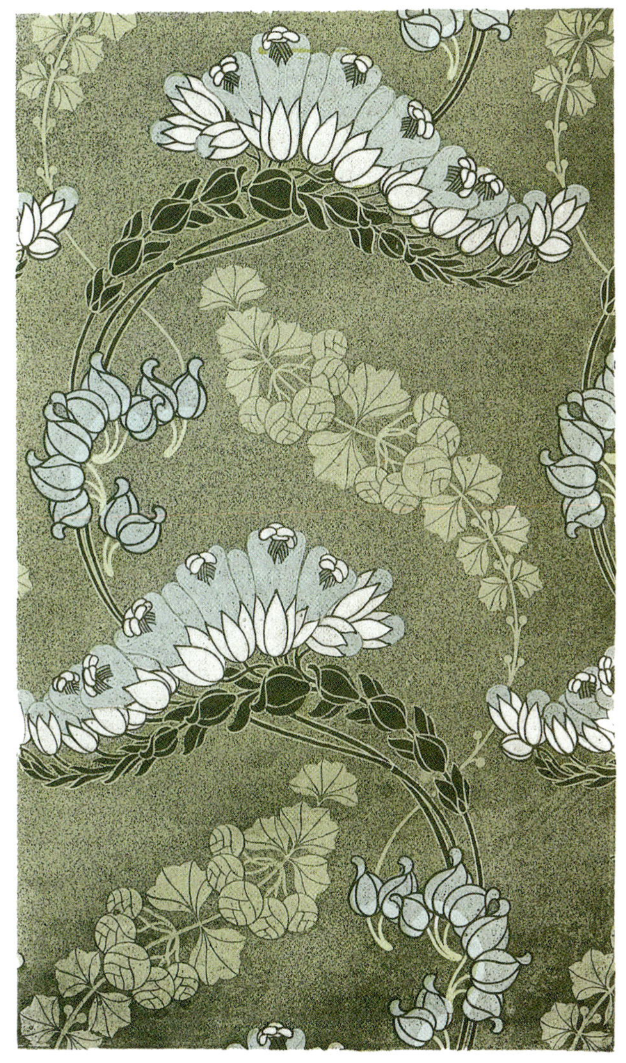
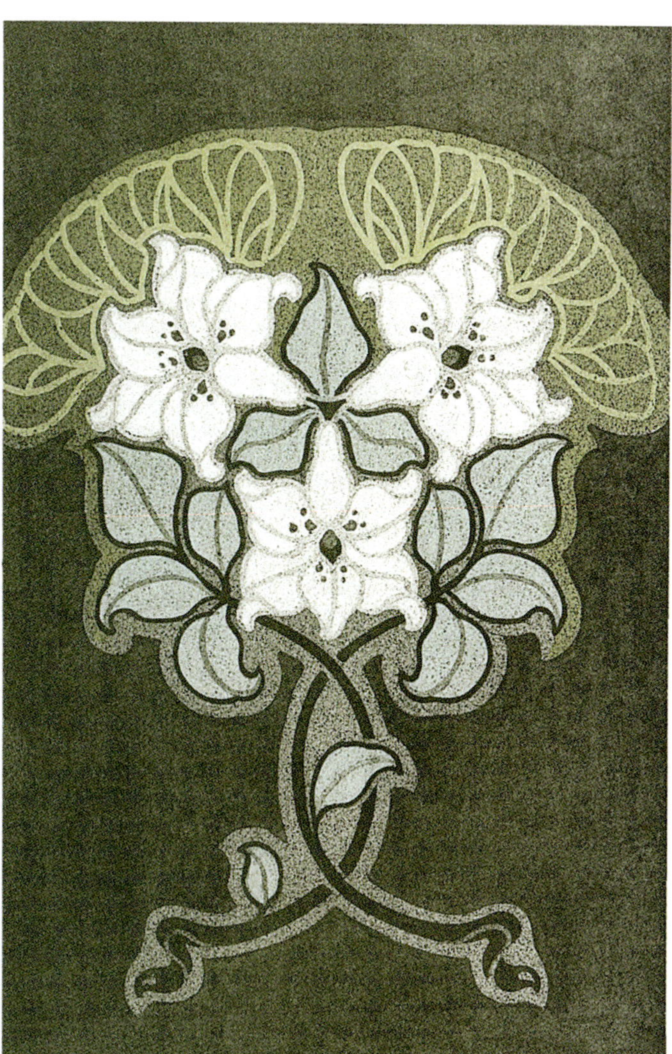
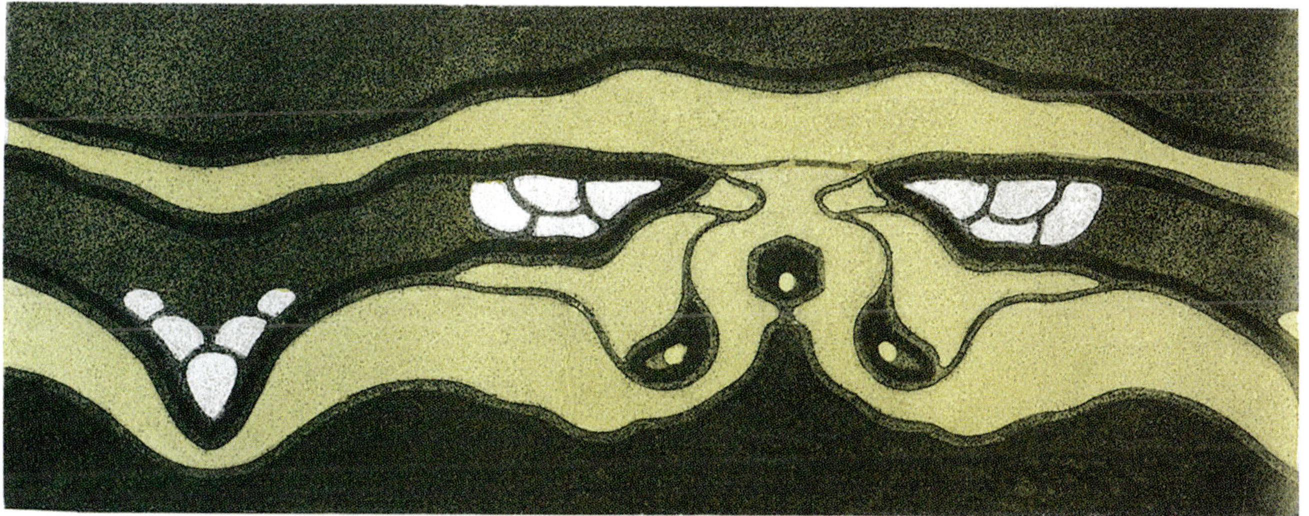
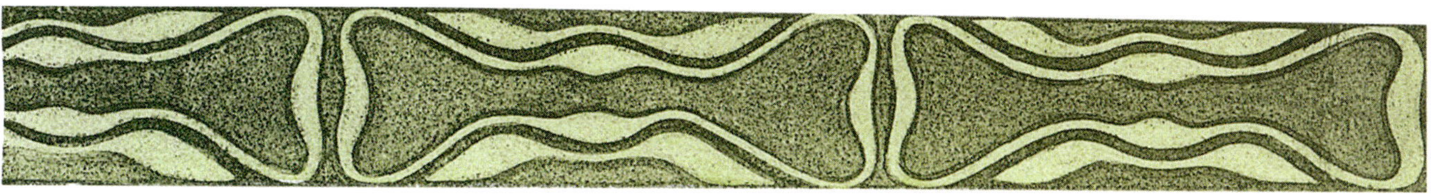

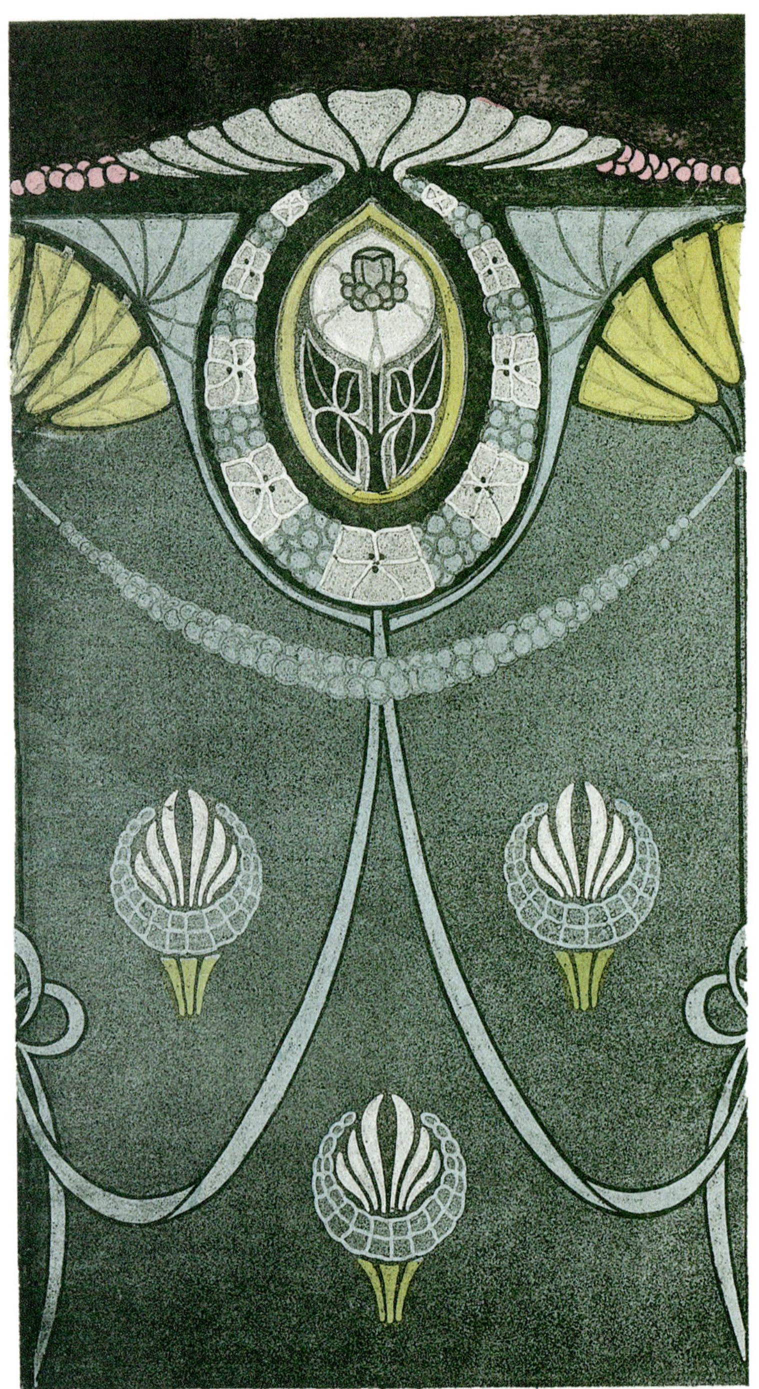
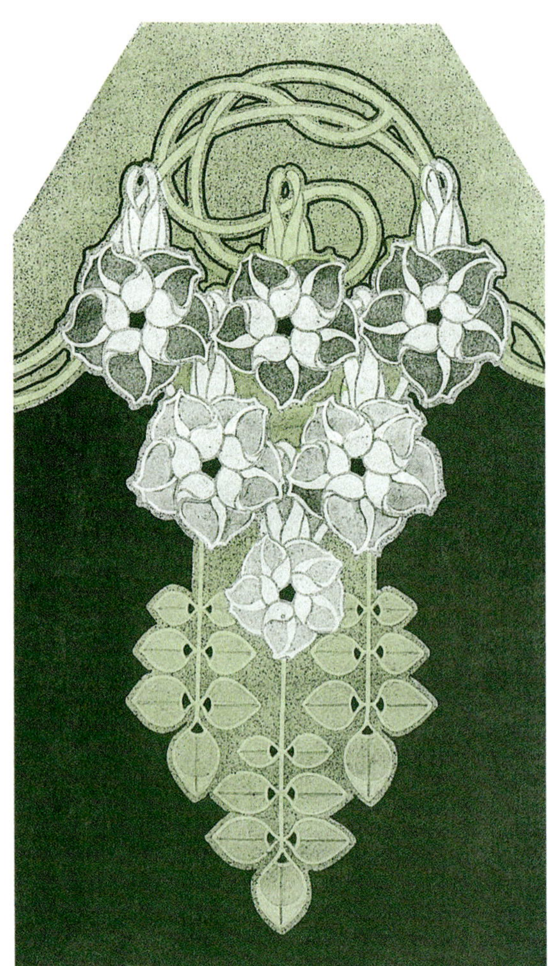
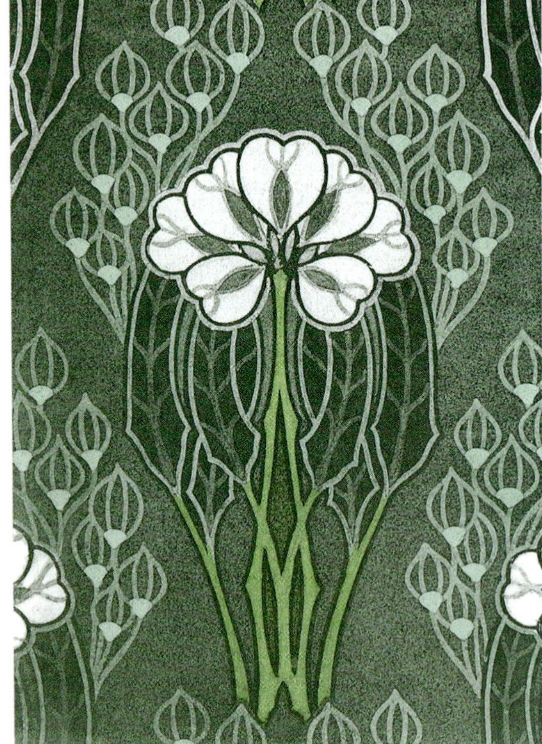
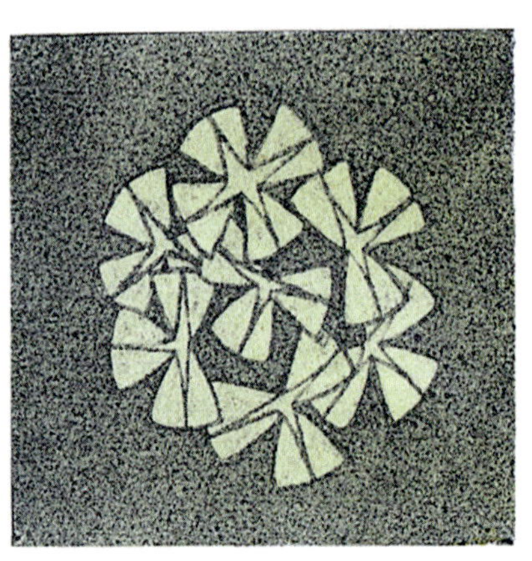
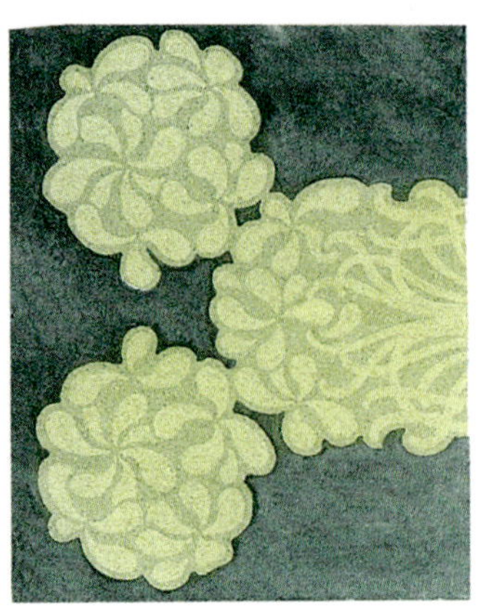

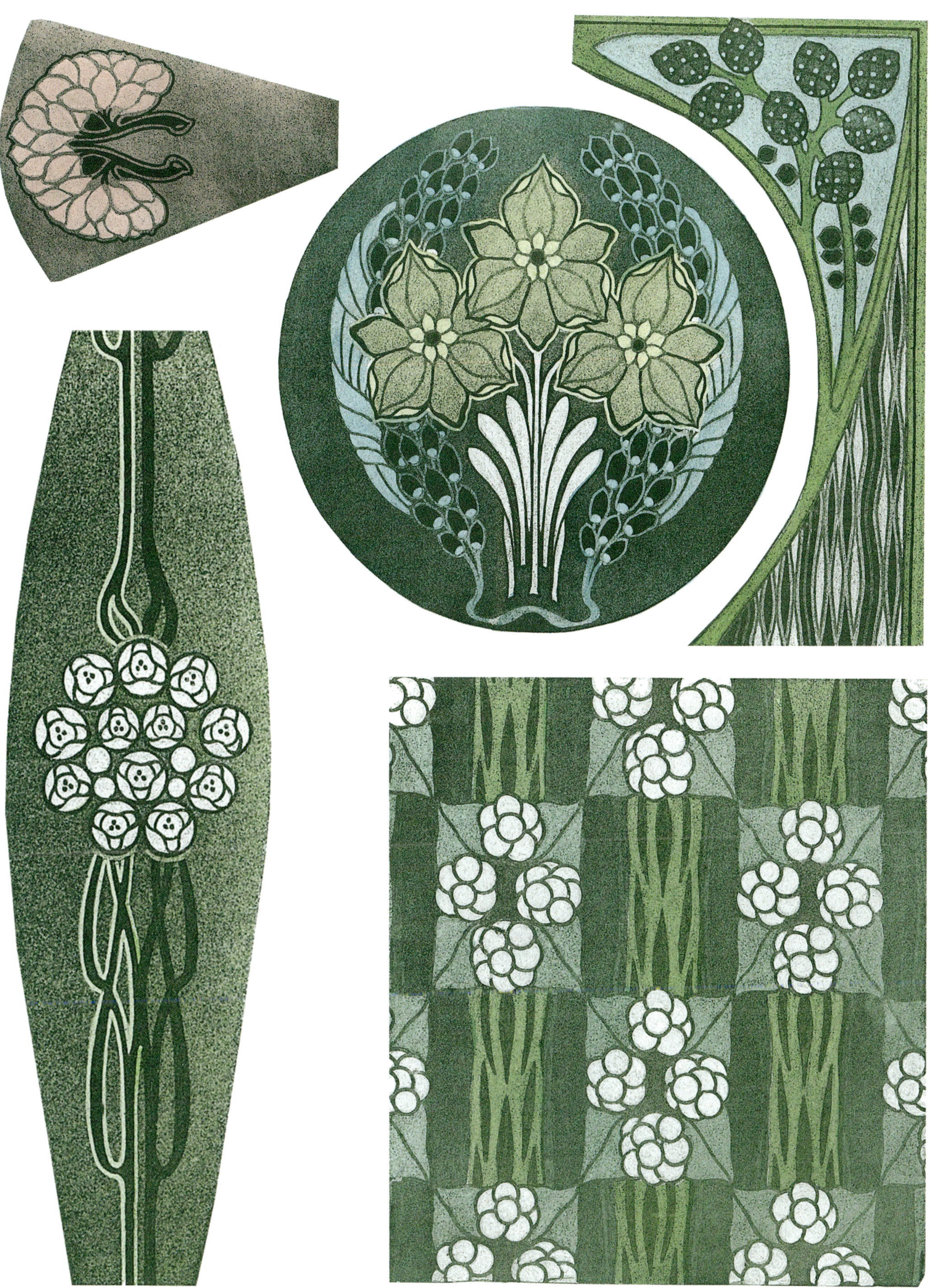

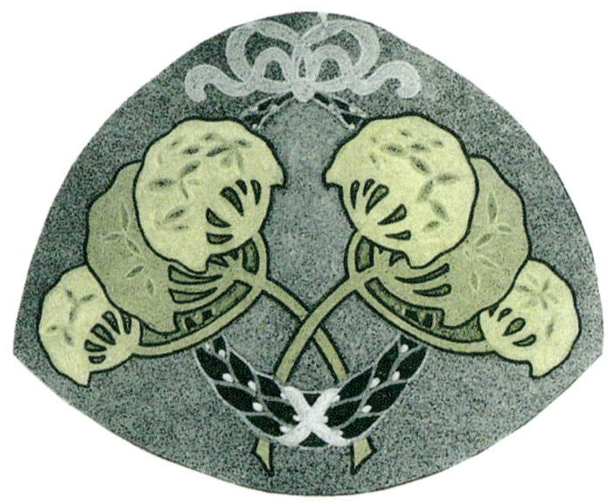

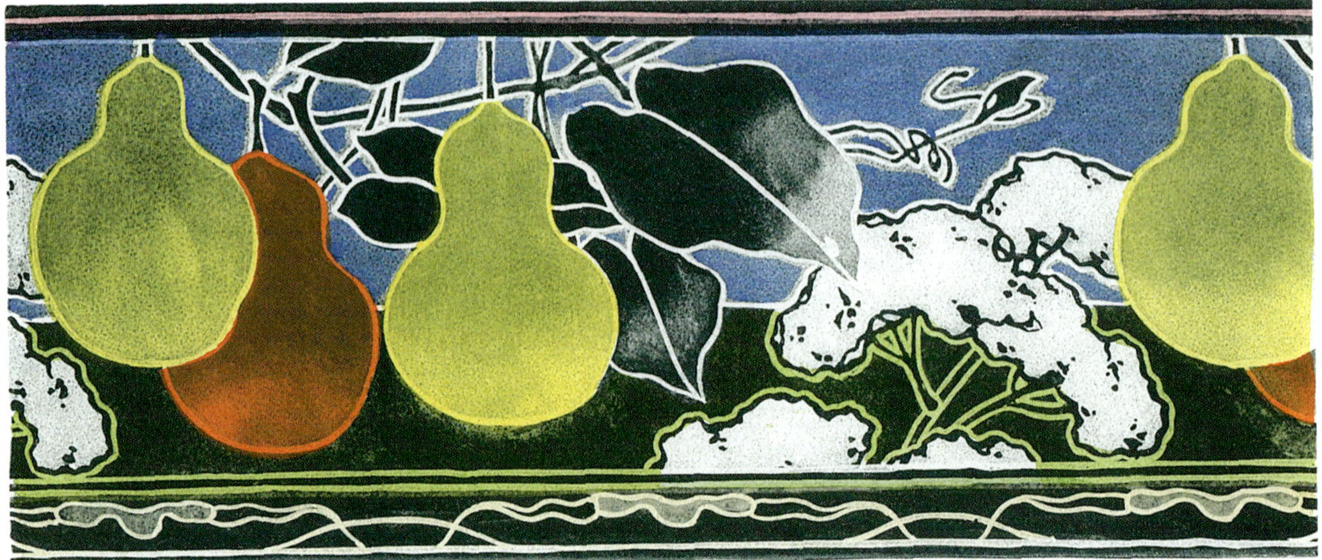

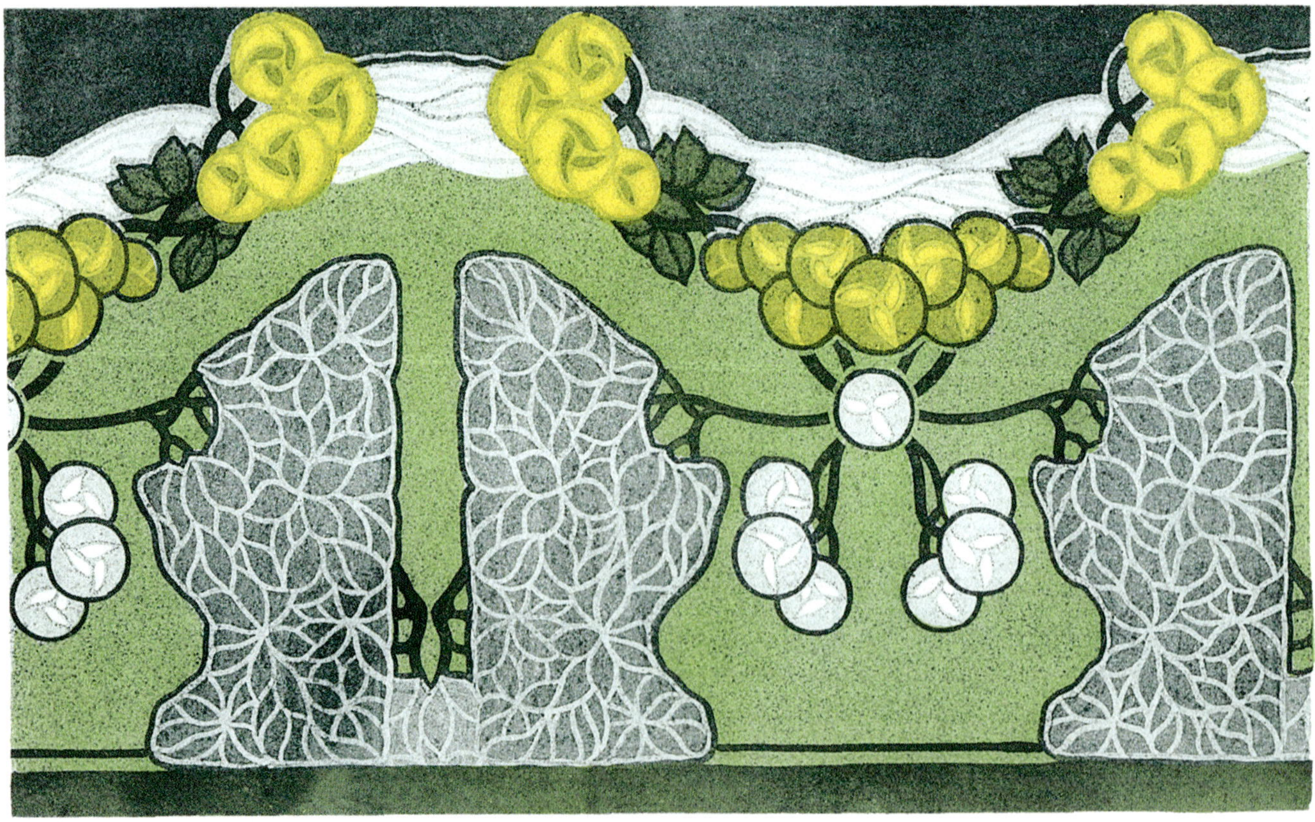

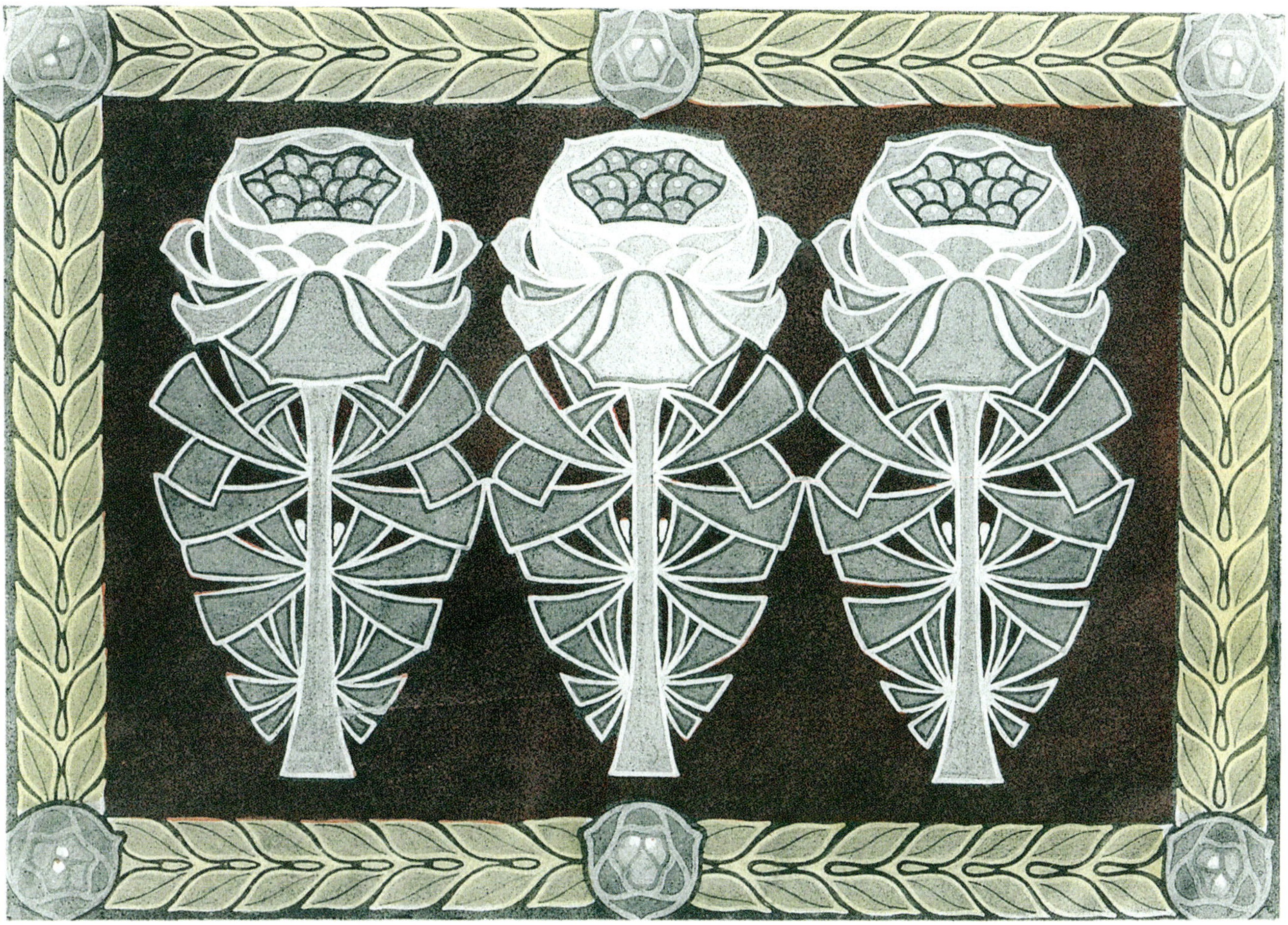

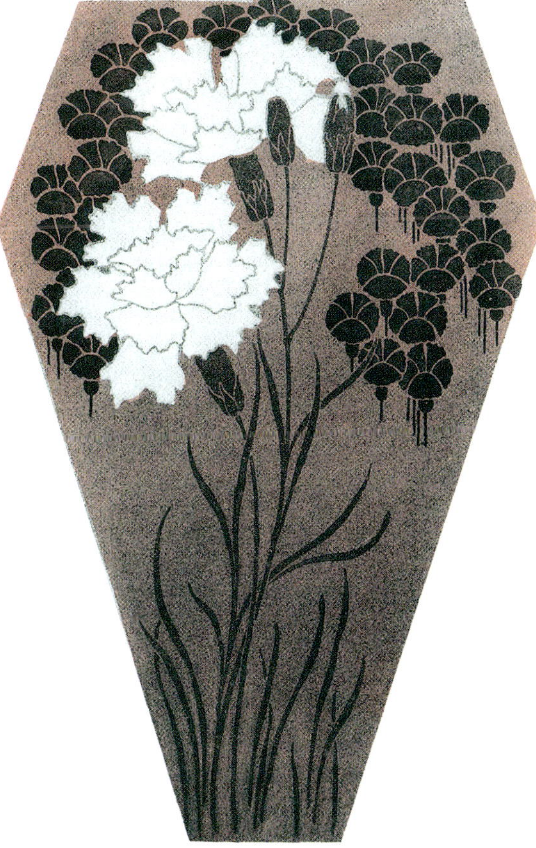

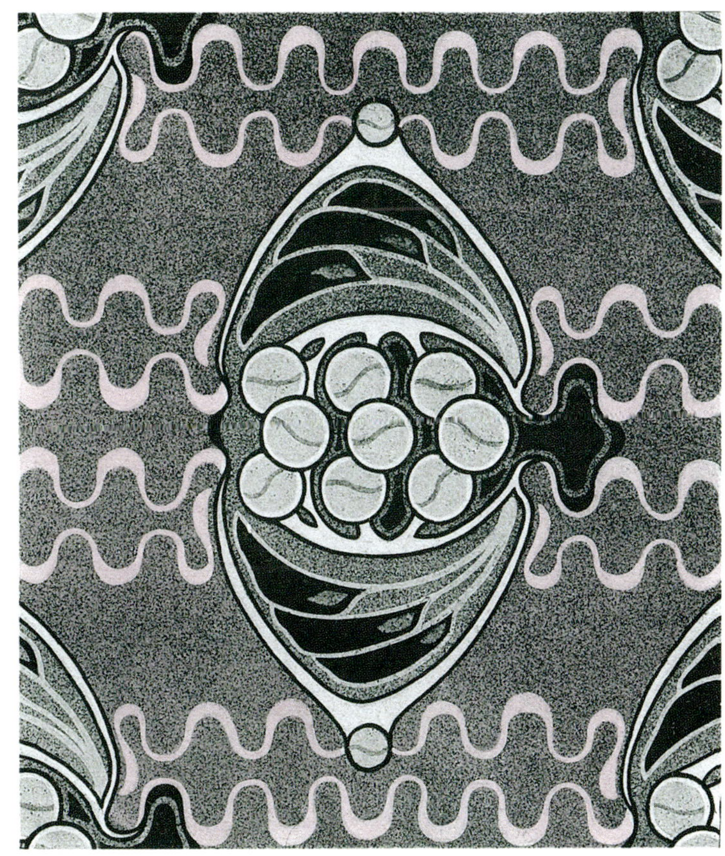

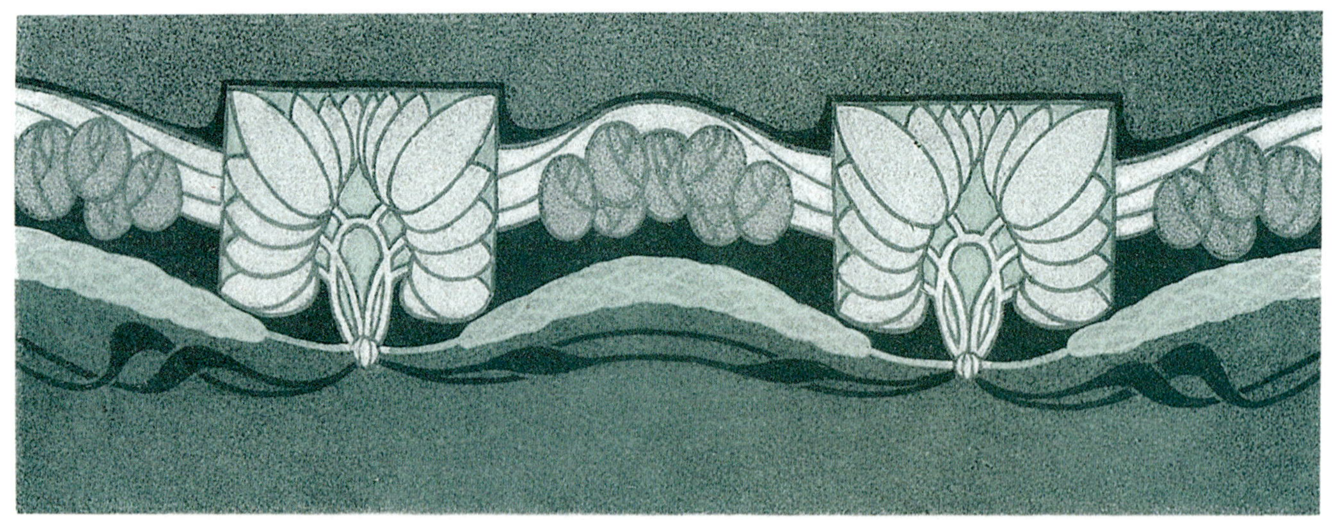

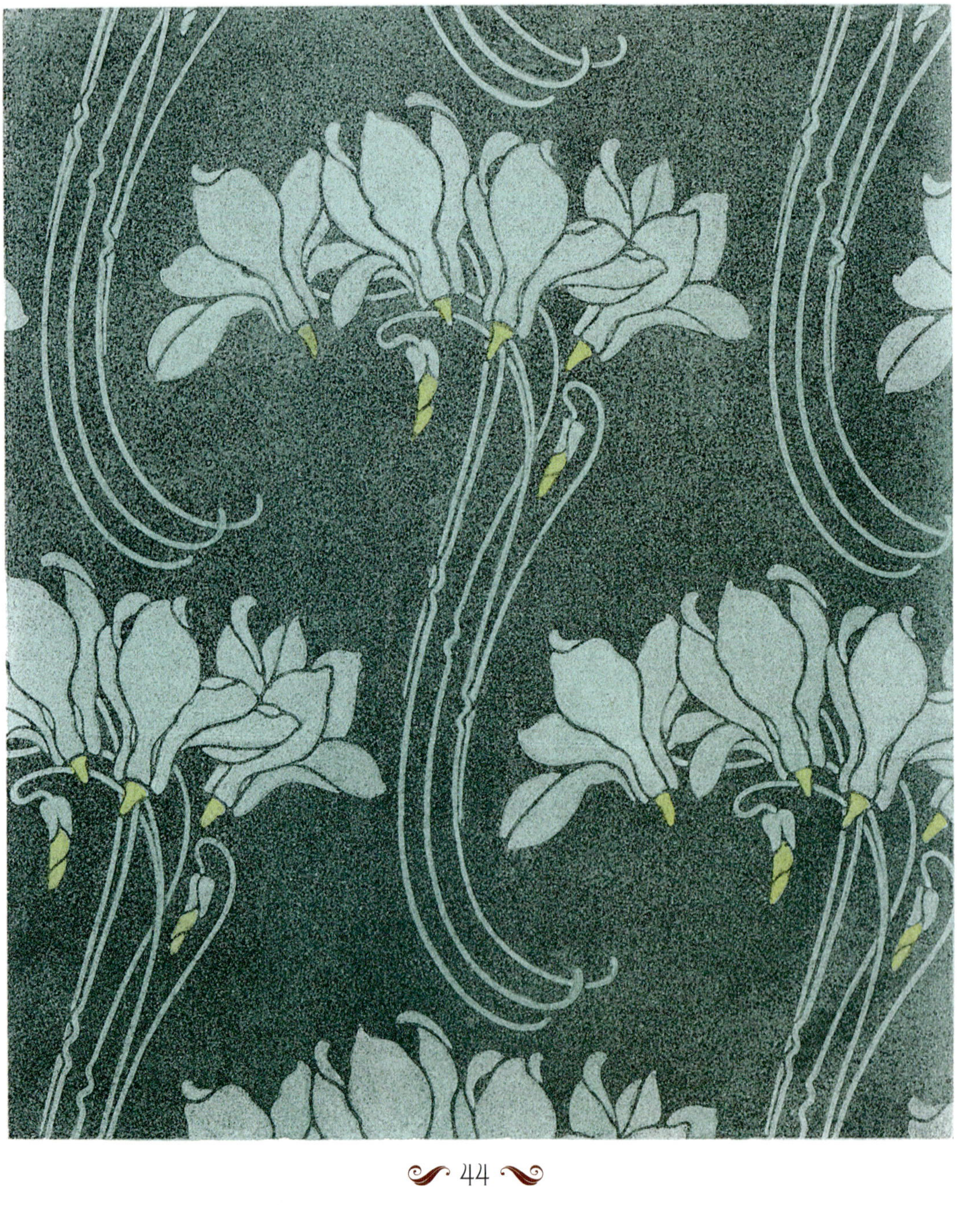

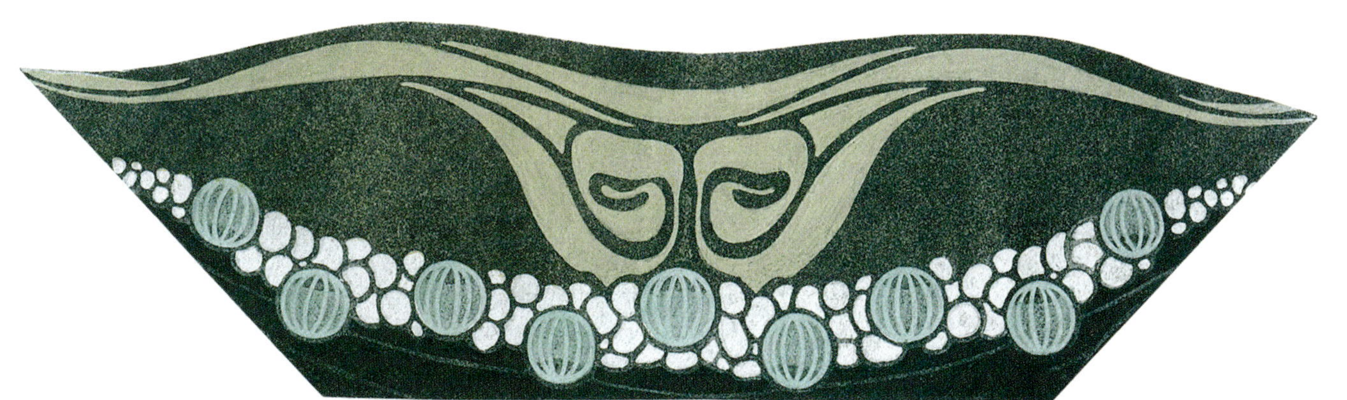

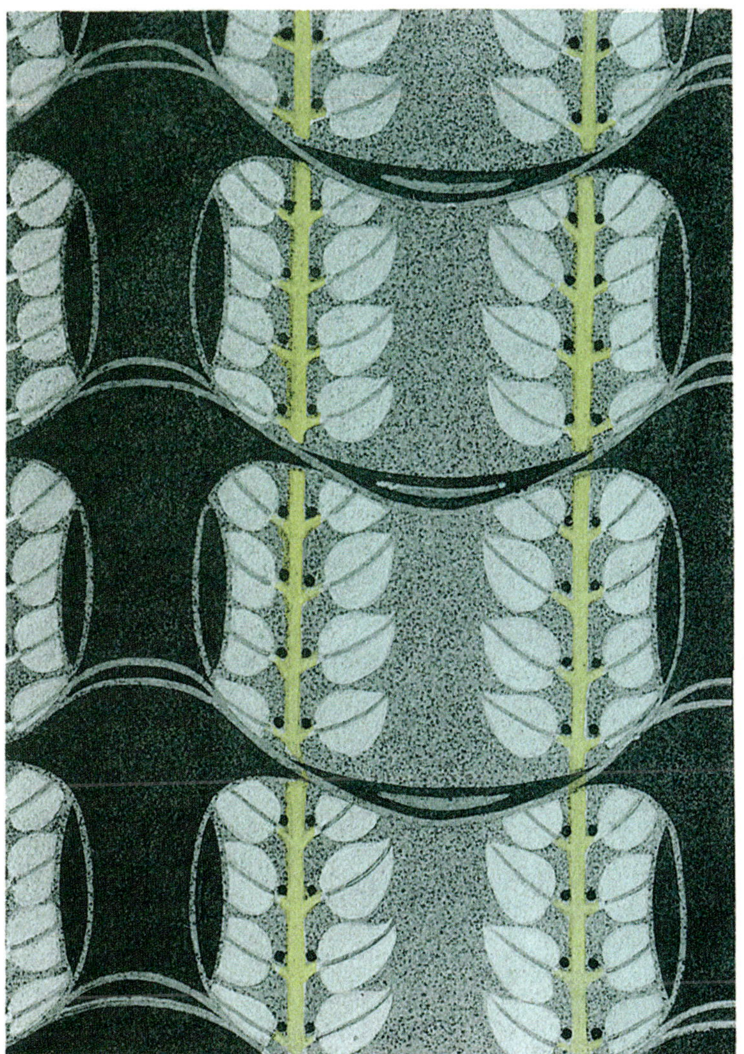

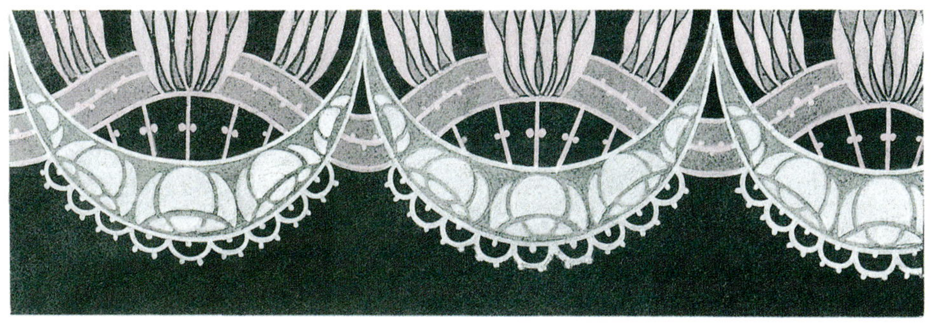

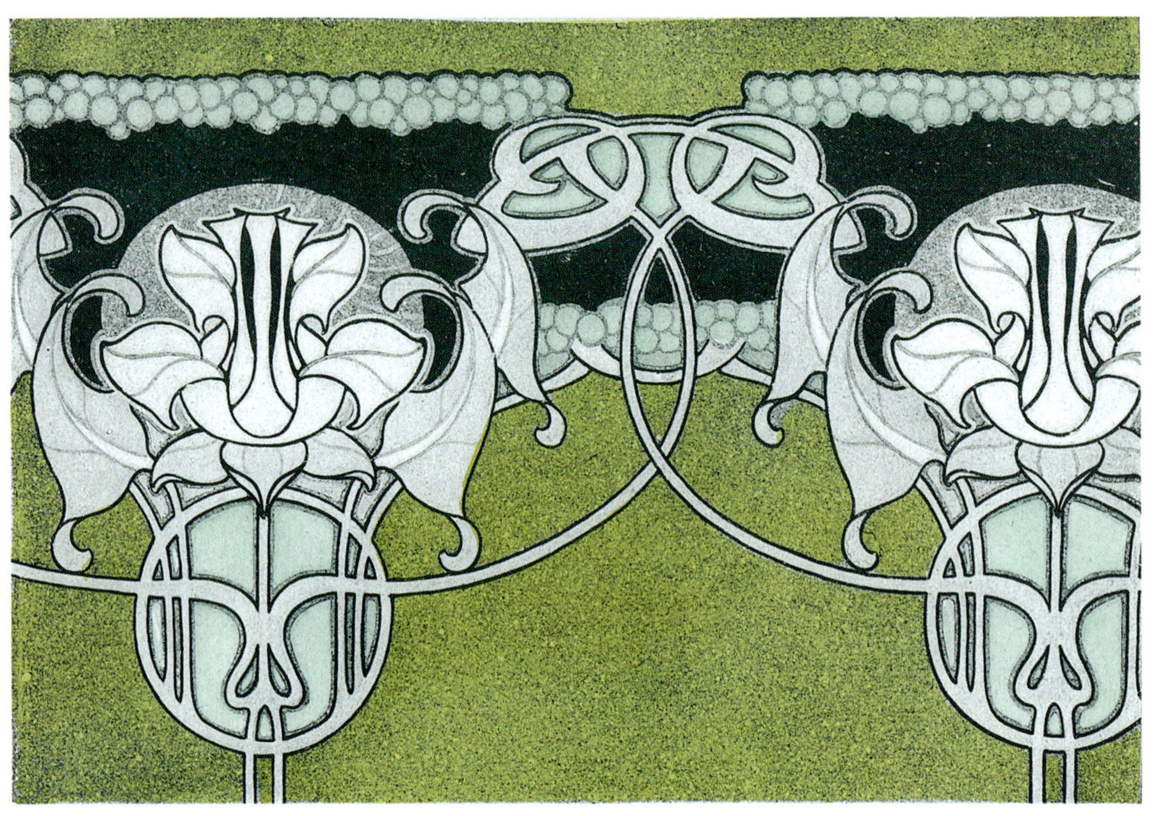

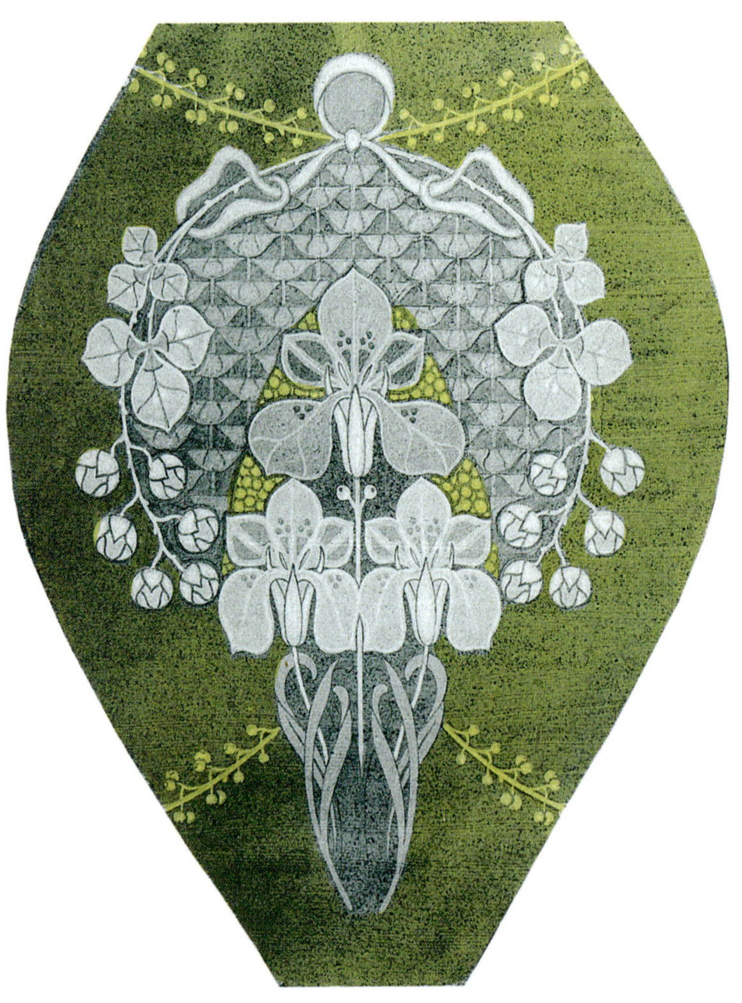

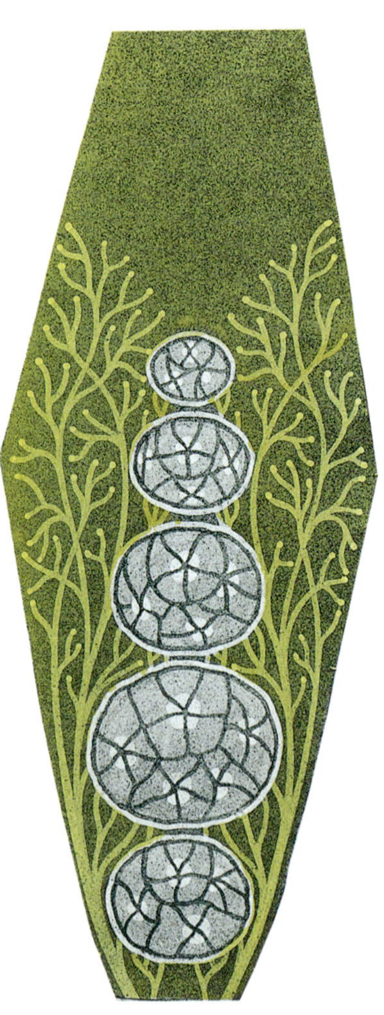

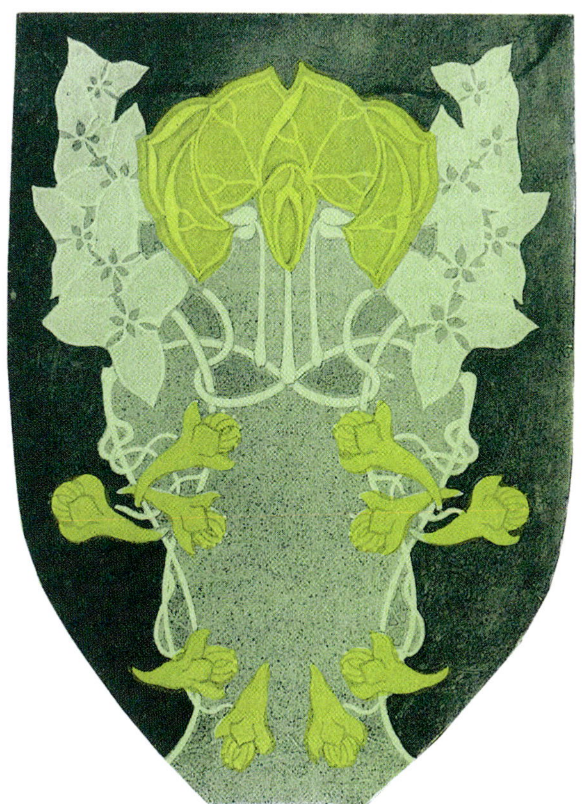
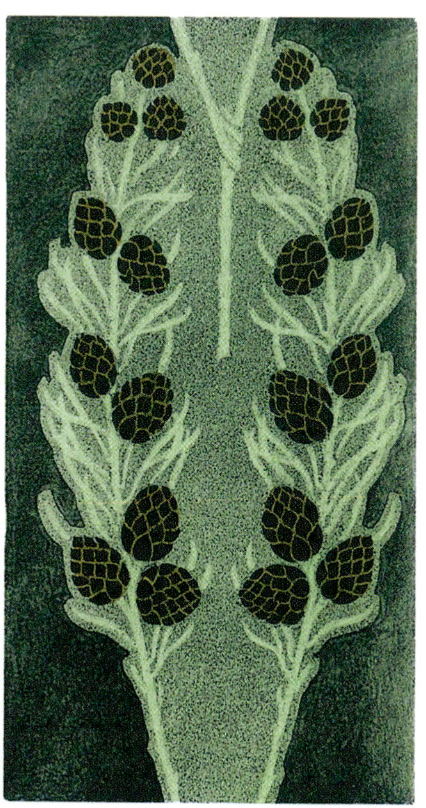
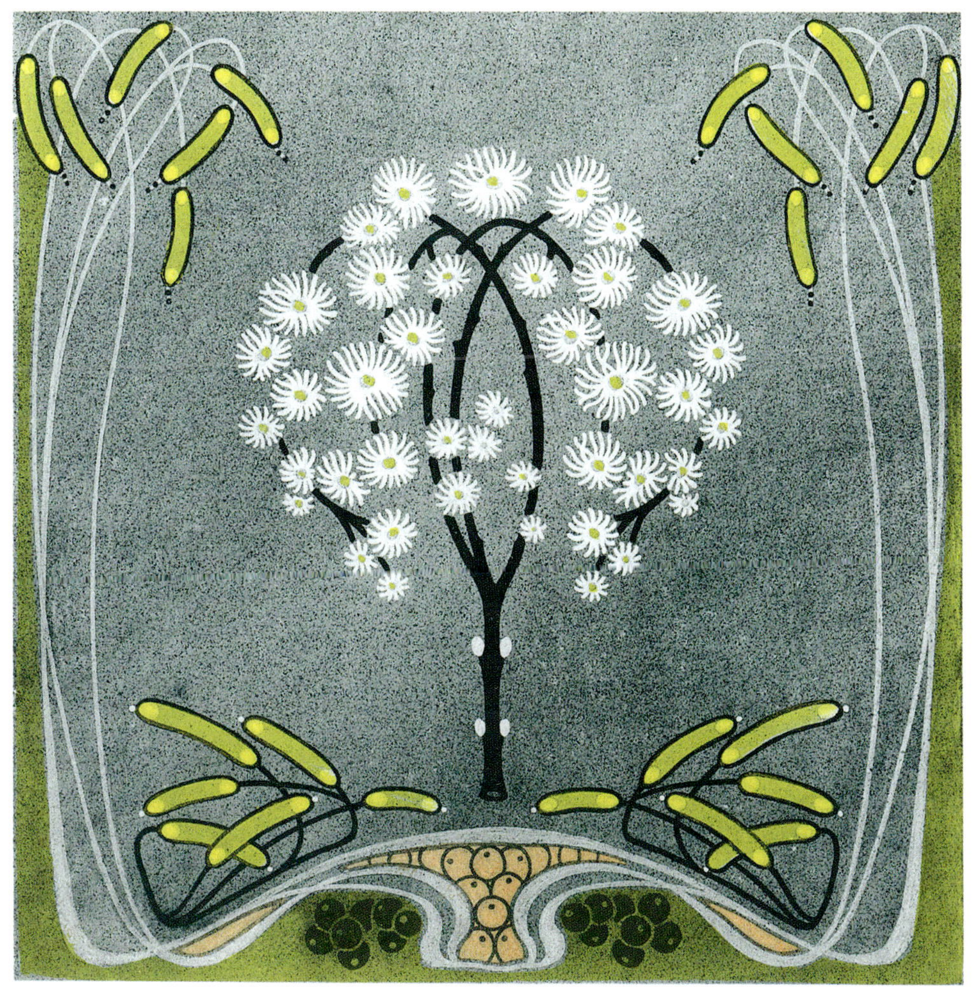

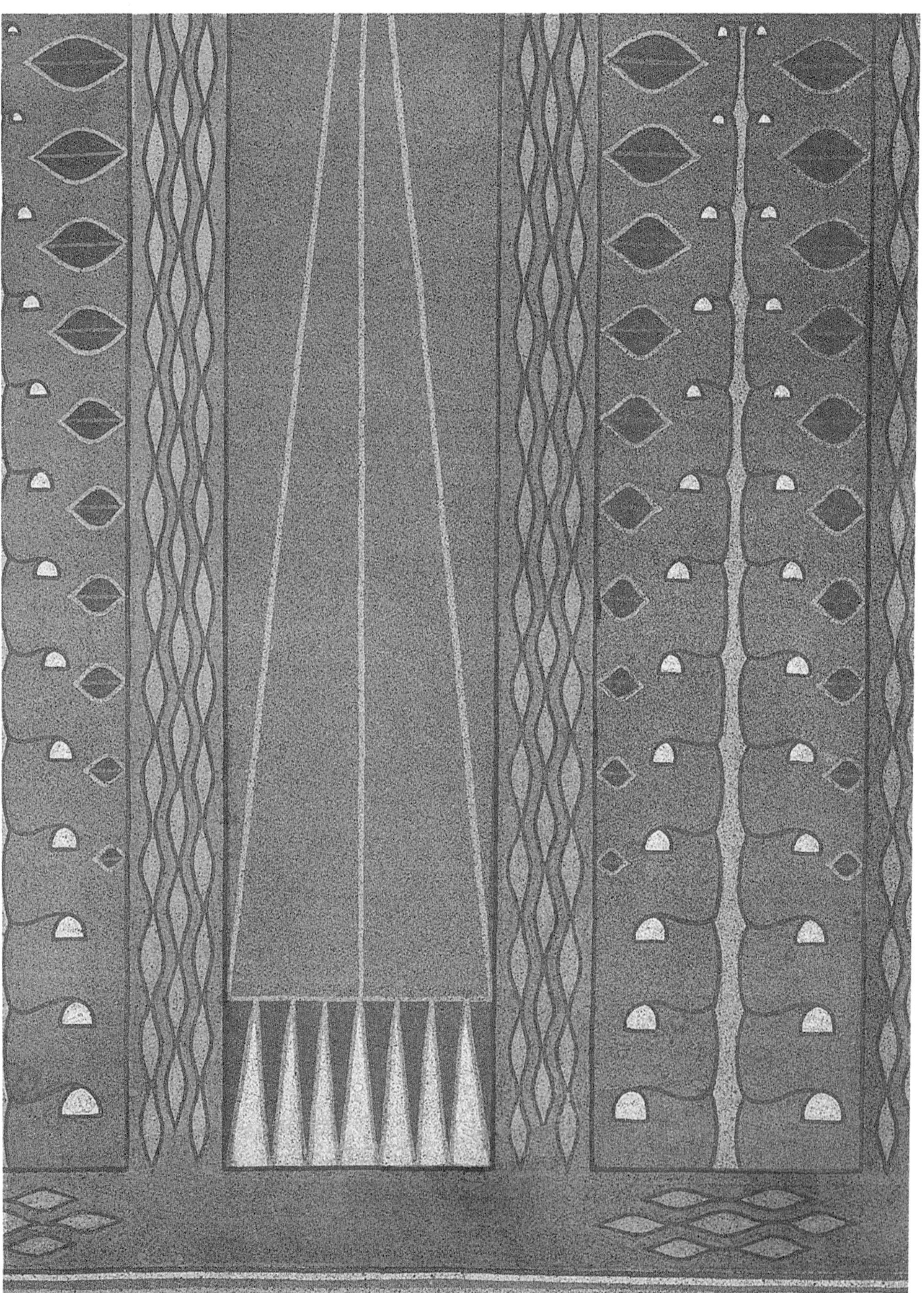

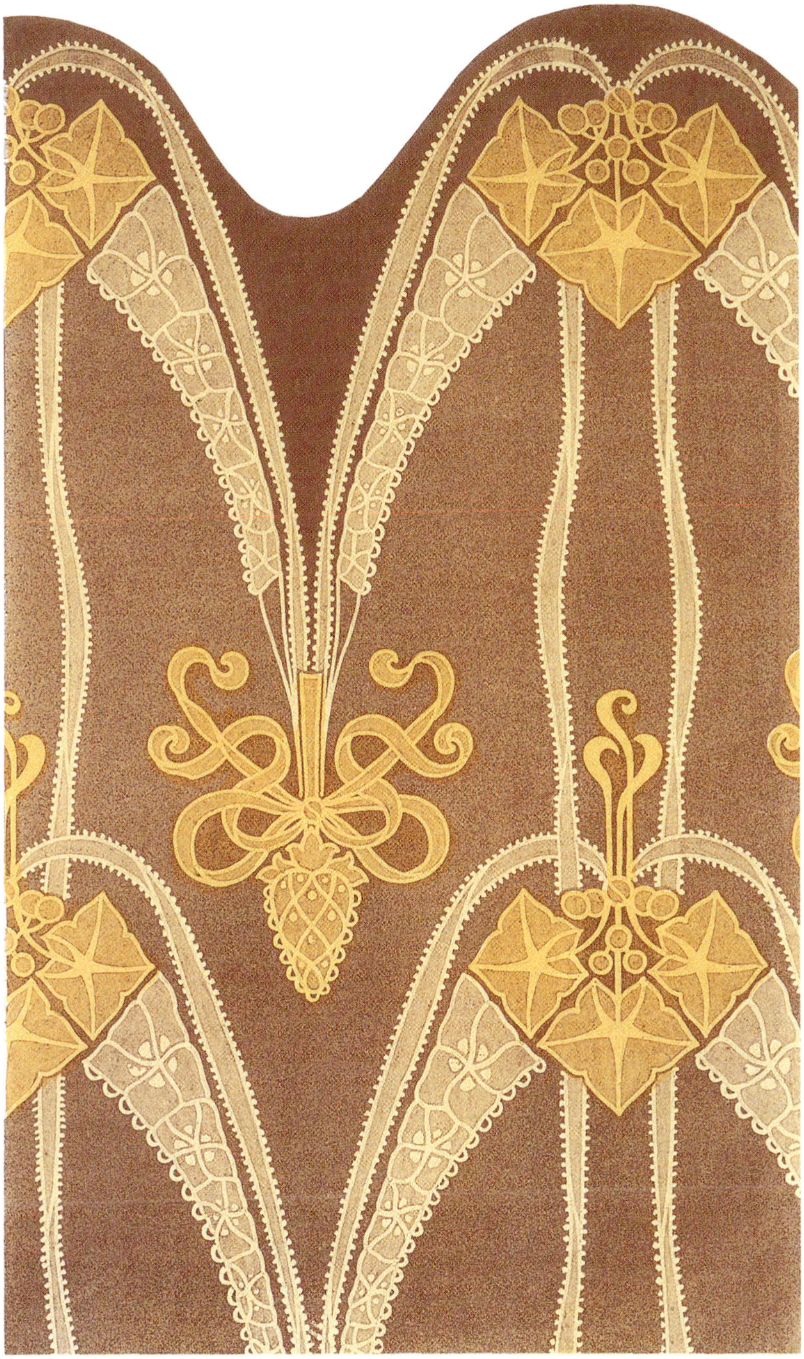

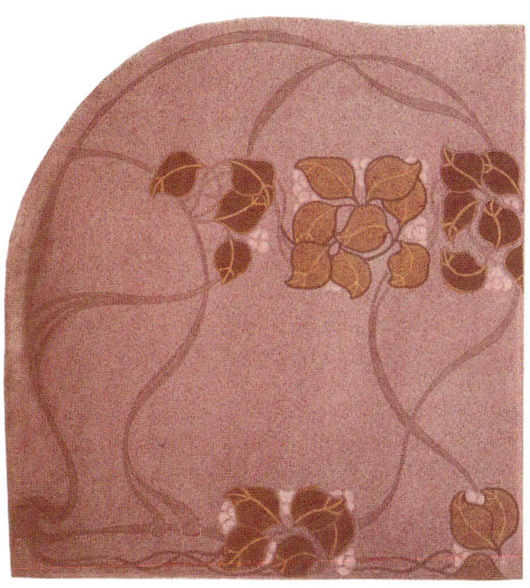

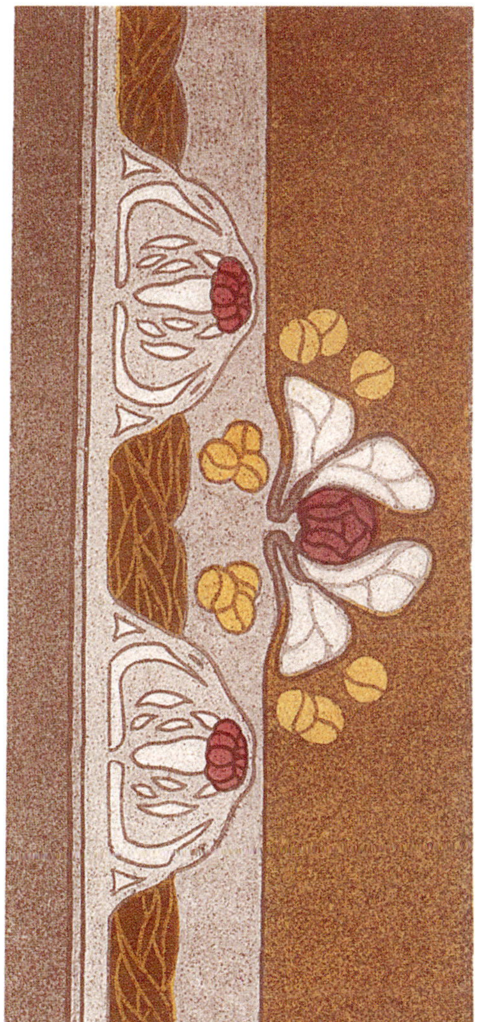

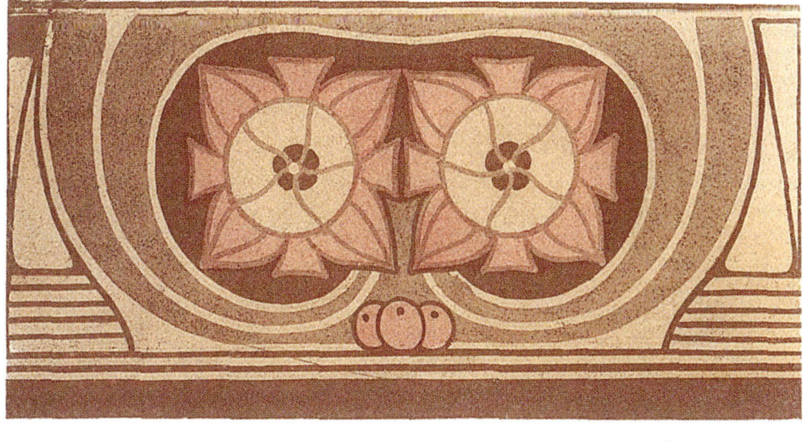

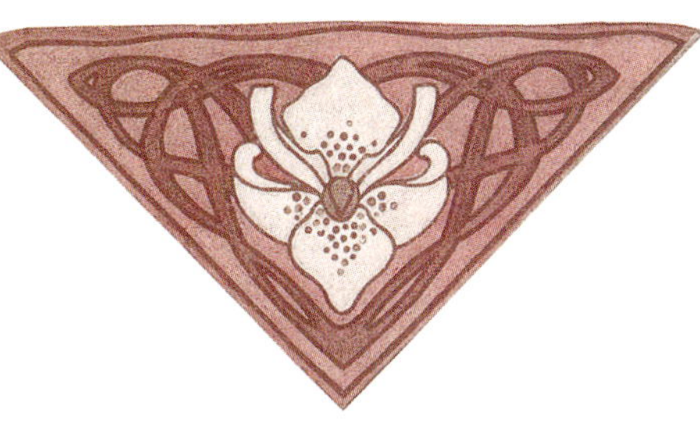

MONOCHROME
PLATES

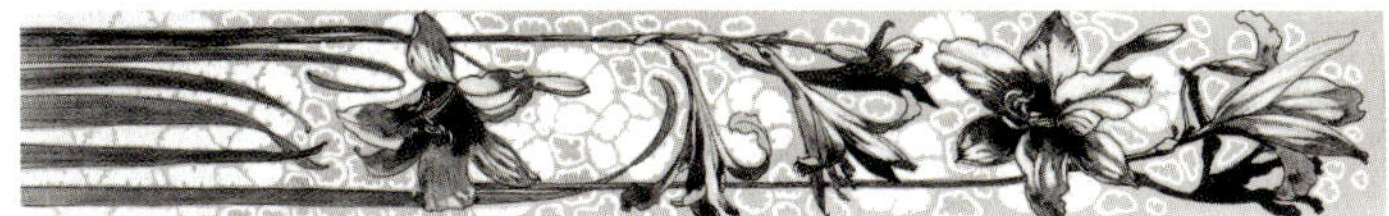

At the dawn of the twentieth century, imagery for decoration and textile usage was dominated by floral forms. Josef Pilters became quite well-known for his floral paintings. Here we can appreciate his raw design abilities with the same organic subject that he found so compelling. Like the full-color plates, these monochrome plates were originally printed as collotypes. They range in shades from warm grays to deep, rich blues. This collection begins with Pilters's attractive renderings and transforms over the decade to reflect the stylistic tastes of the day.

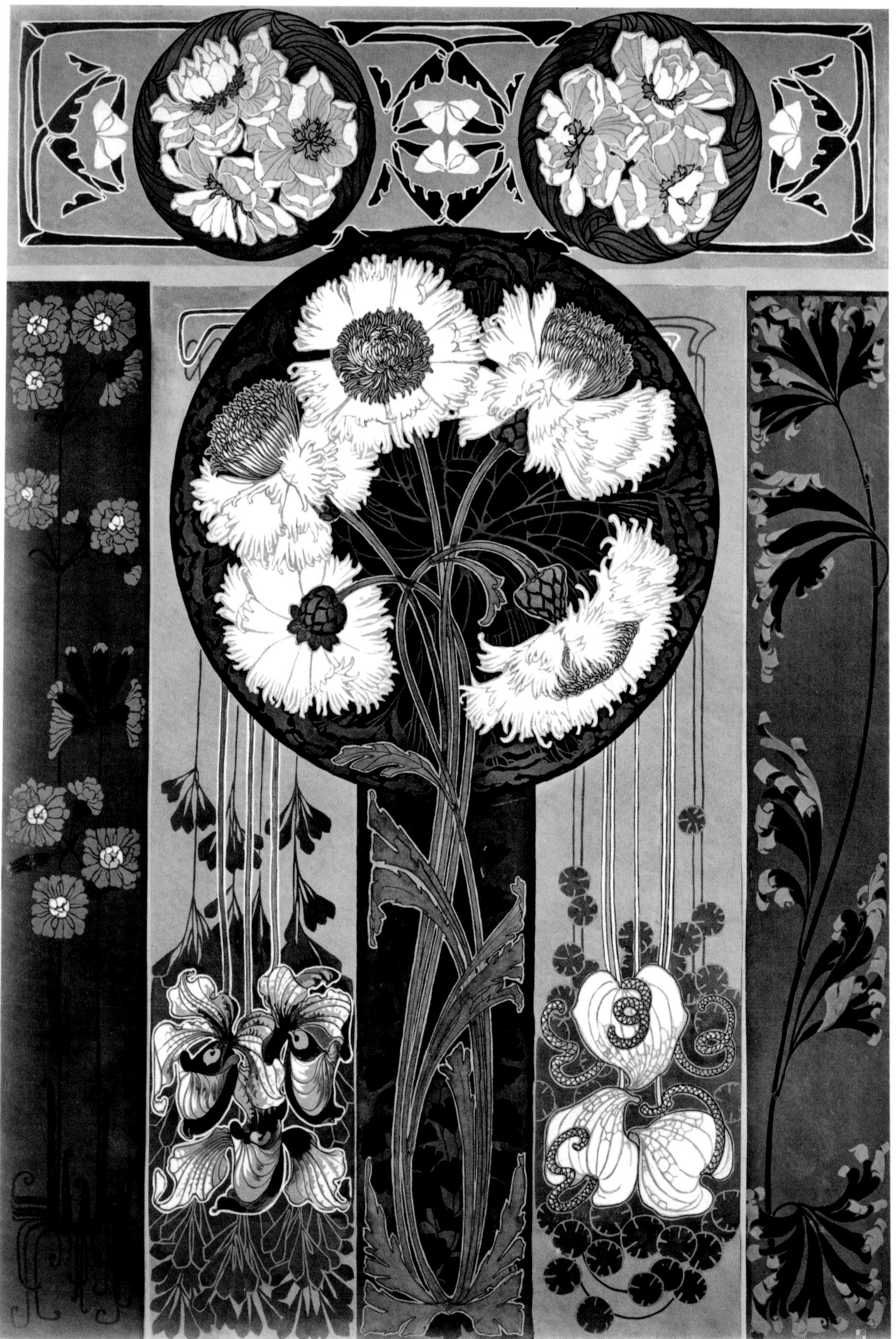

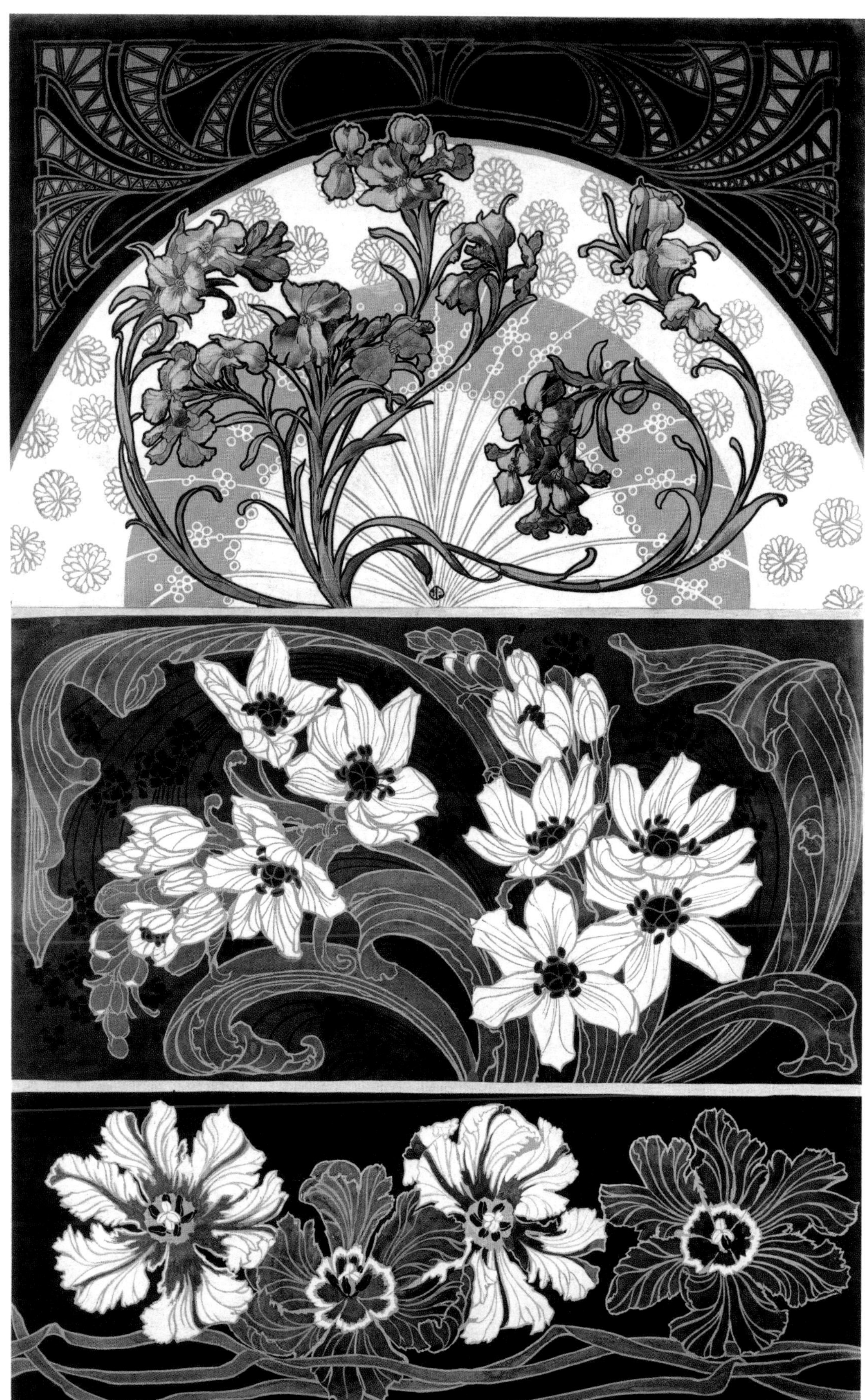

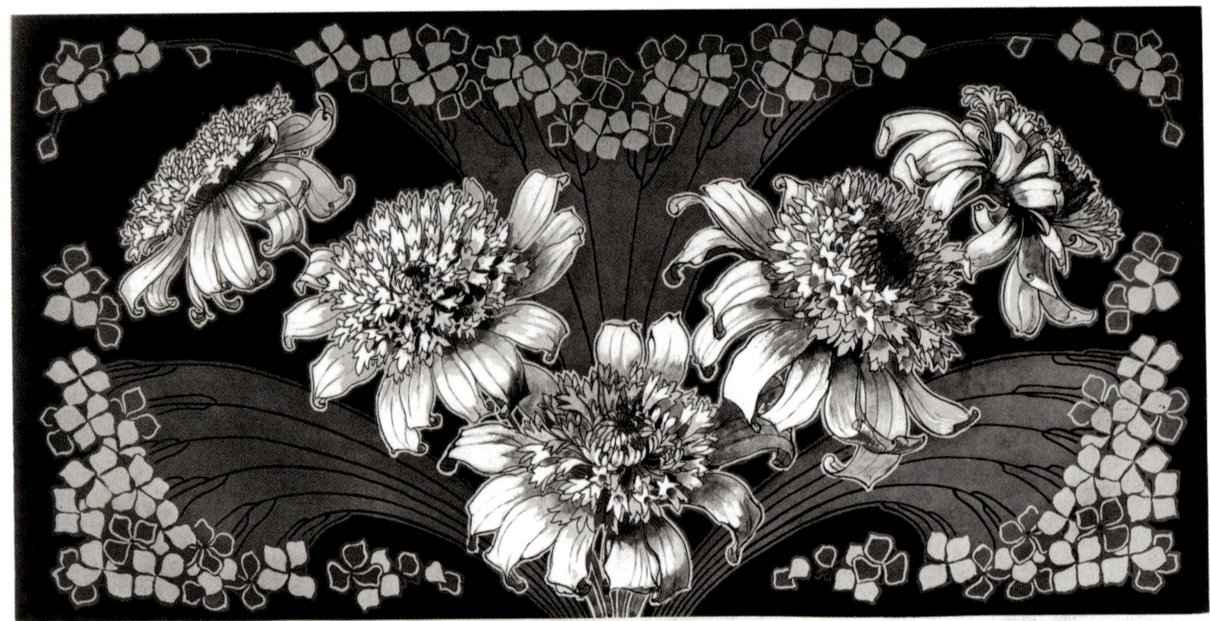

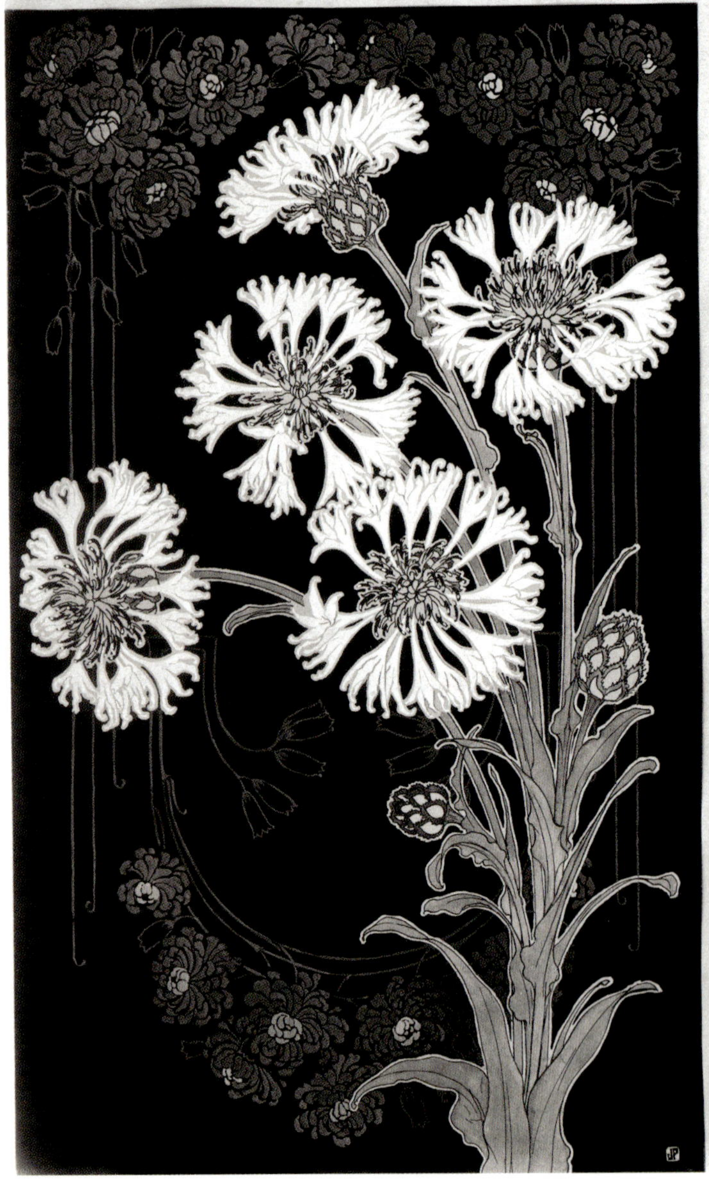

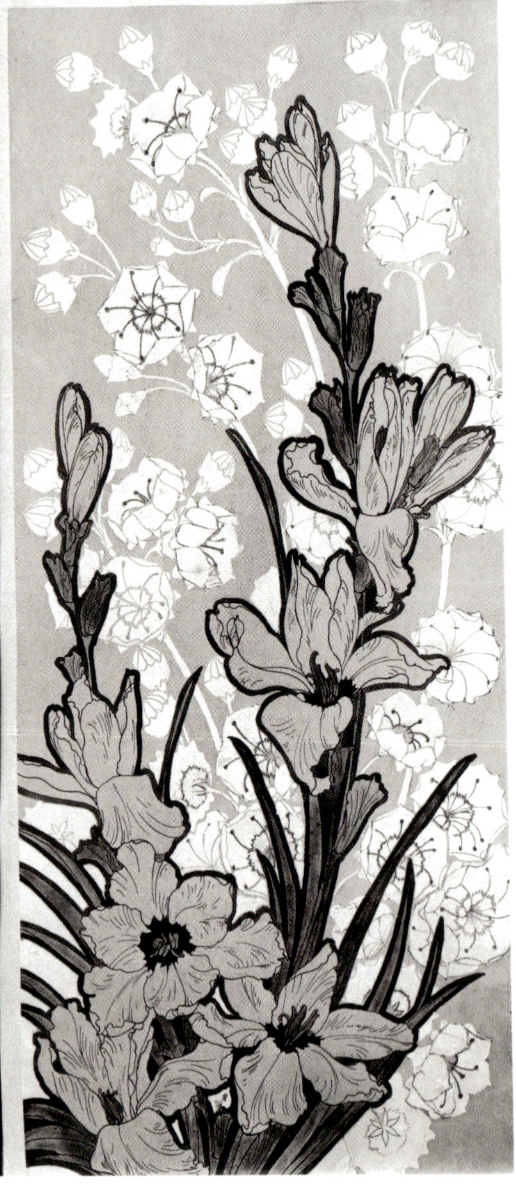

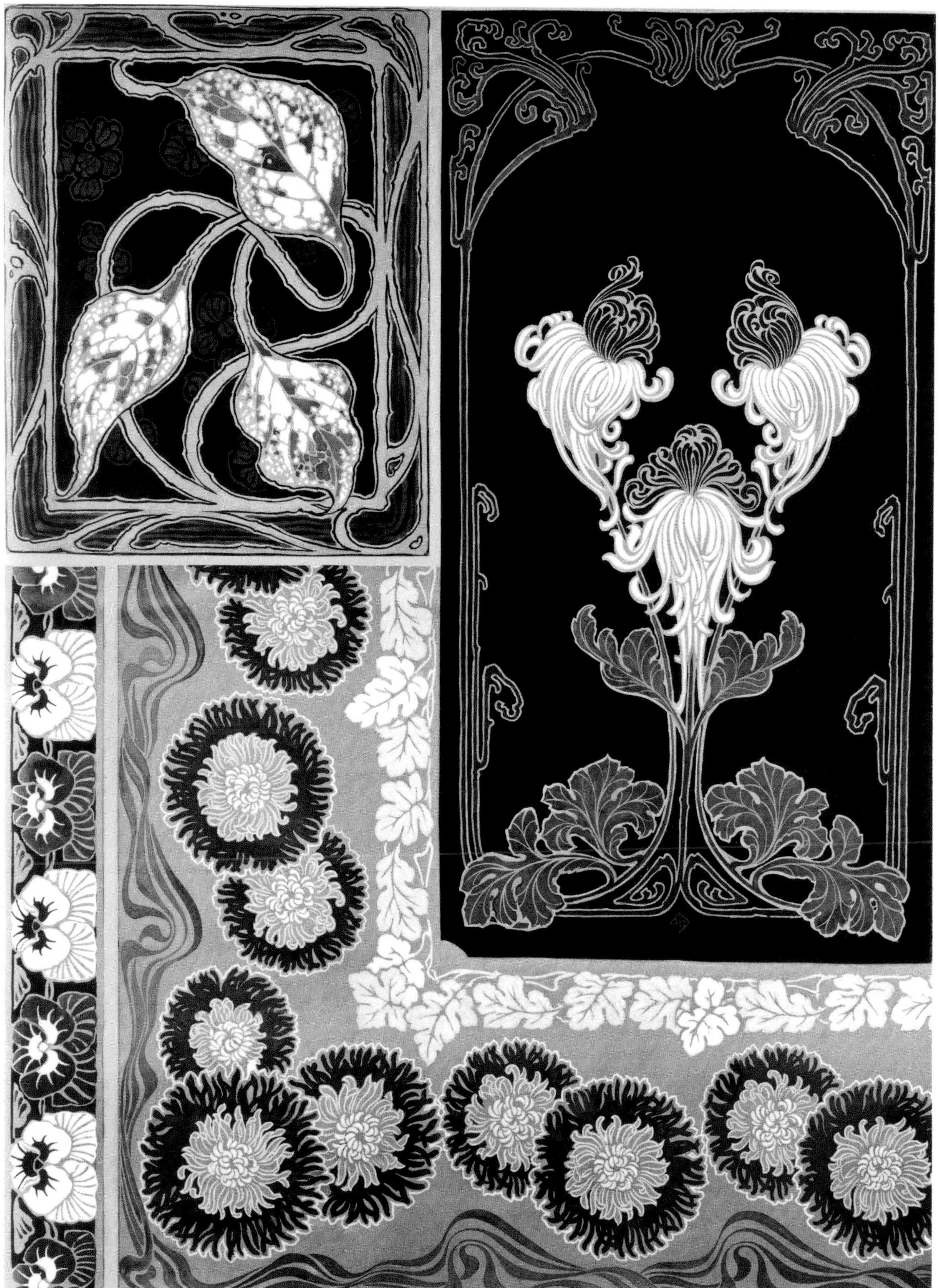

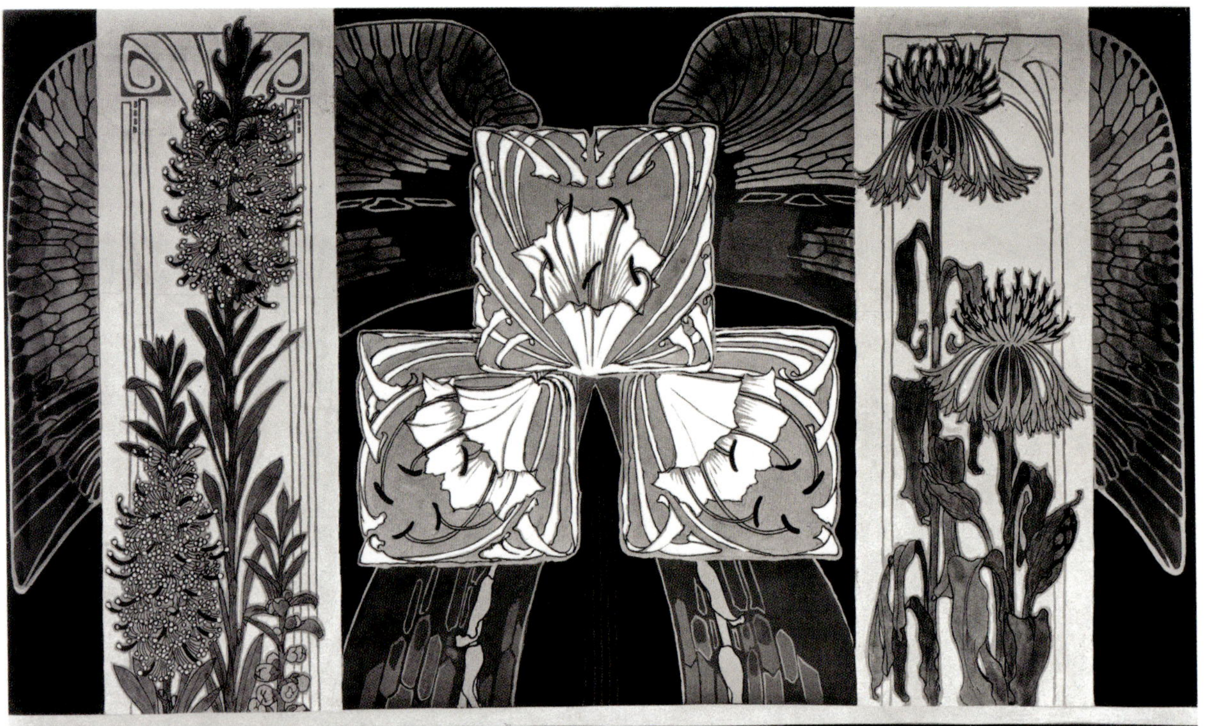

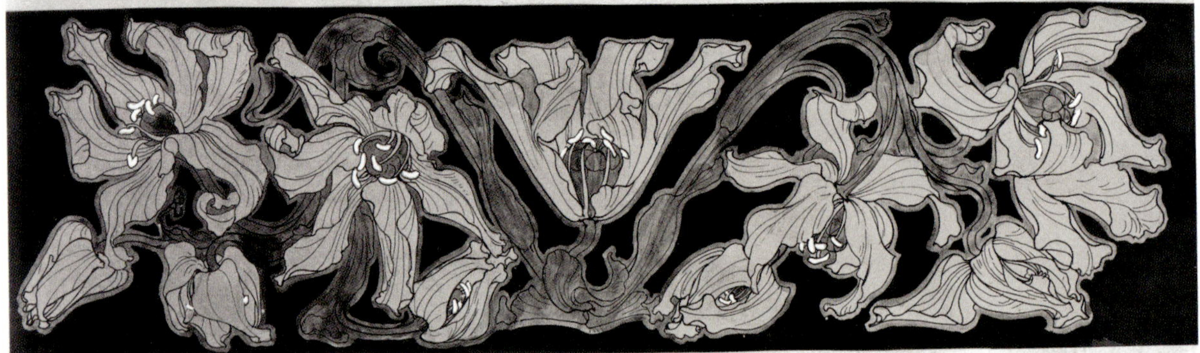

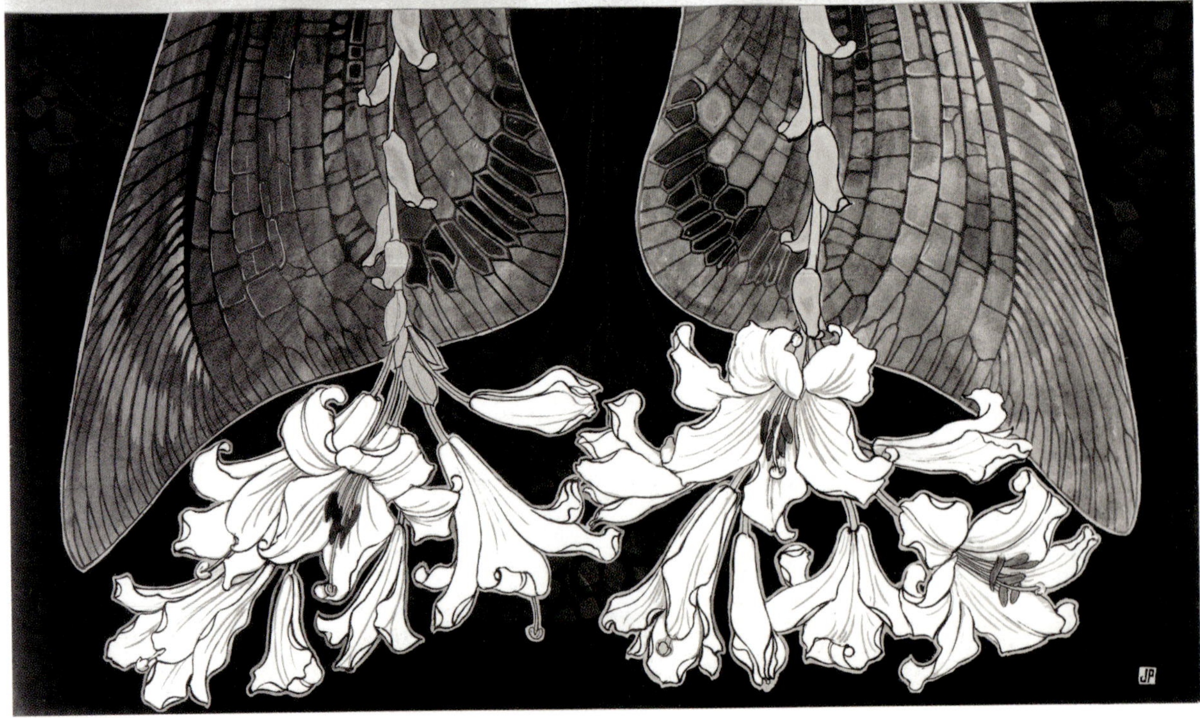
JP

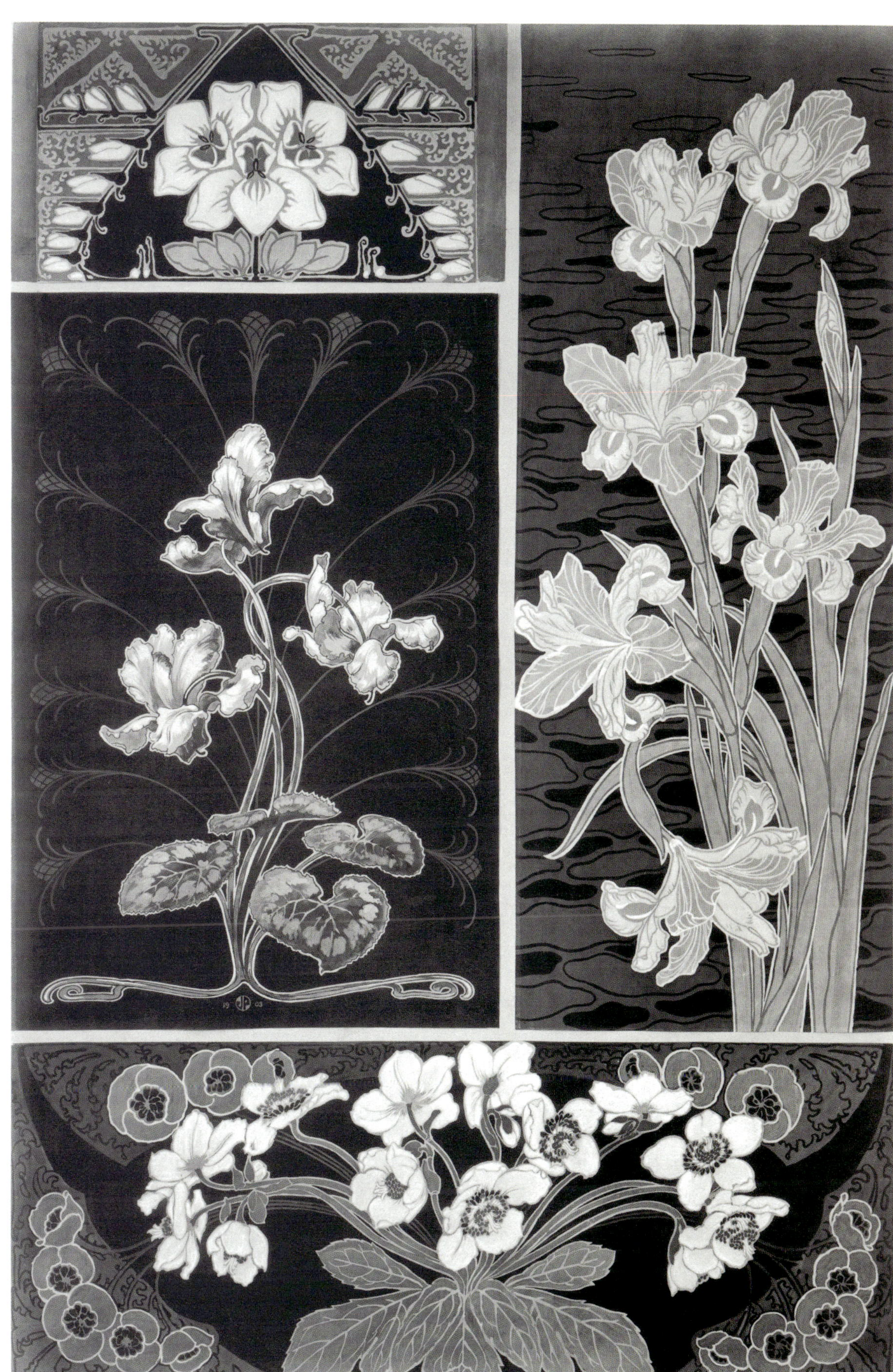

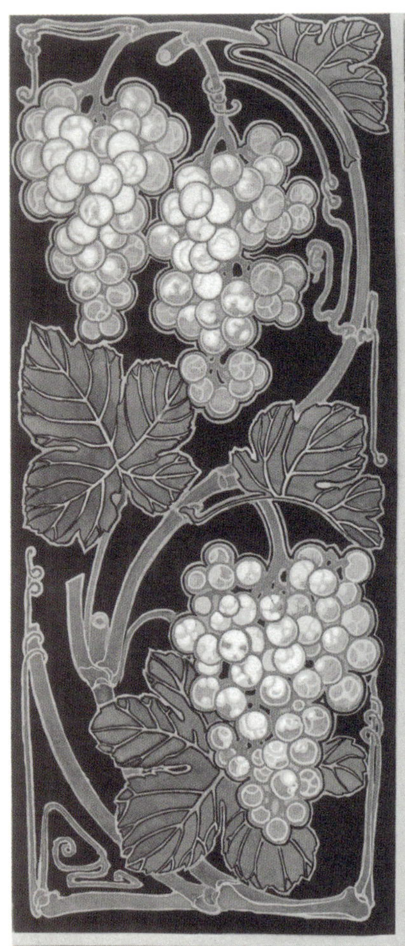
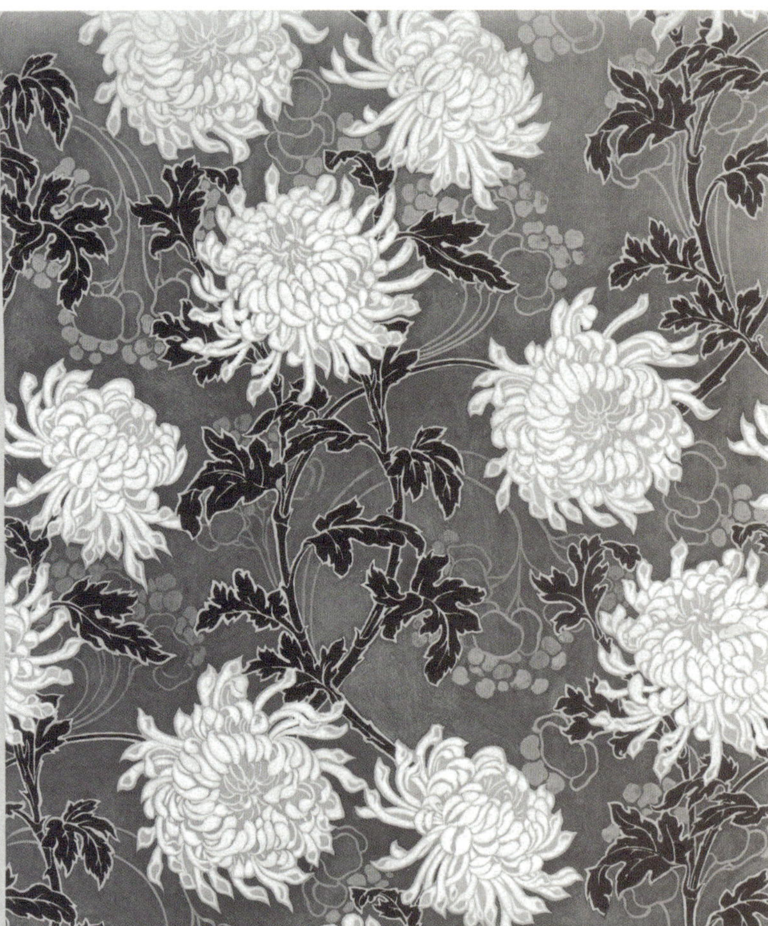
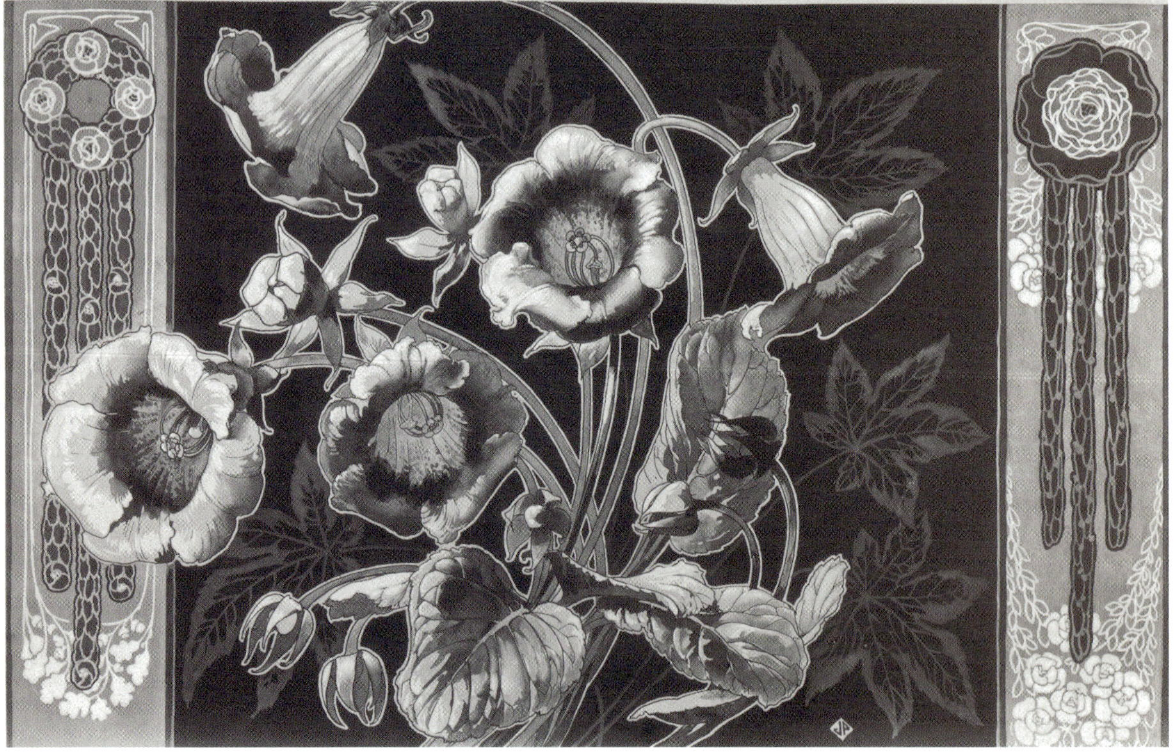

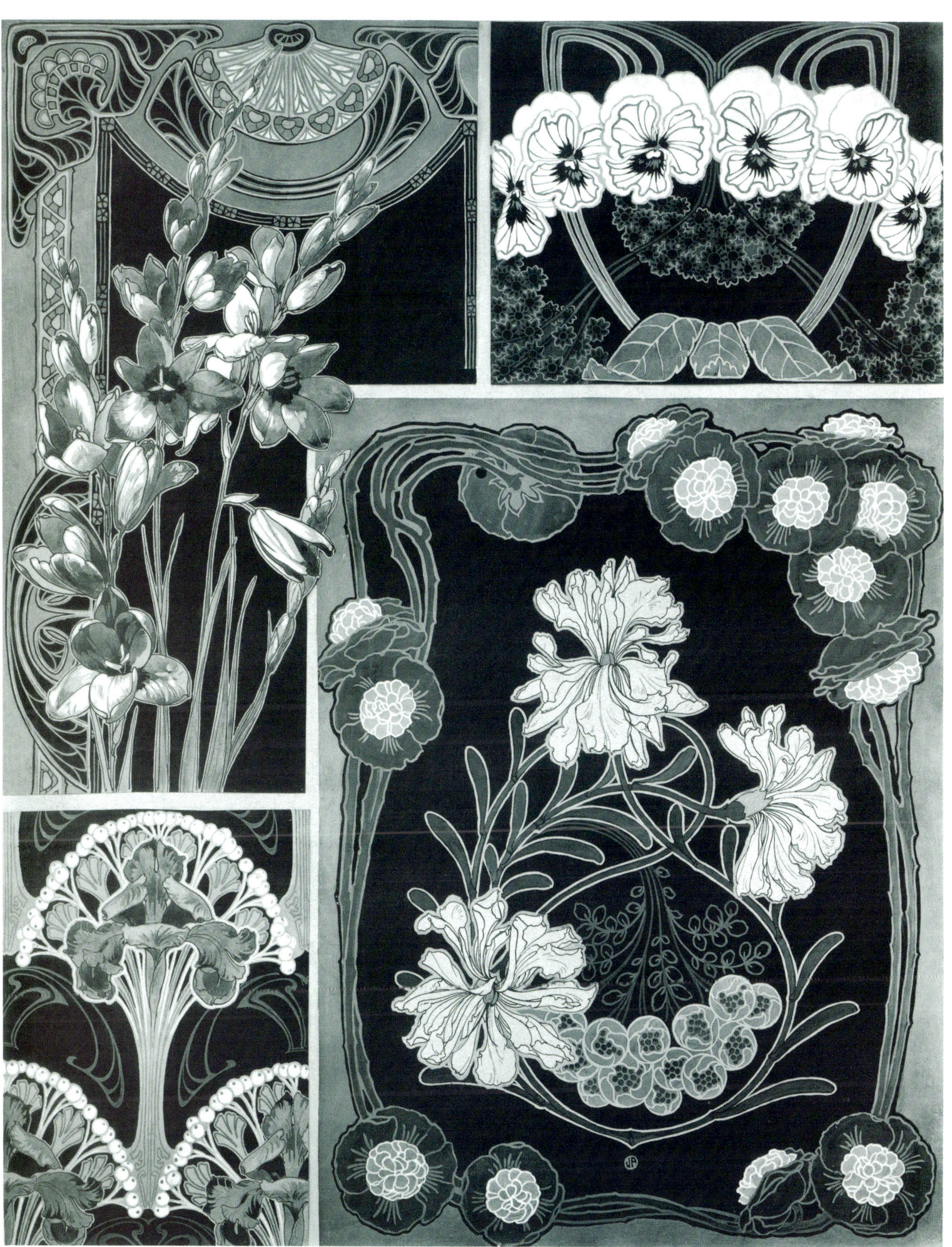

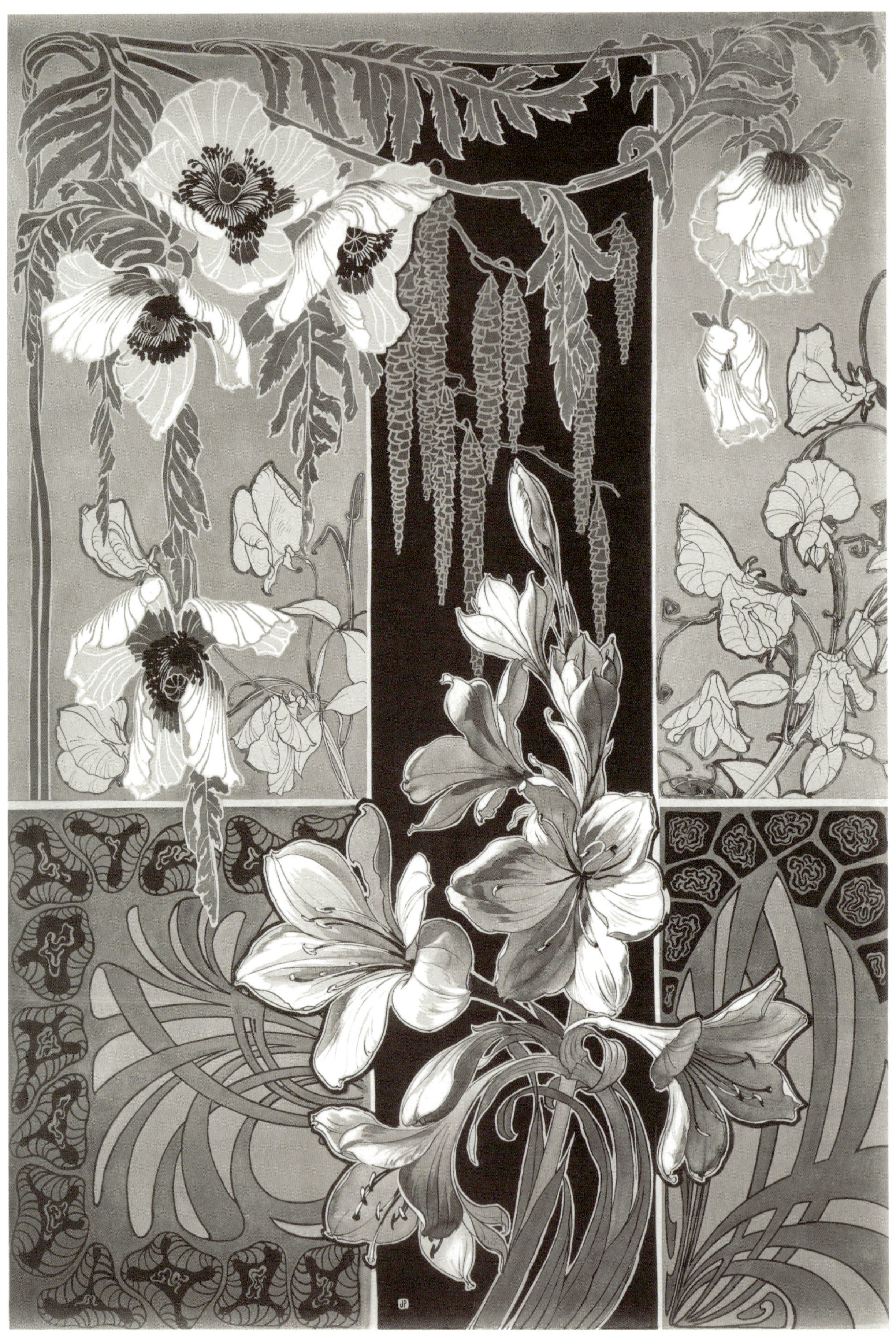

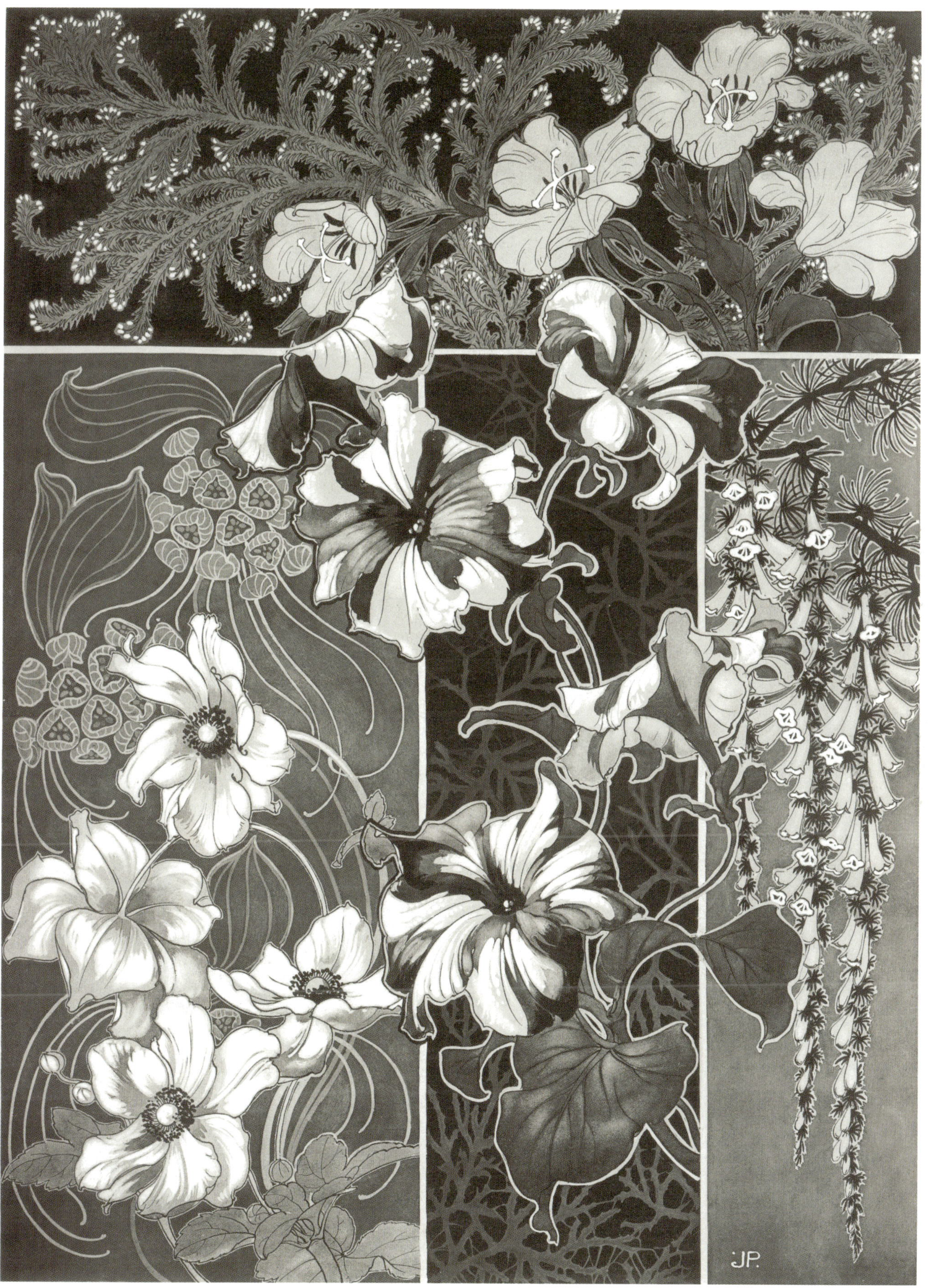
JP.

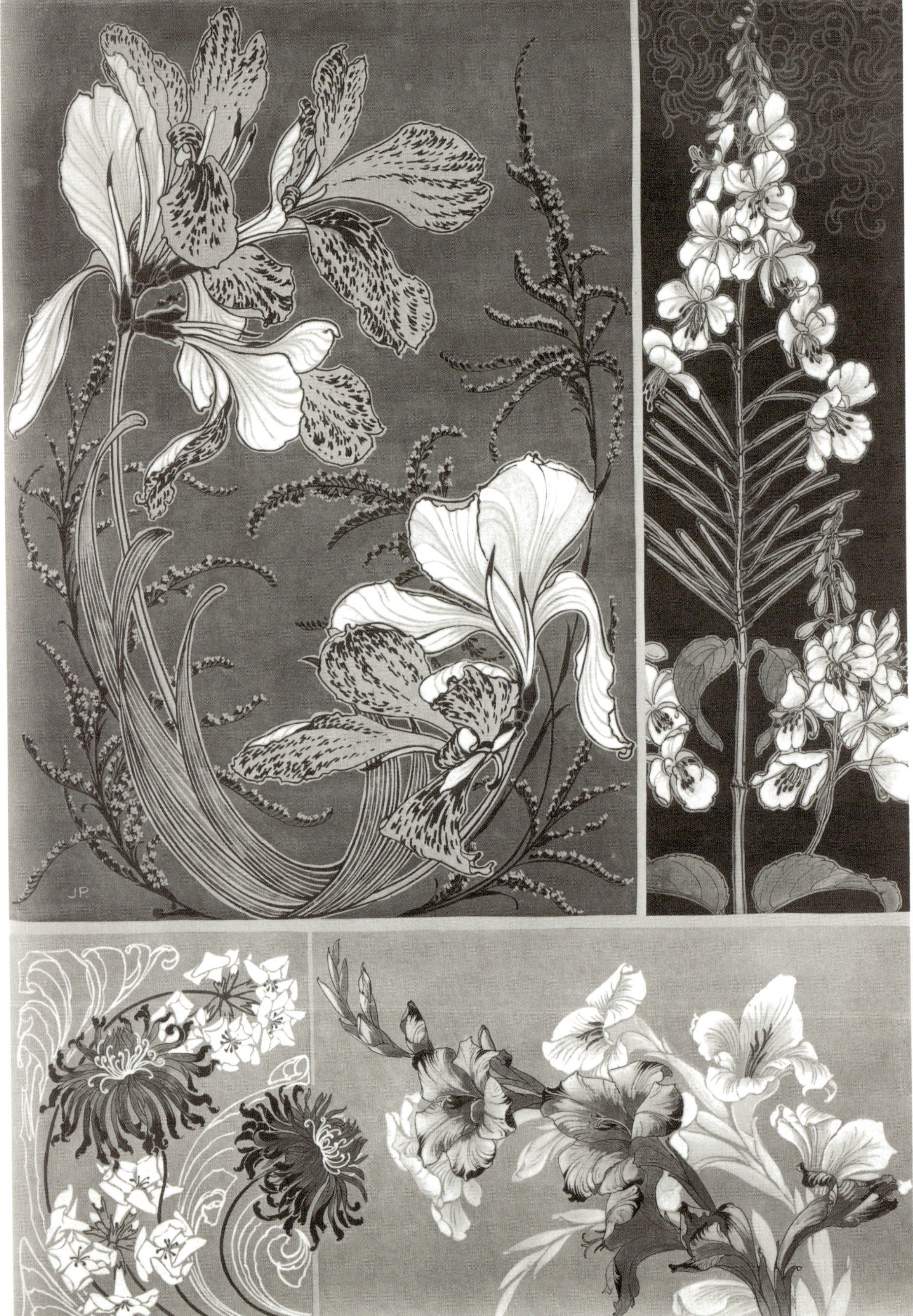
J.P.

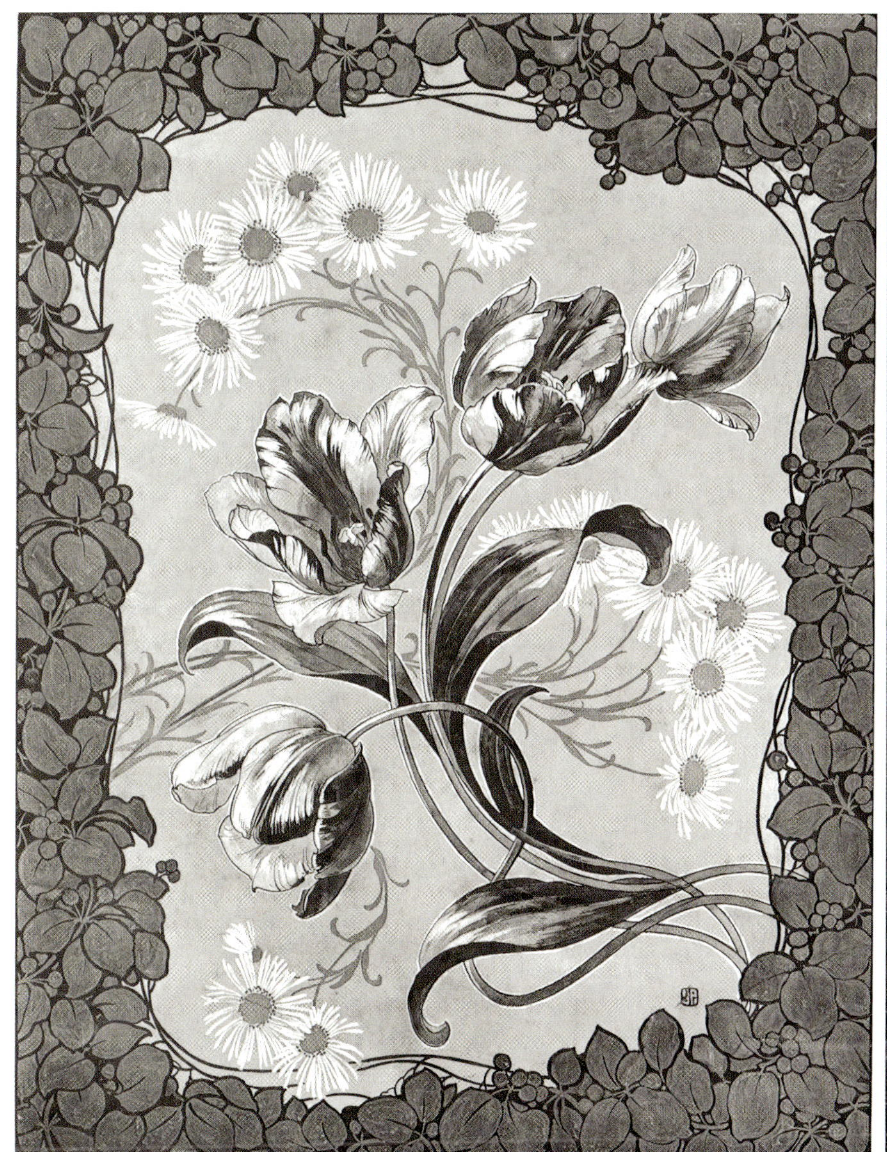
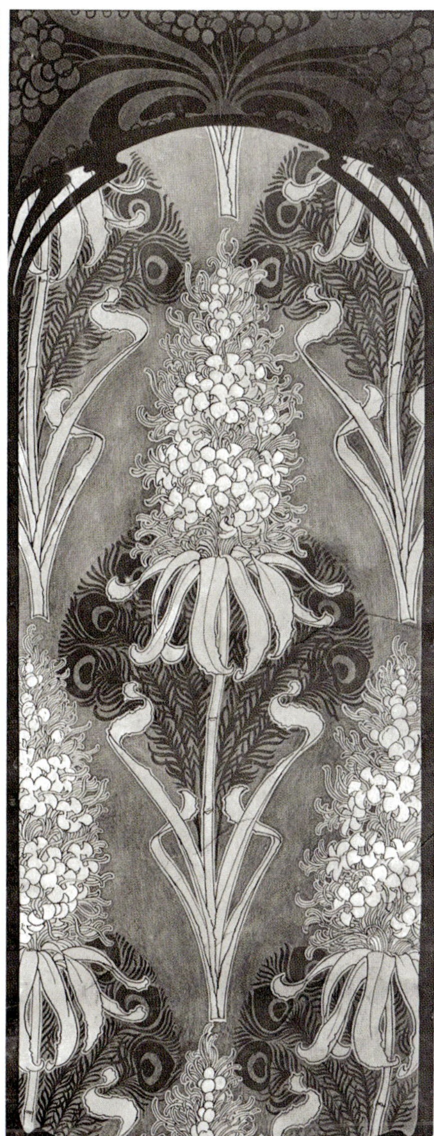
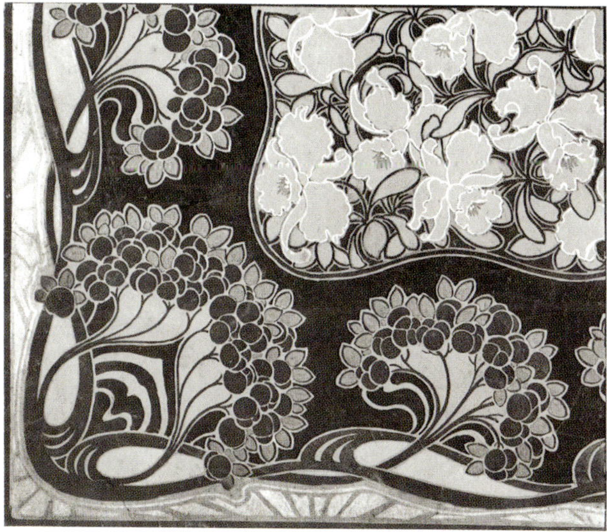
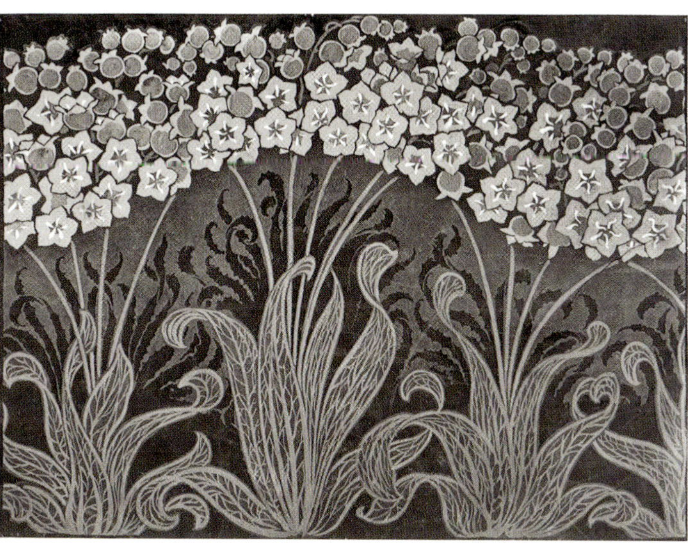

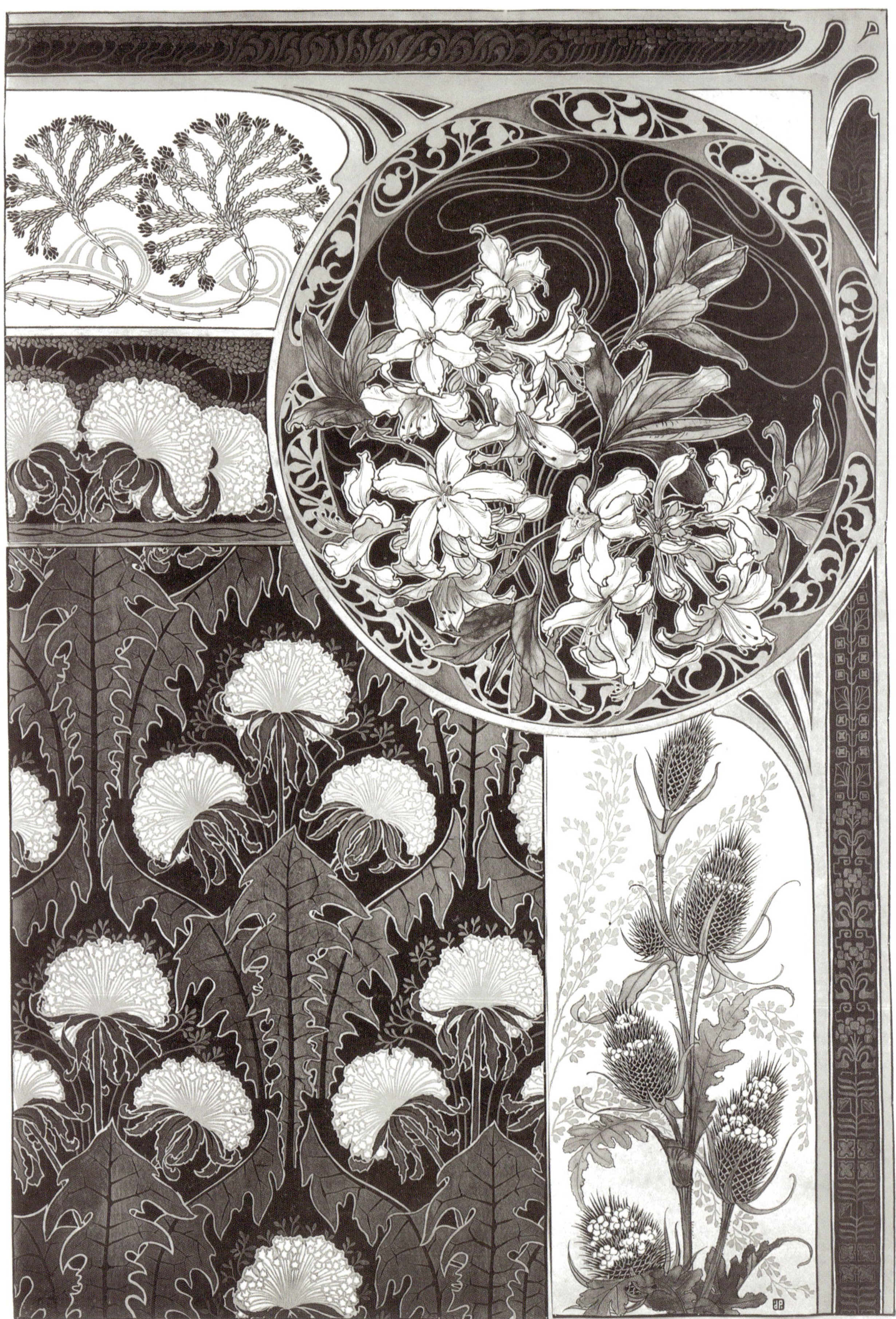

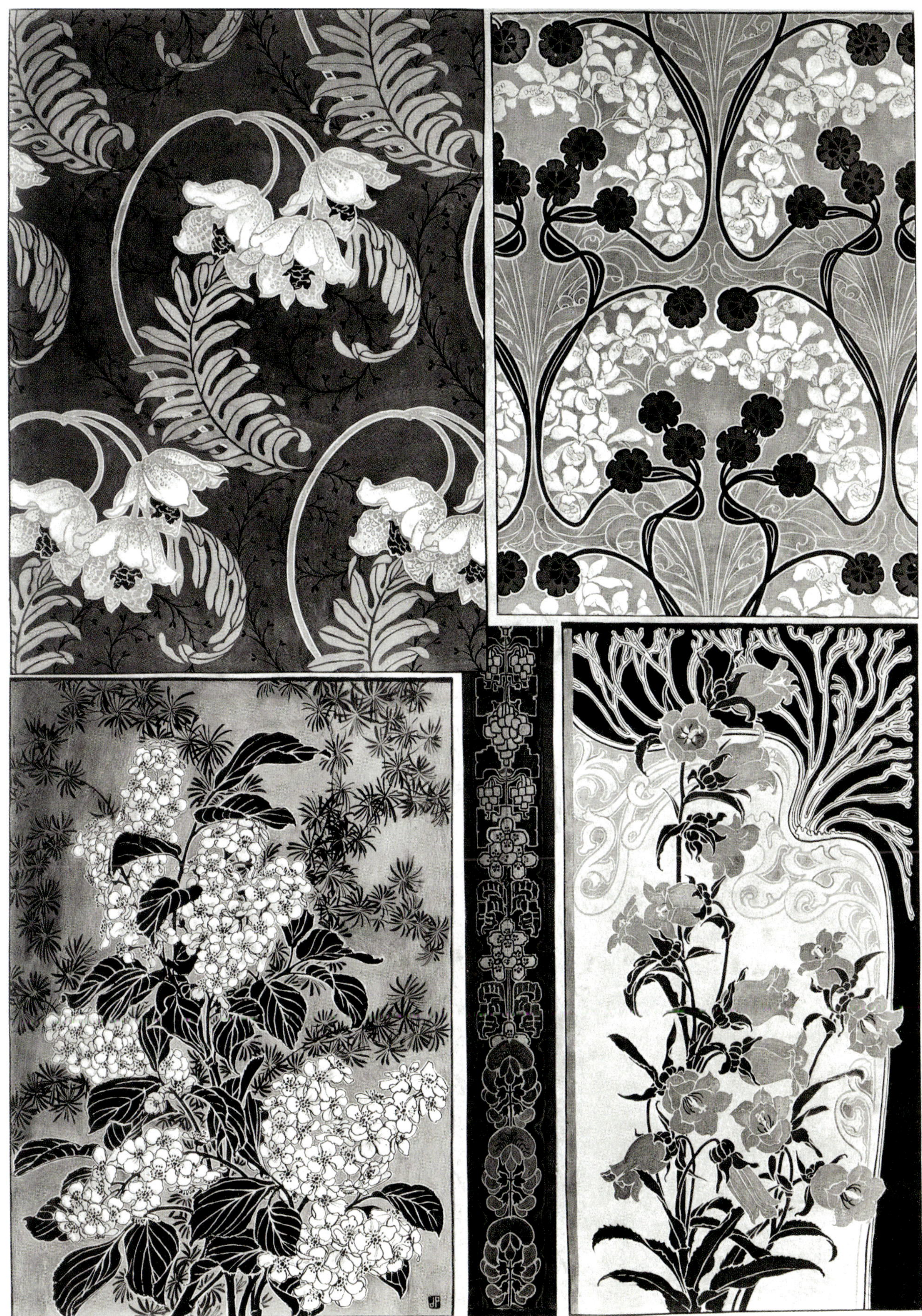

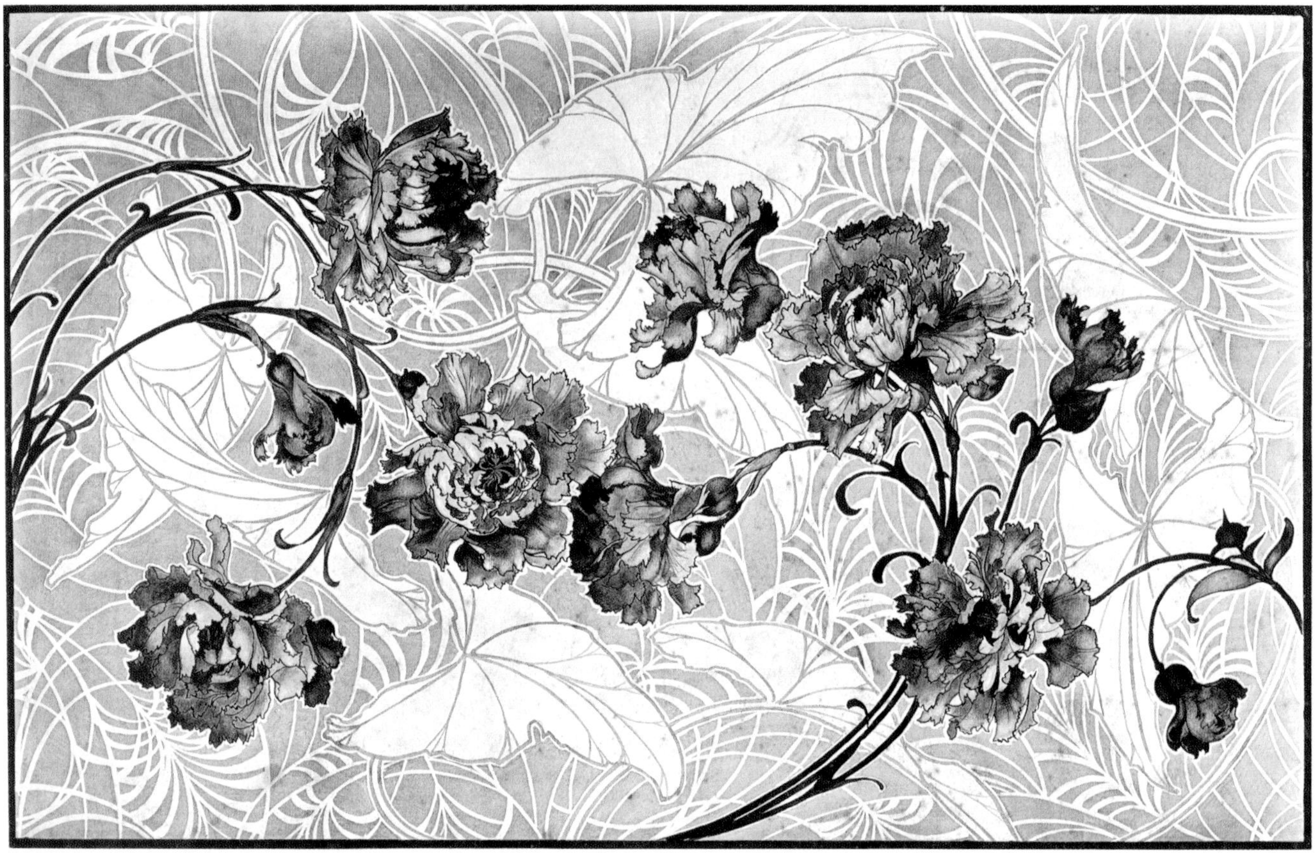

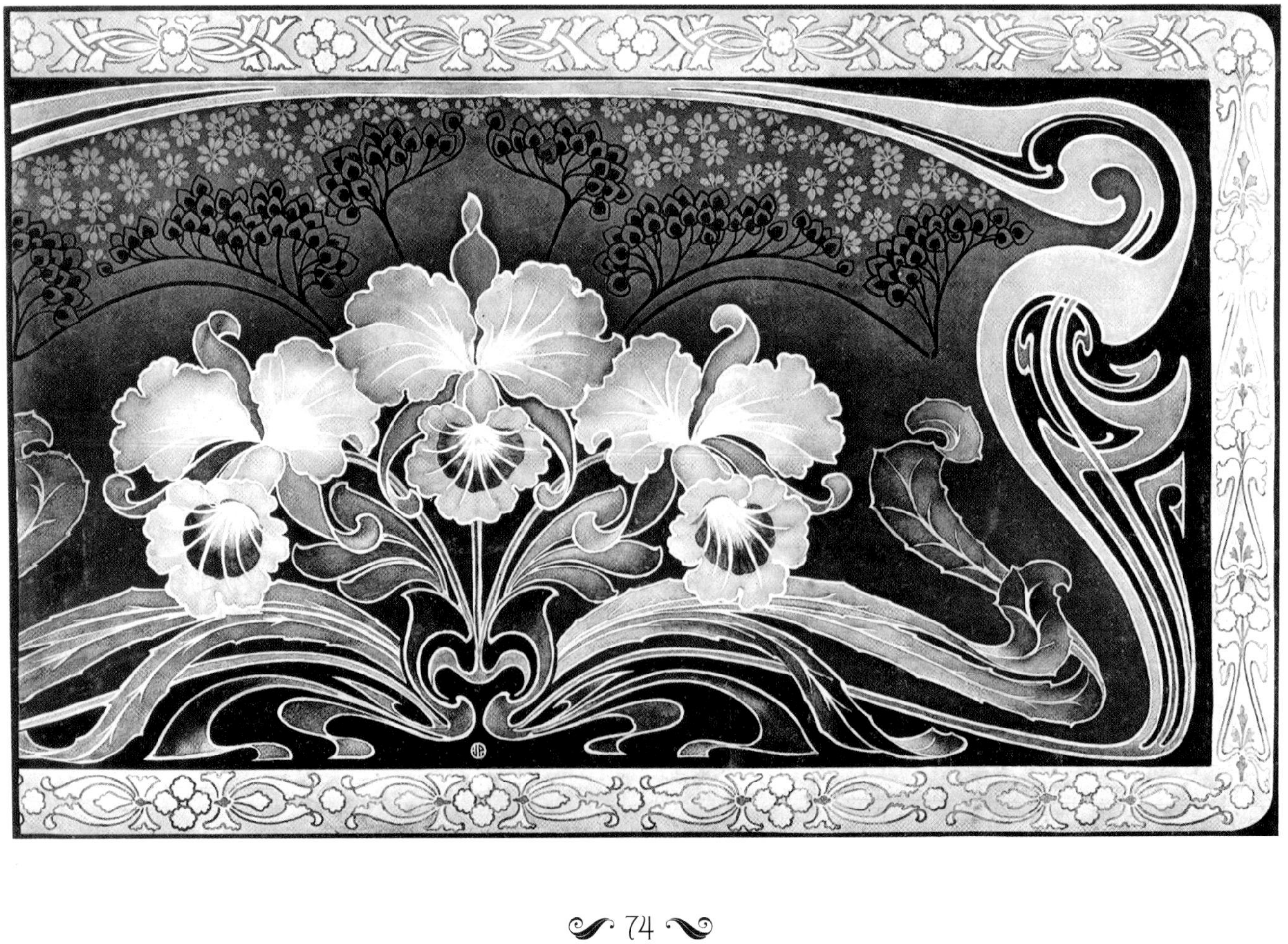

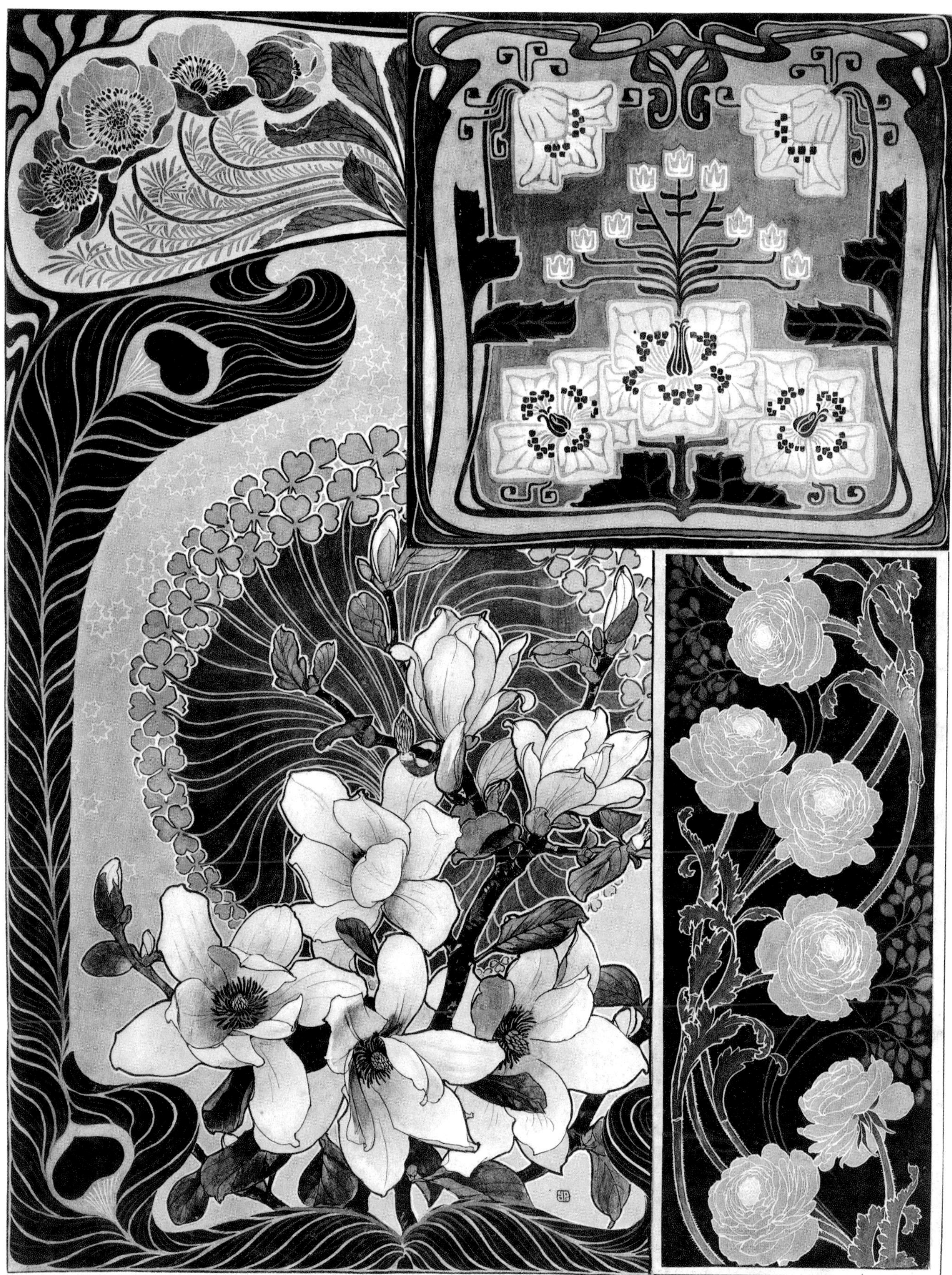

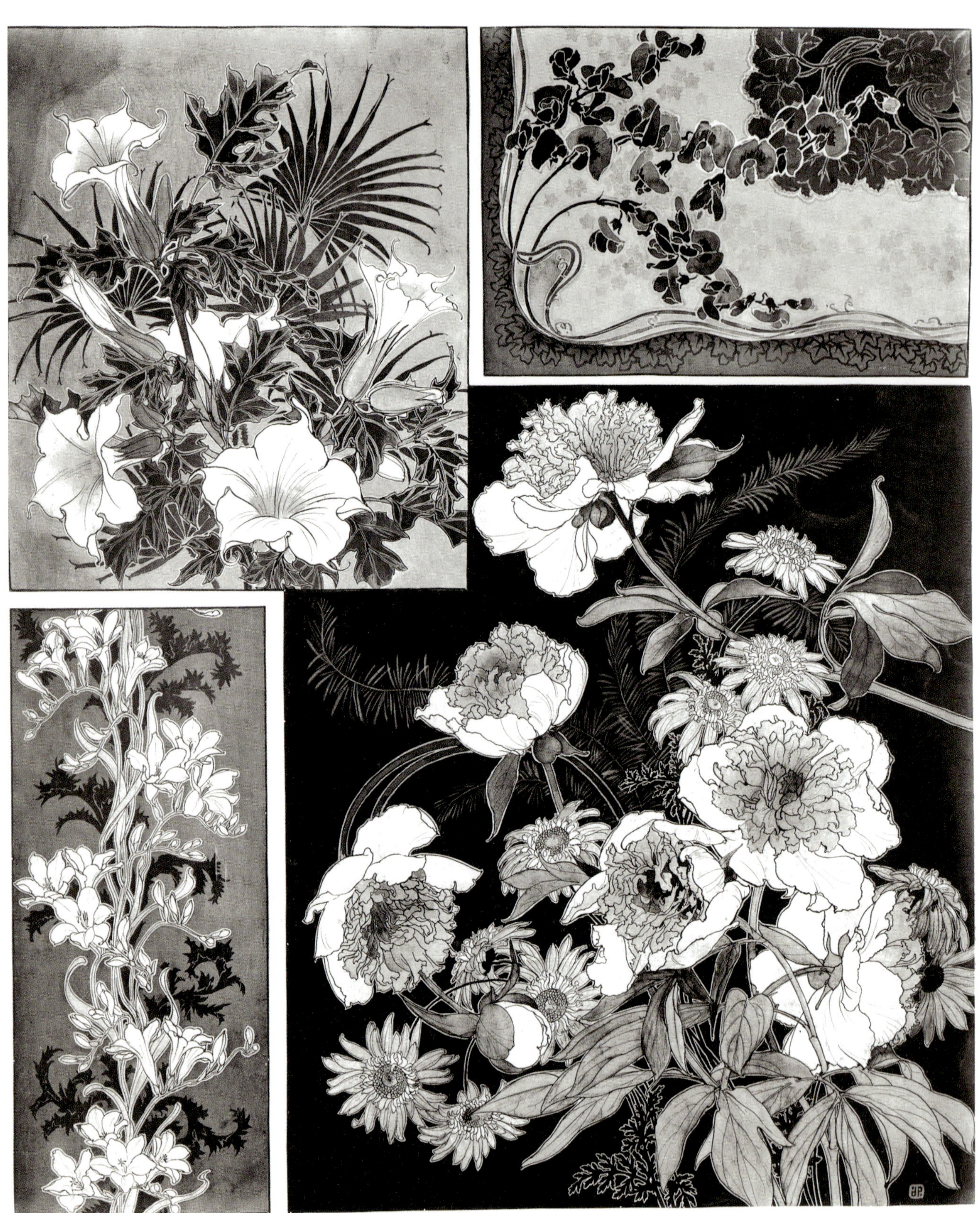

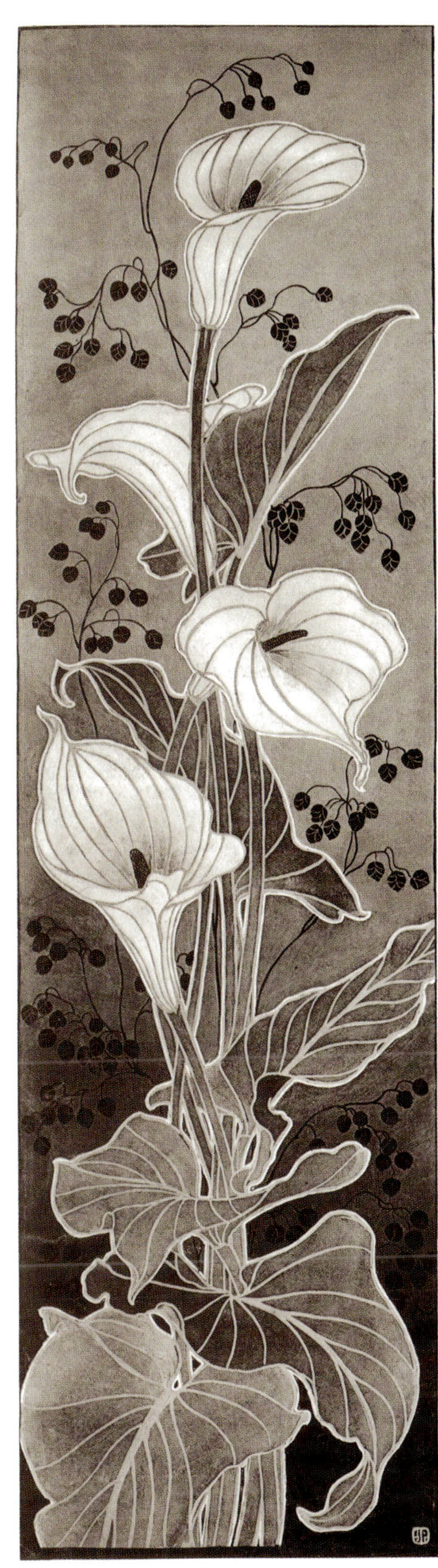

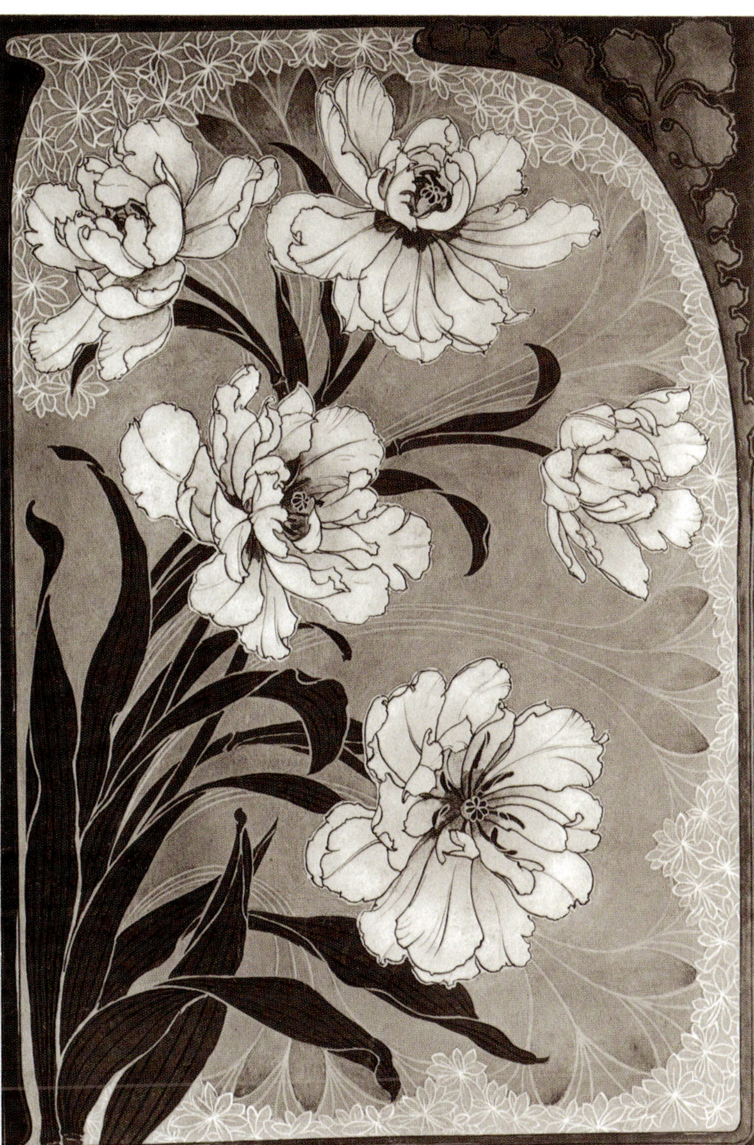

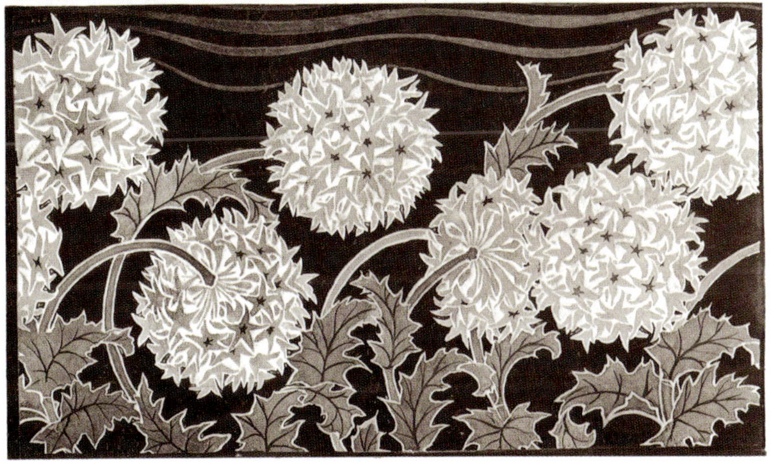

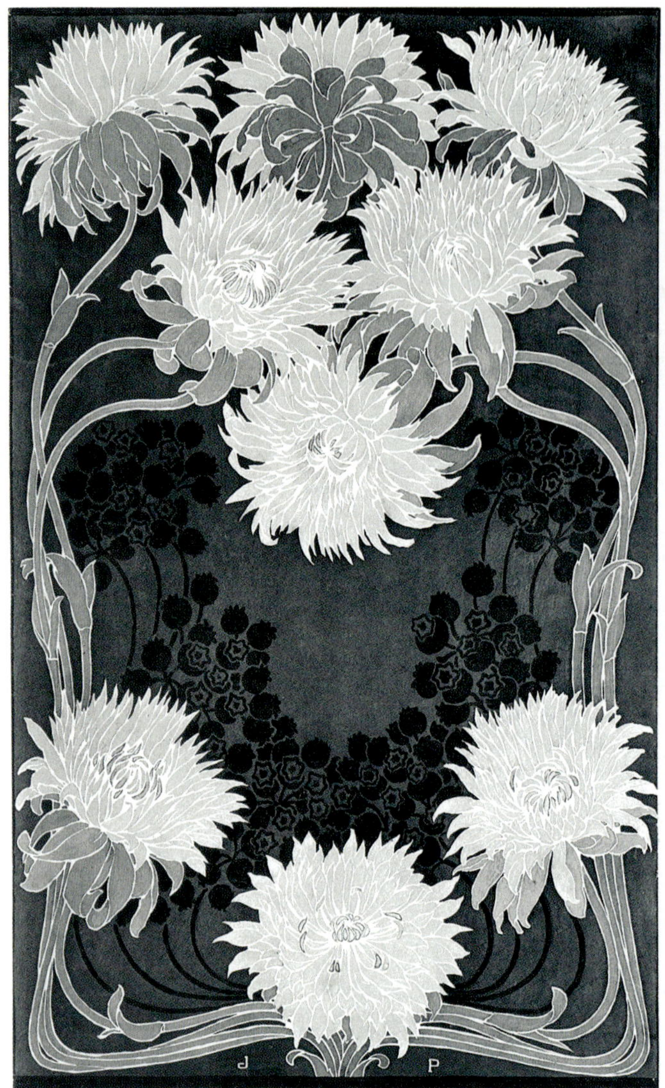

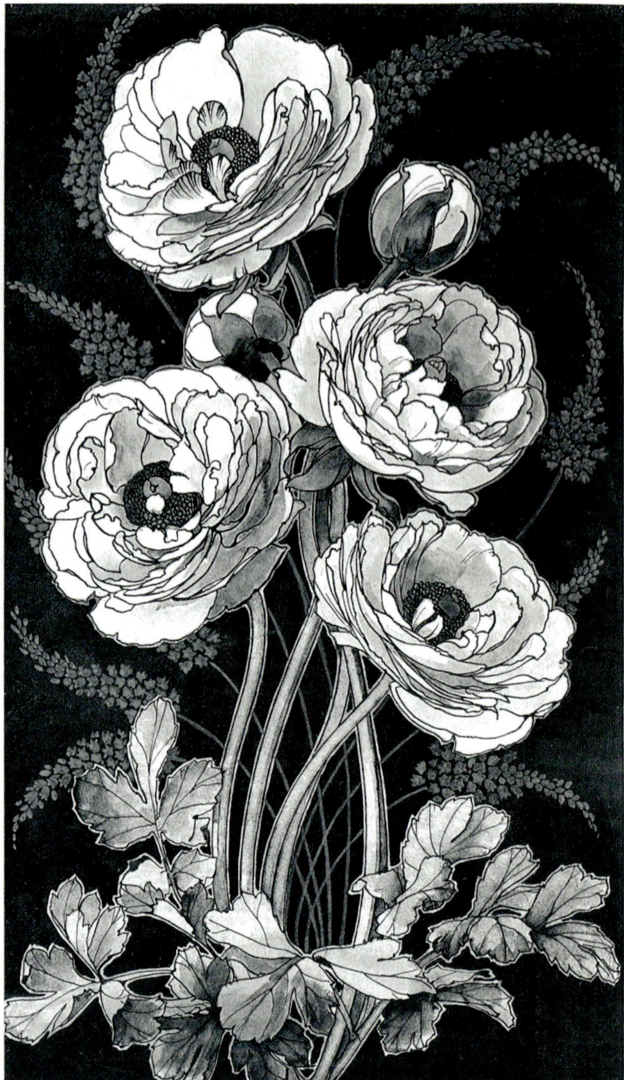

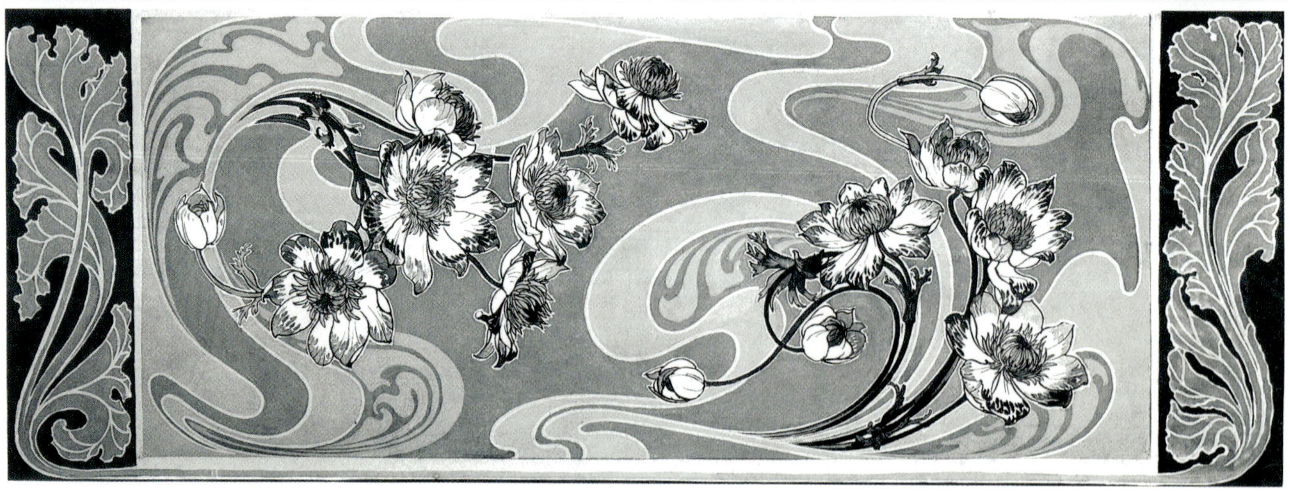

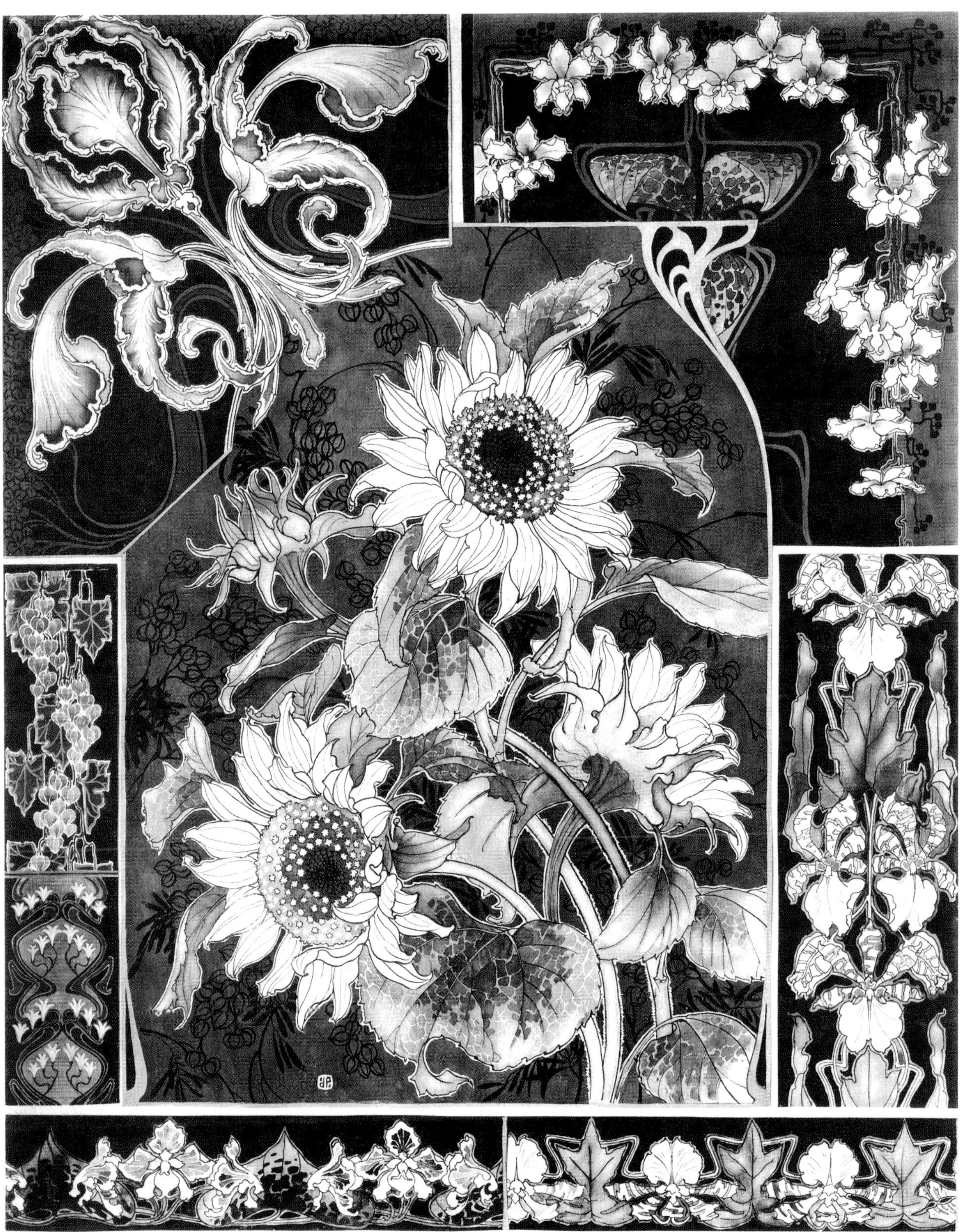

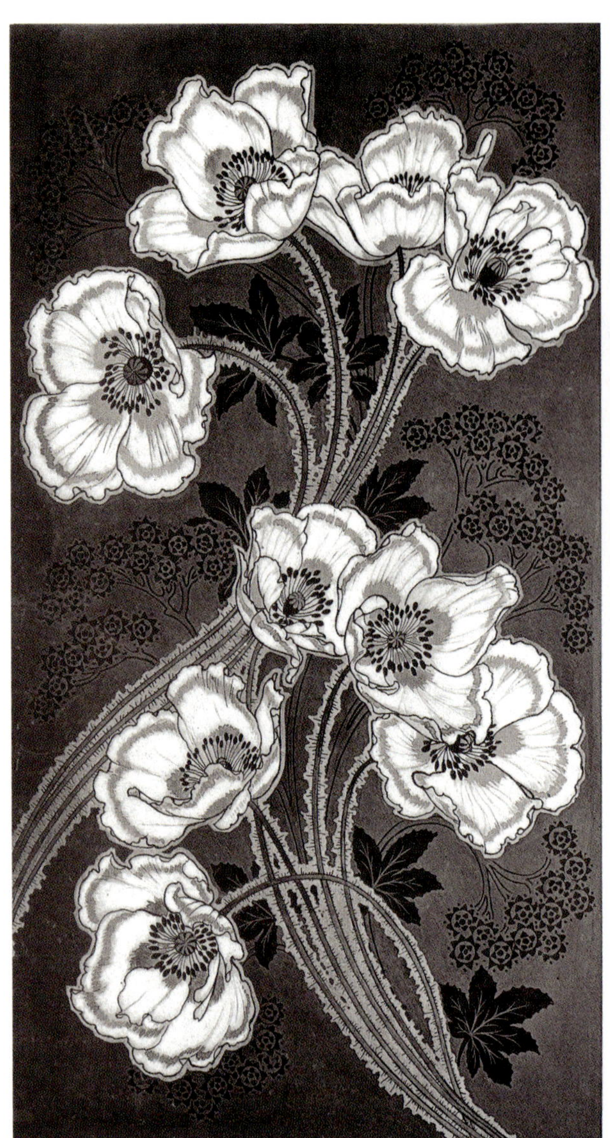

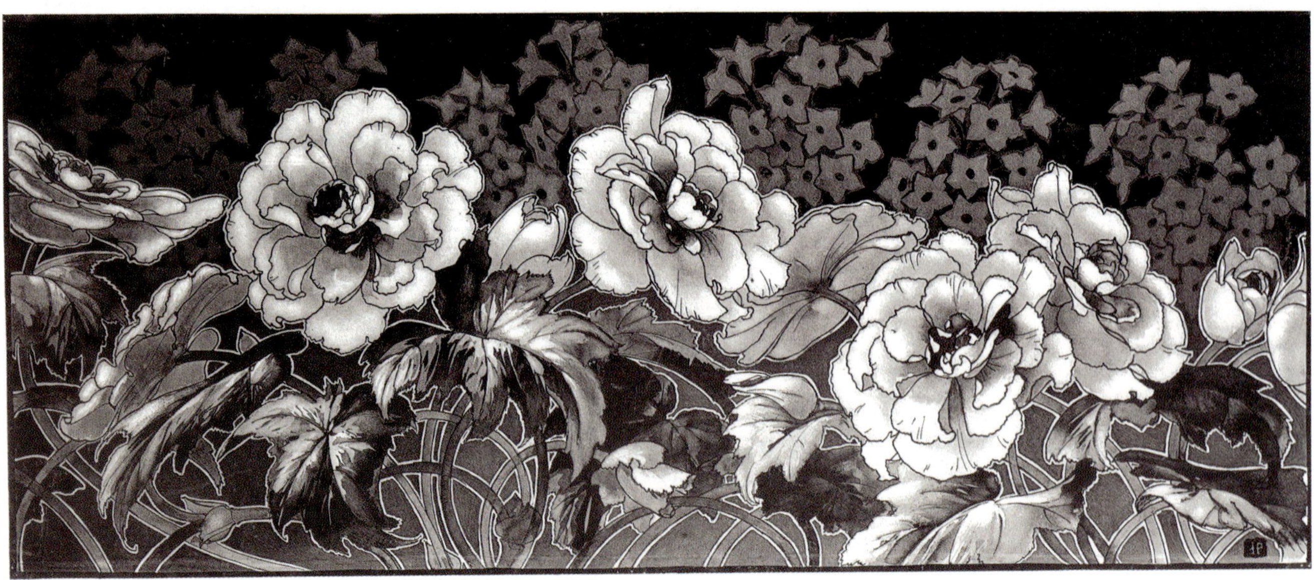

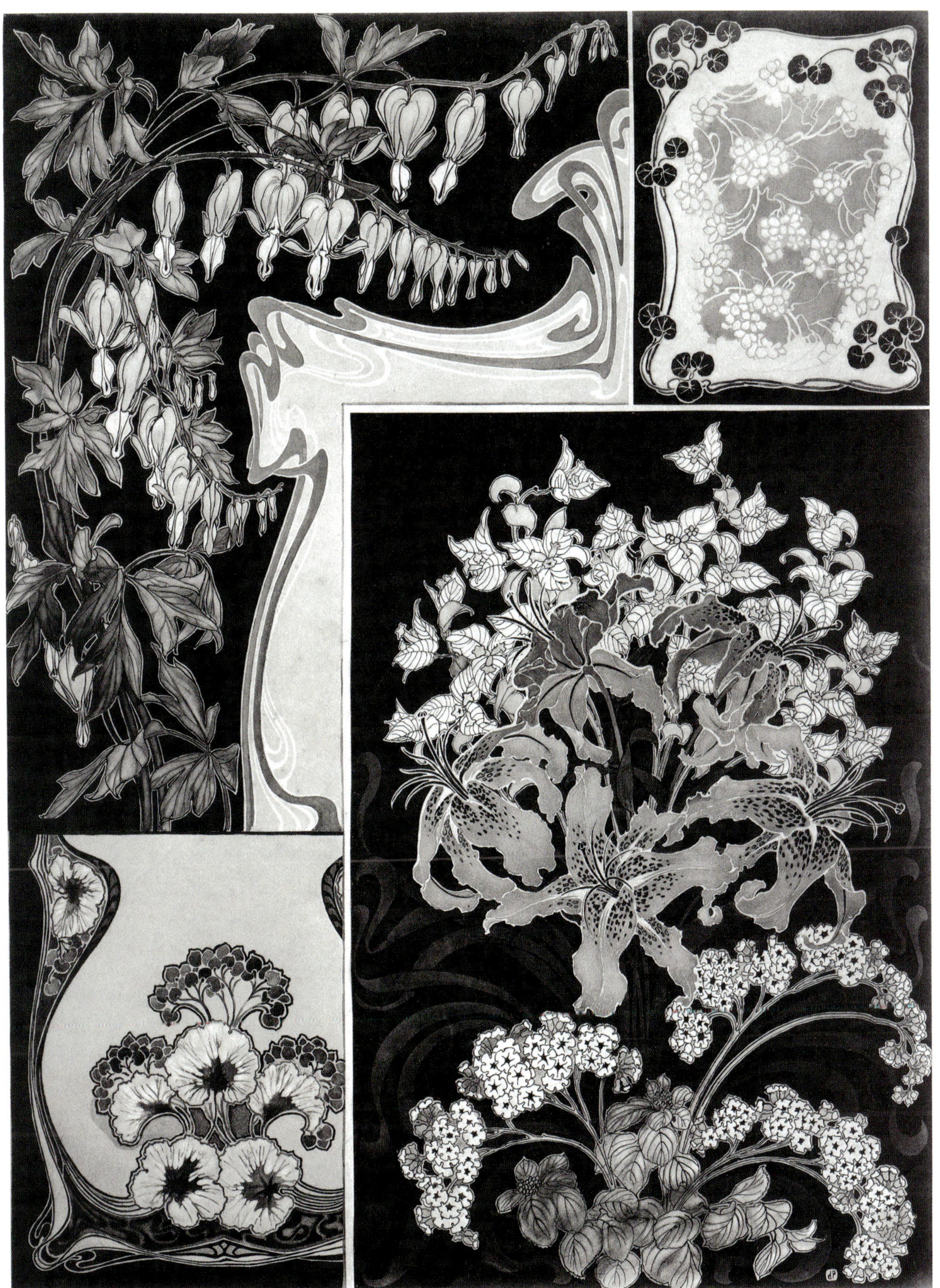

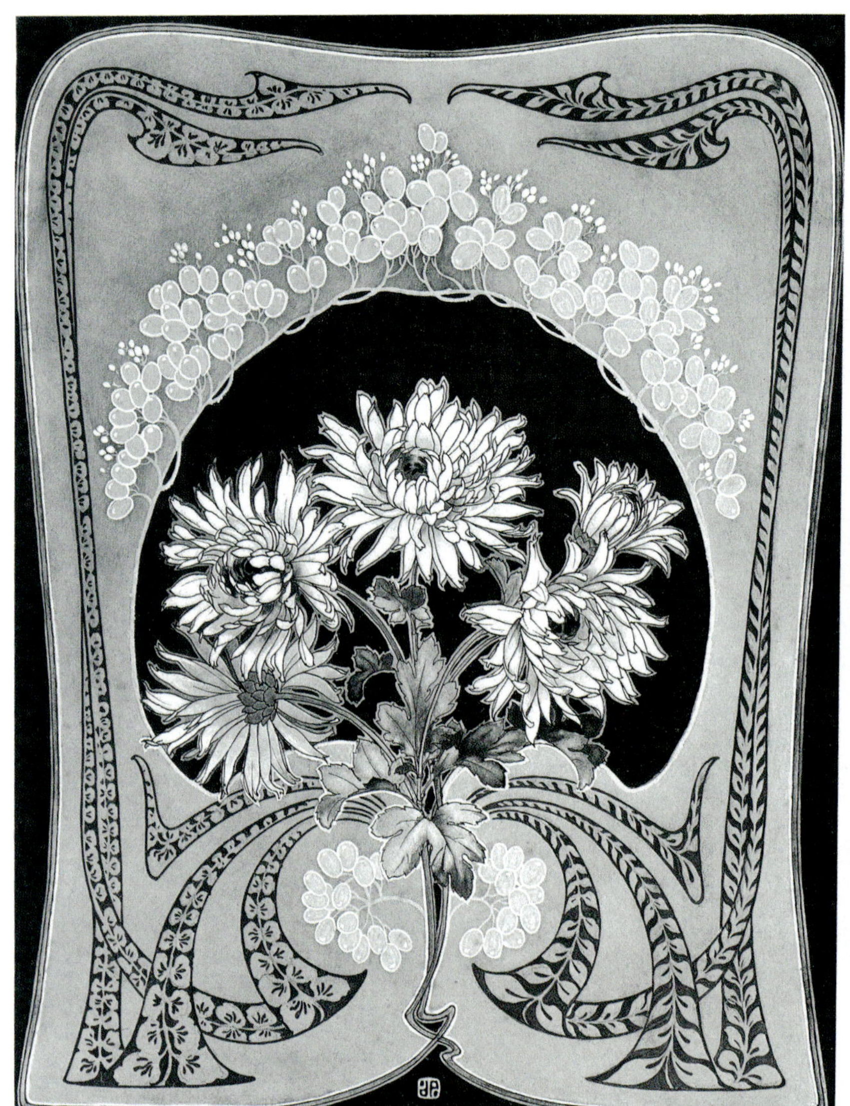

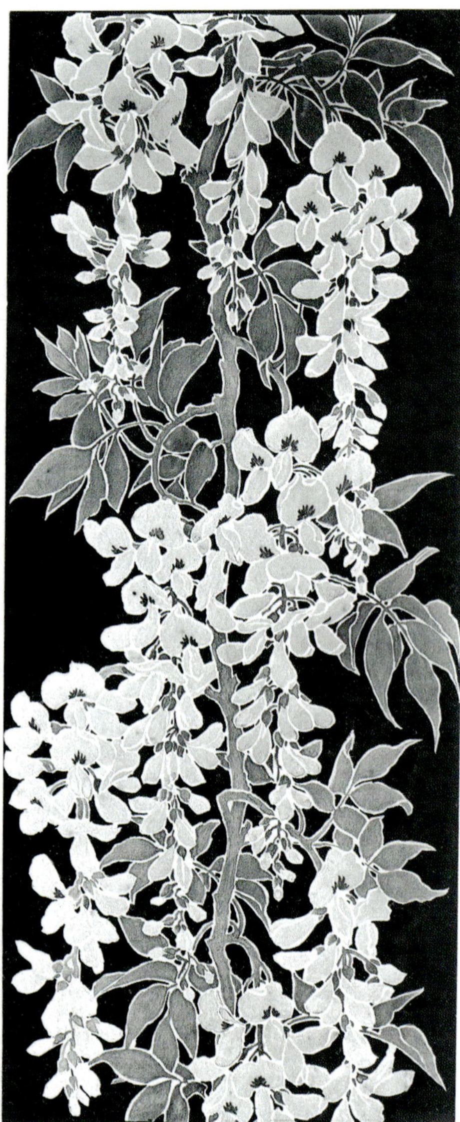

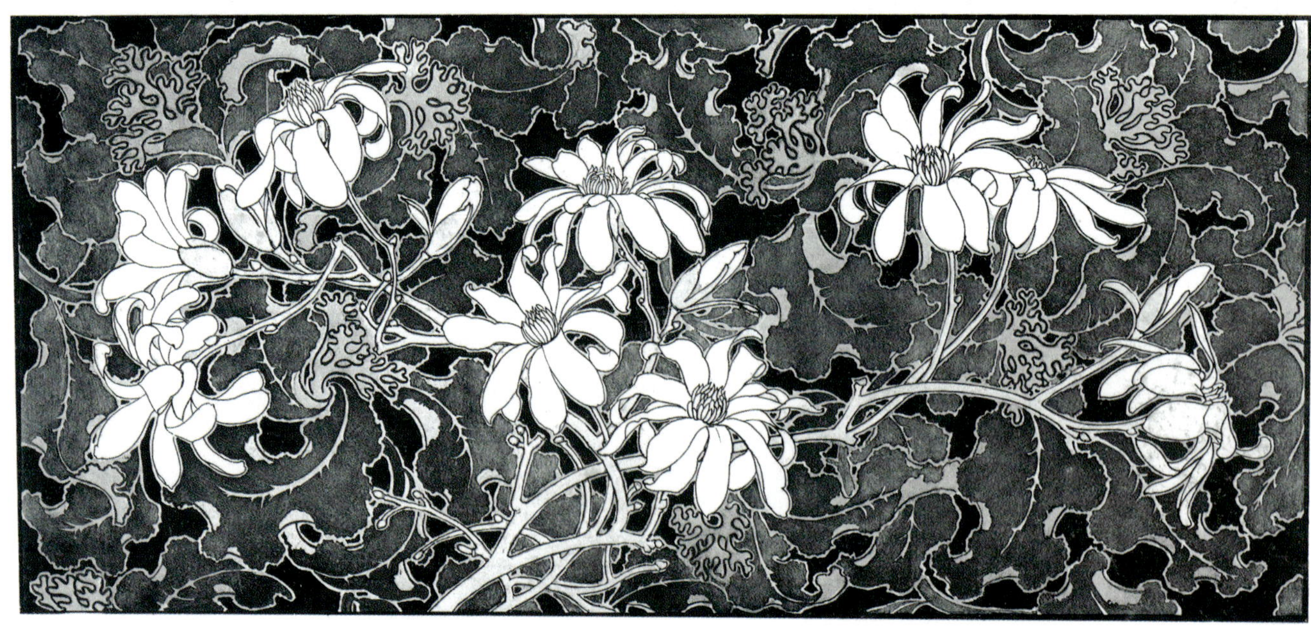

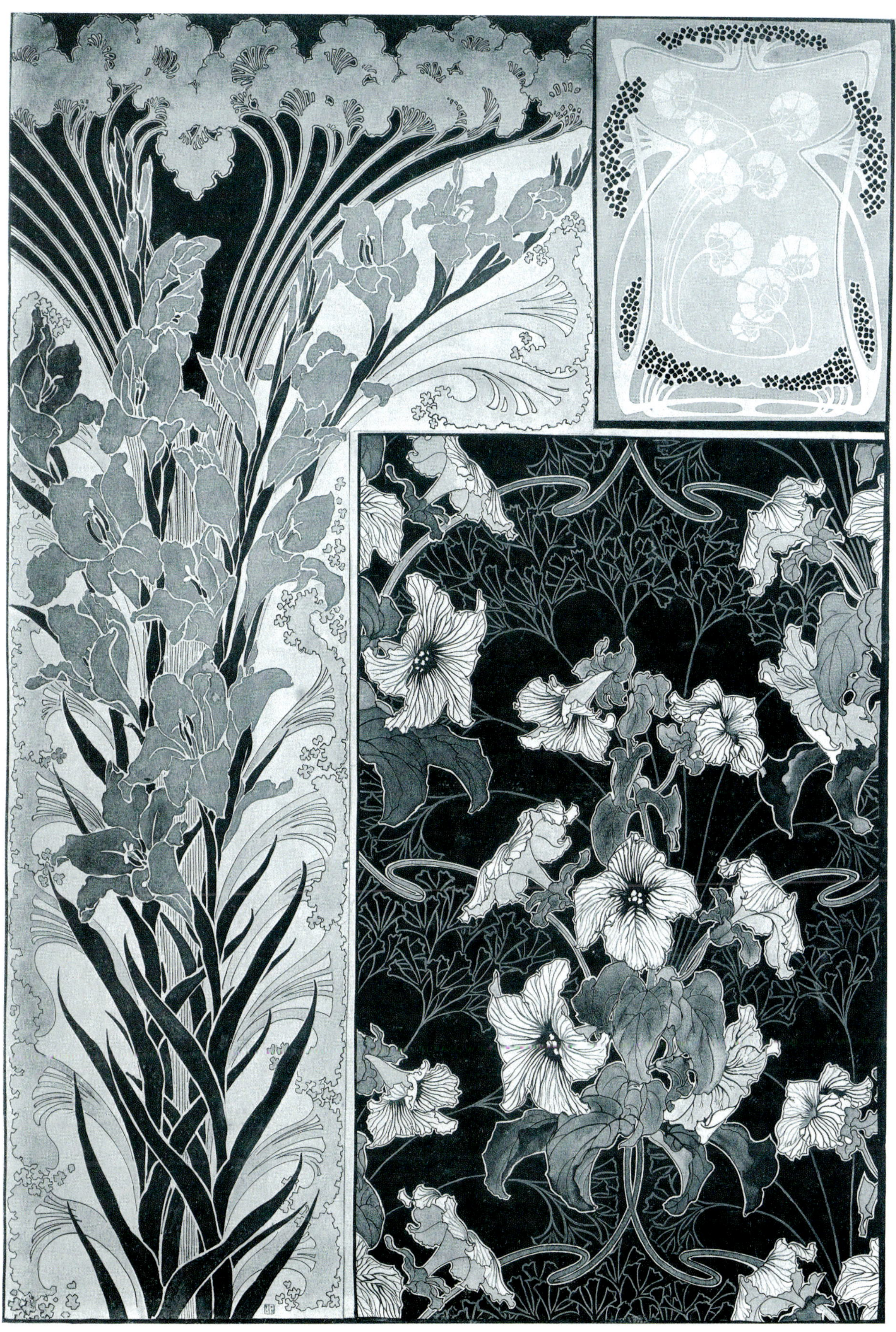

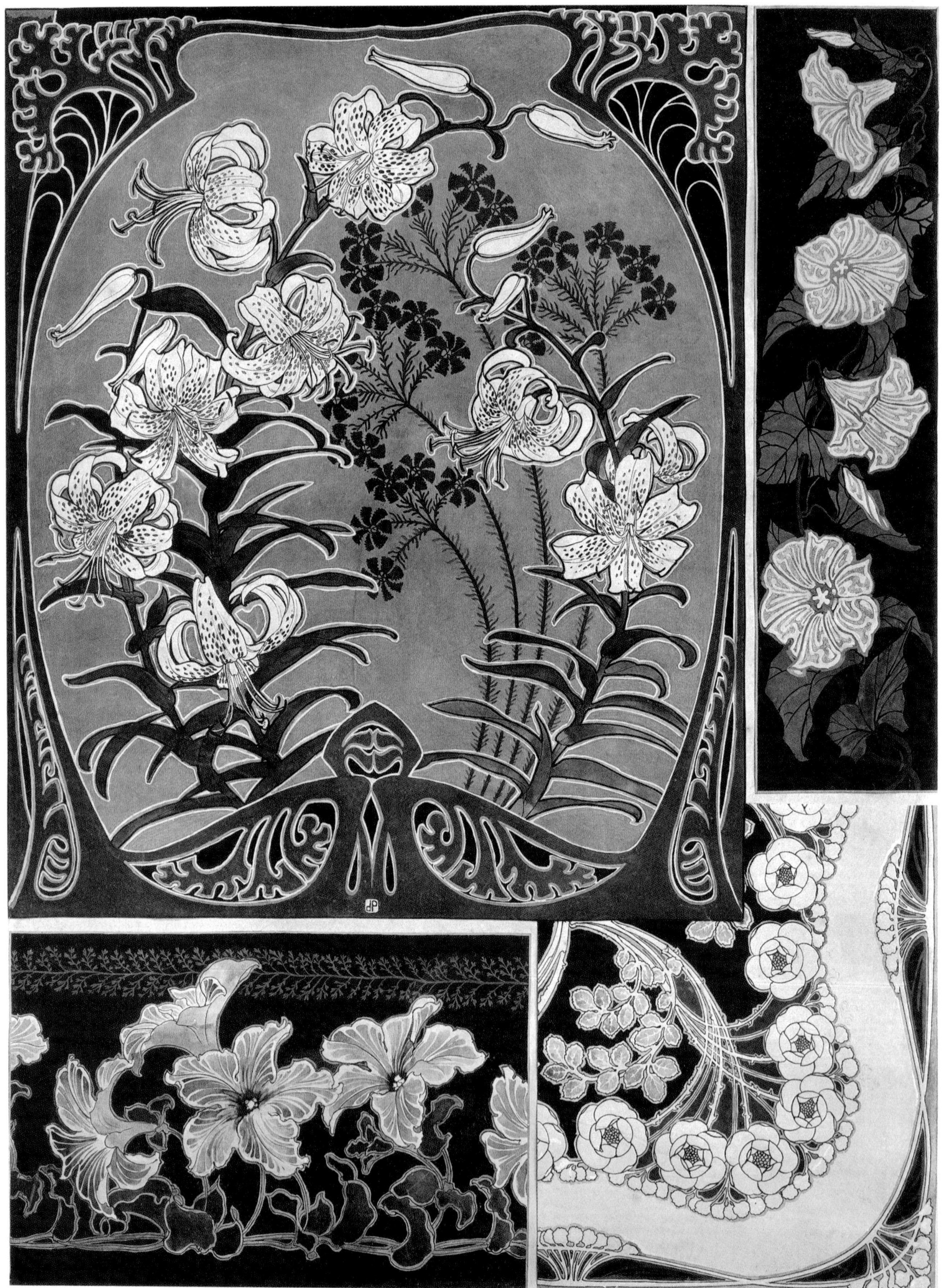

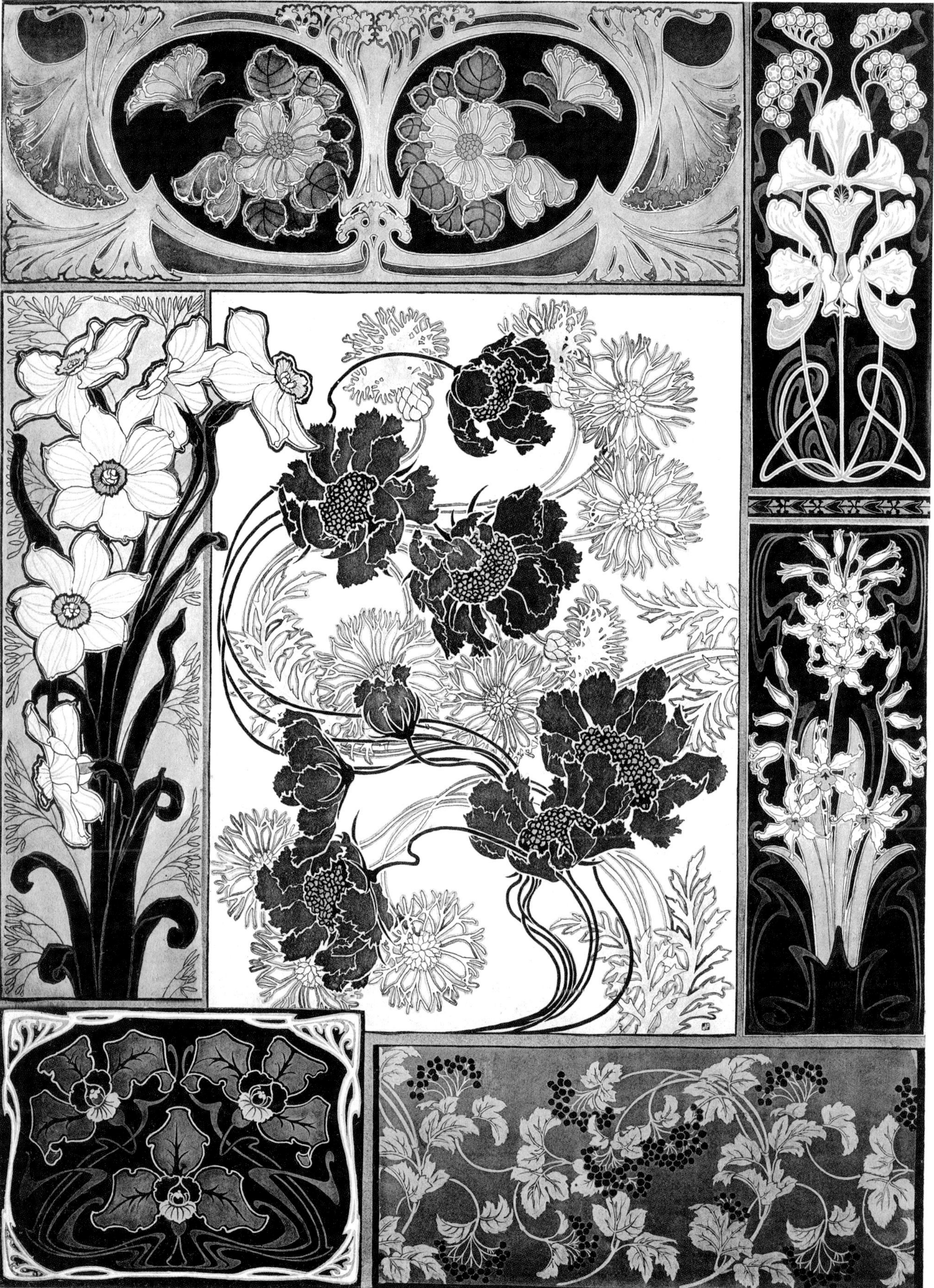

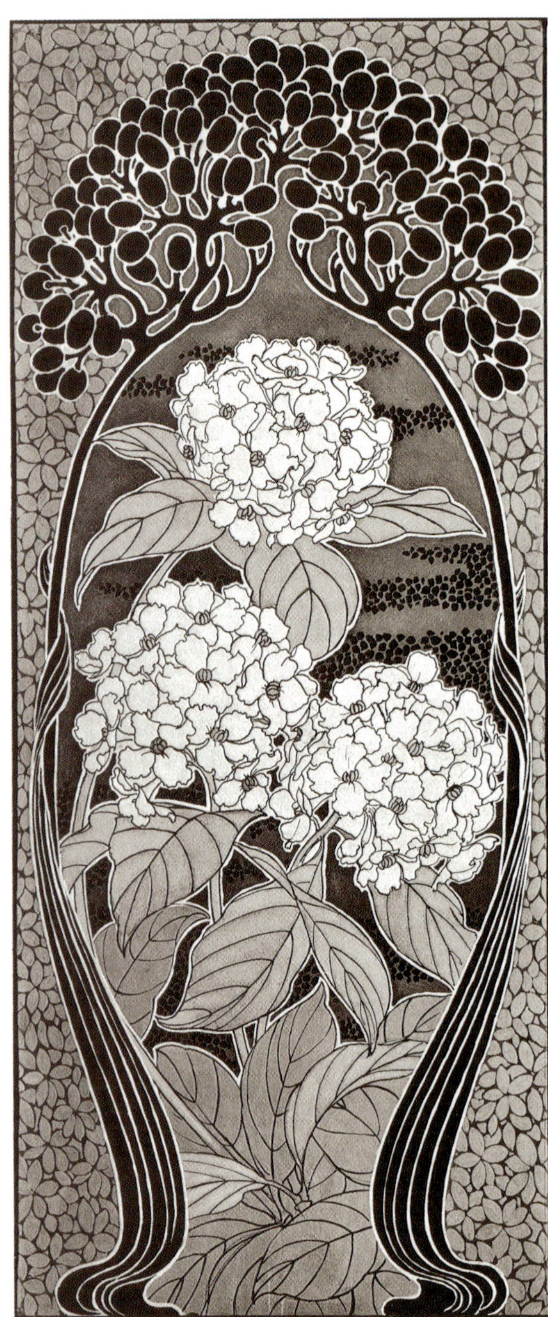

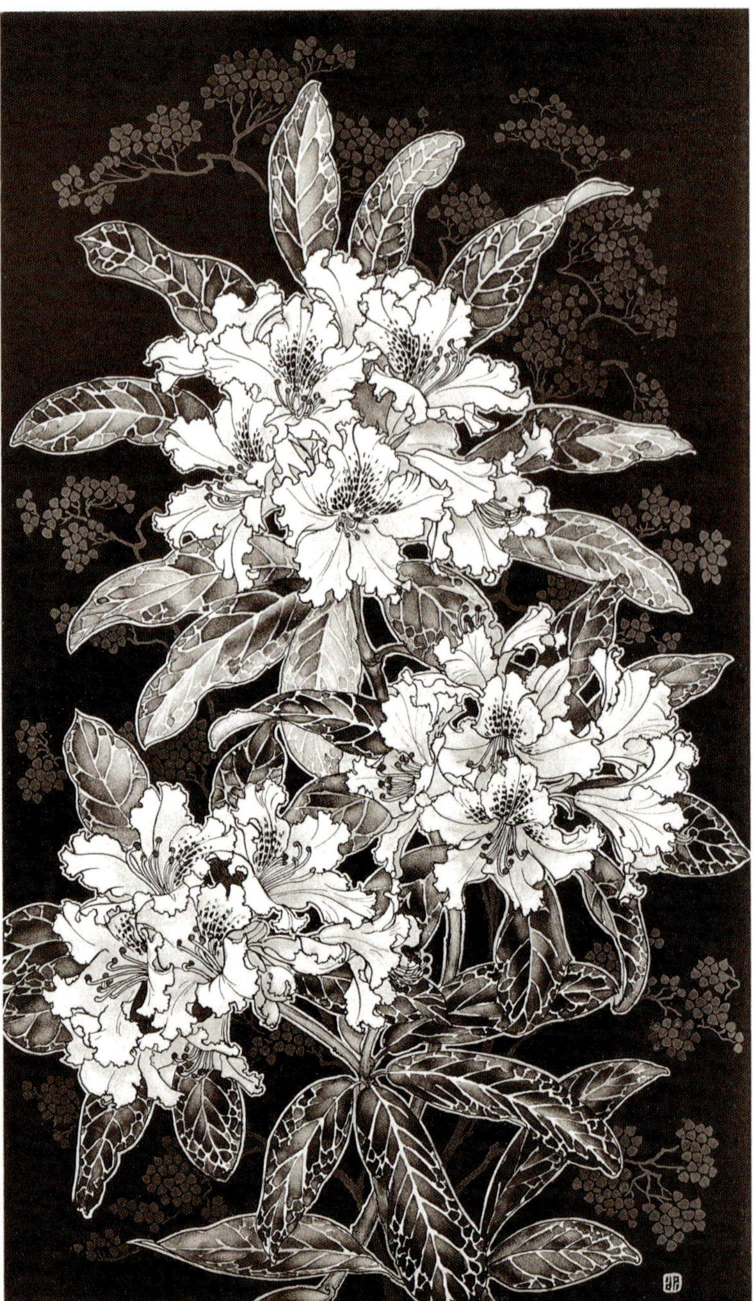

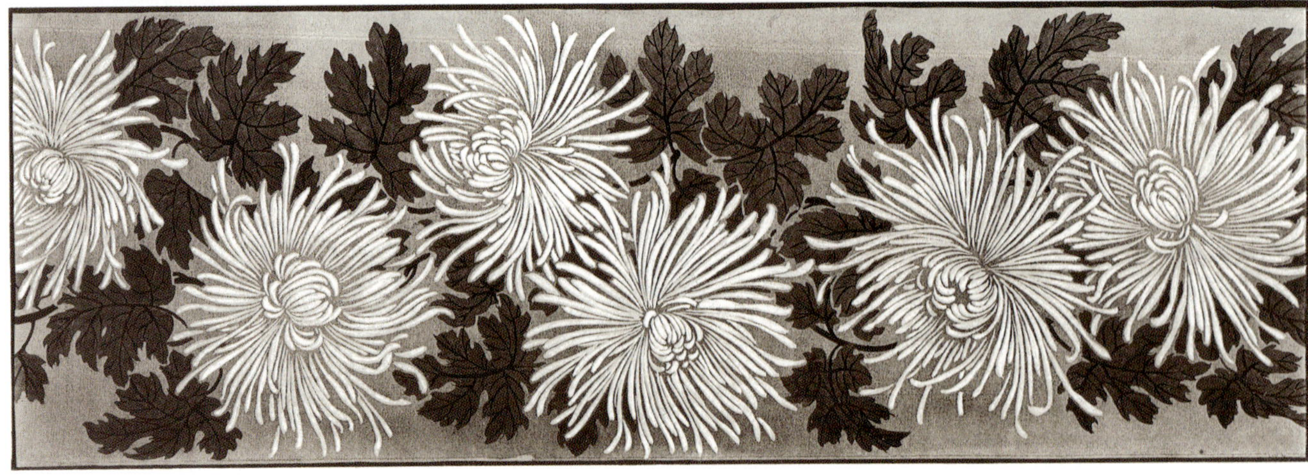

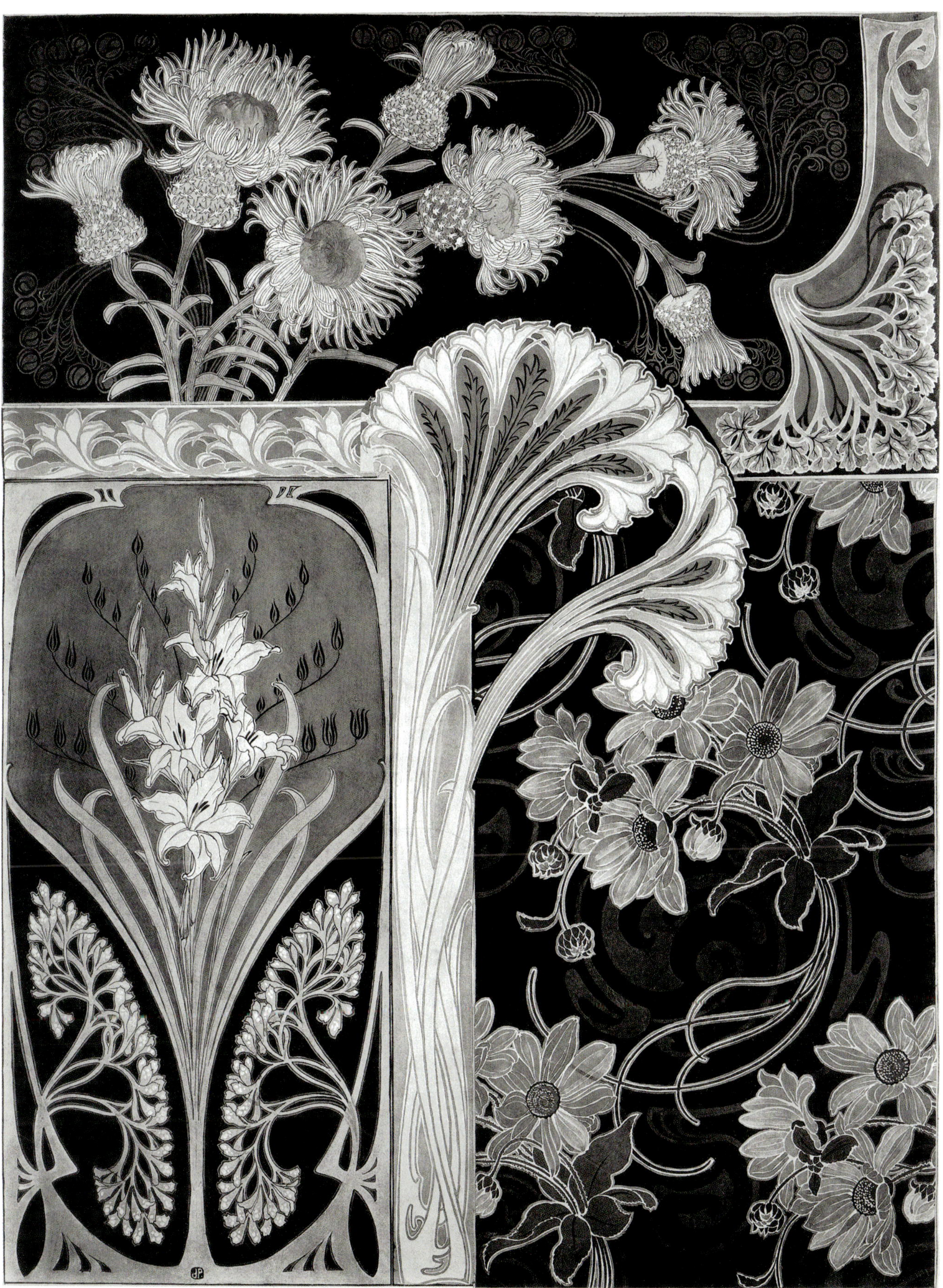

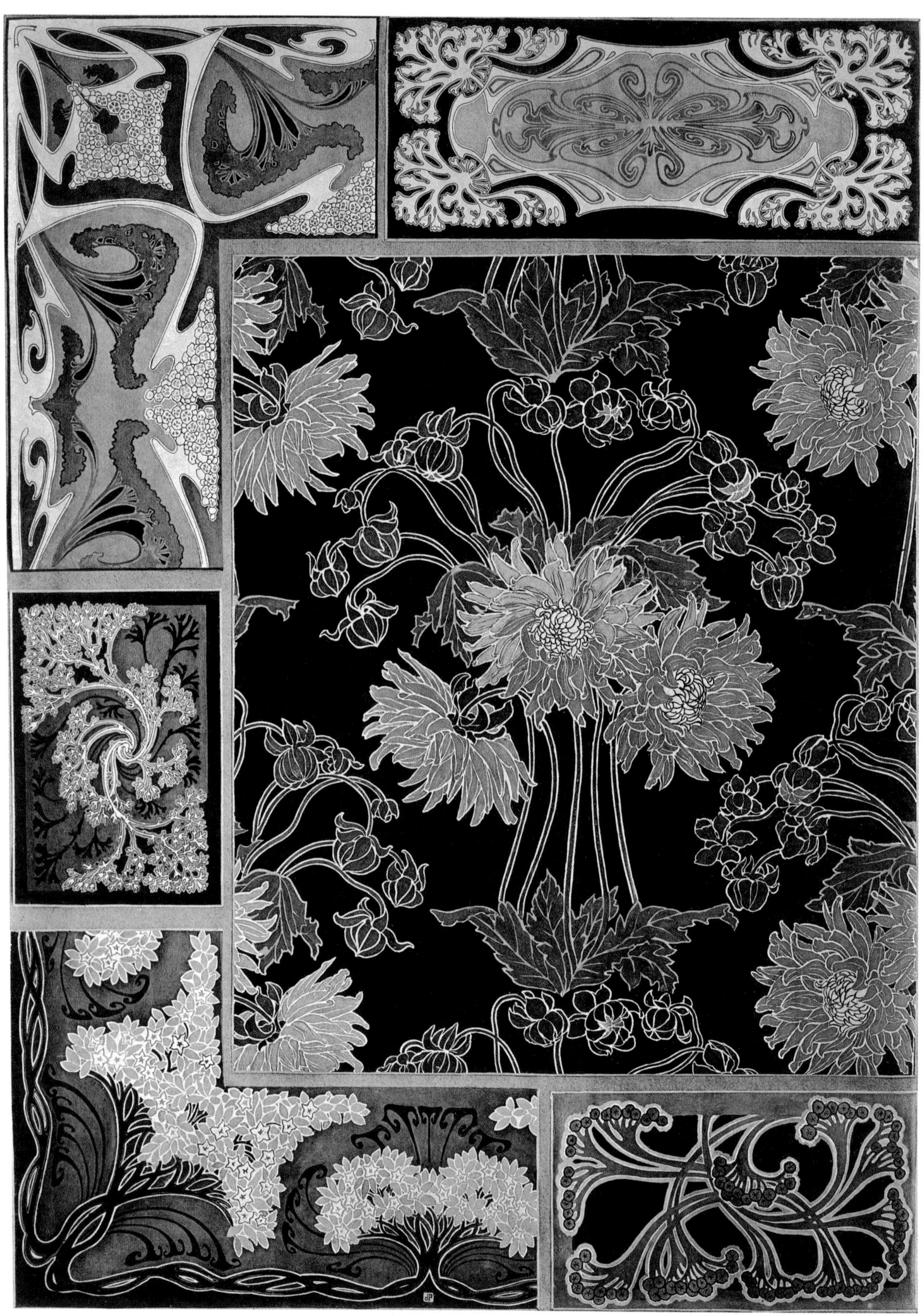

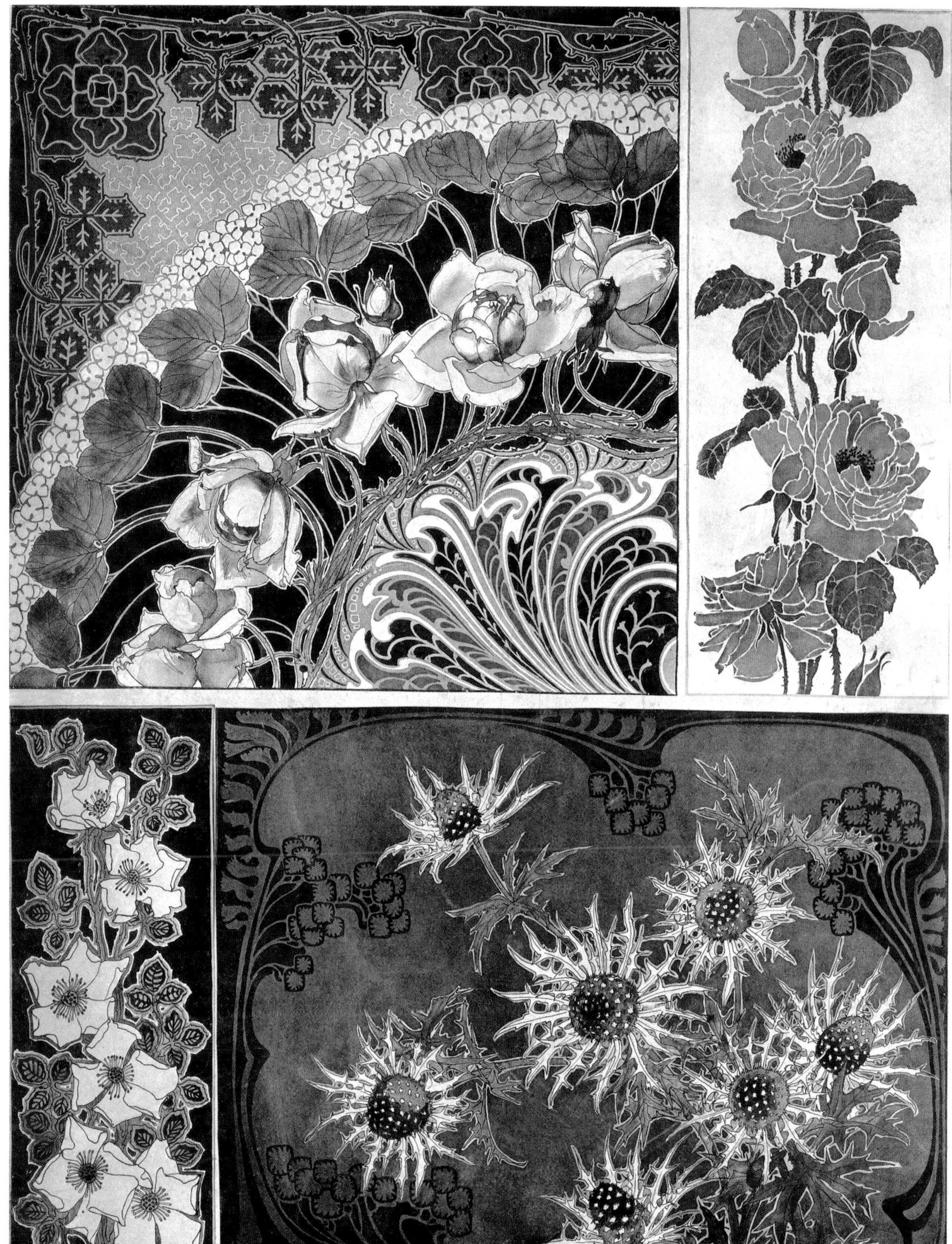

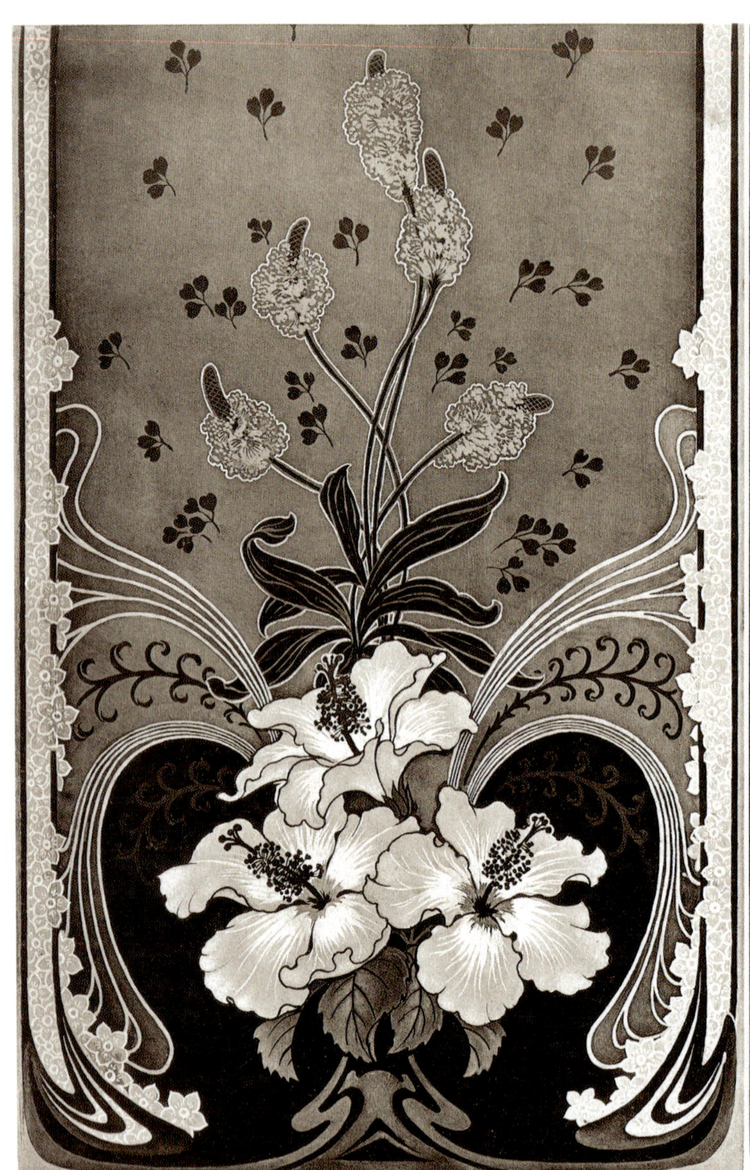
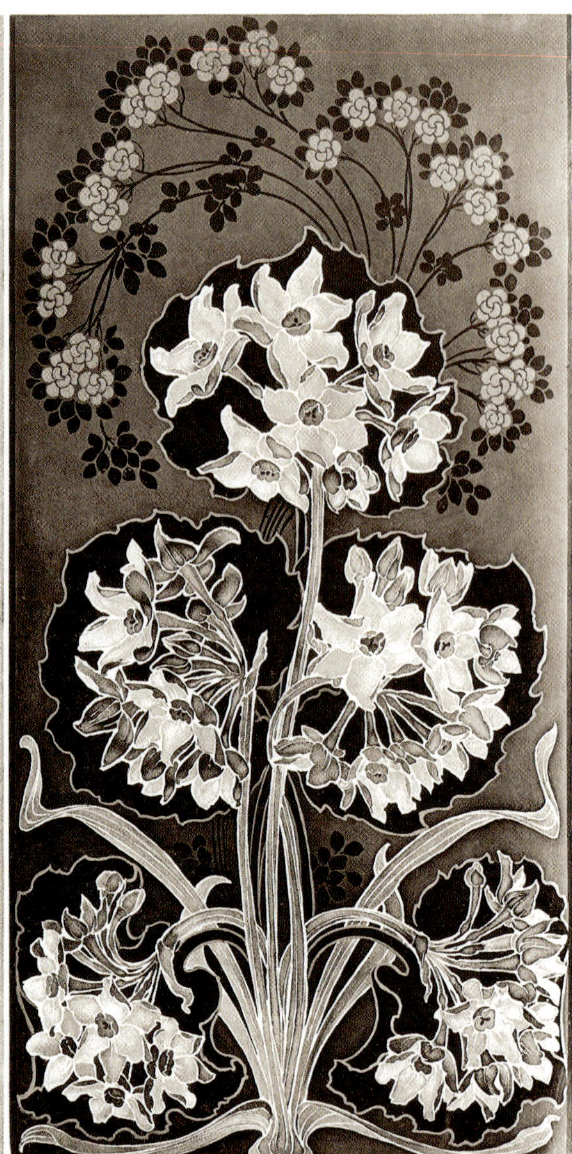
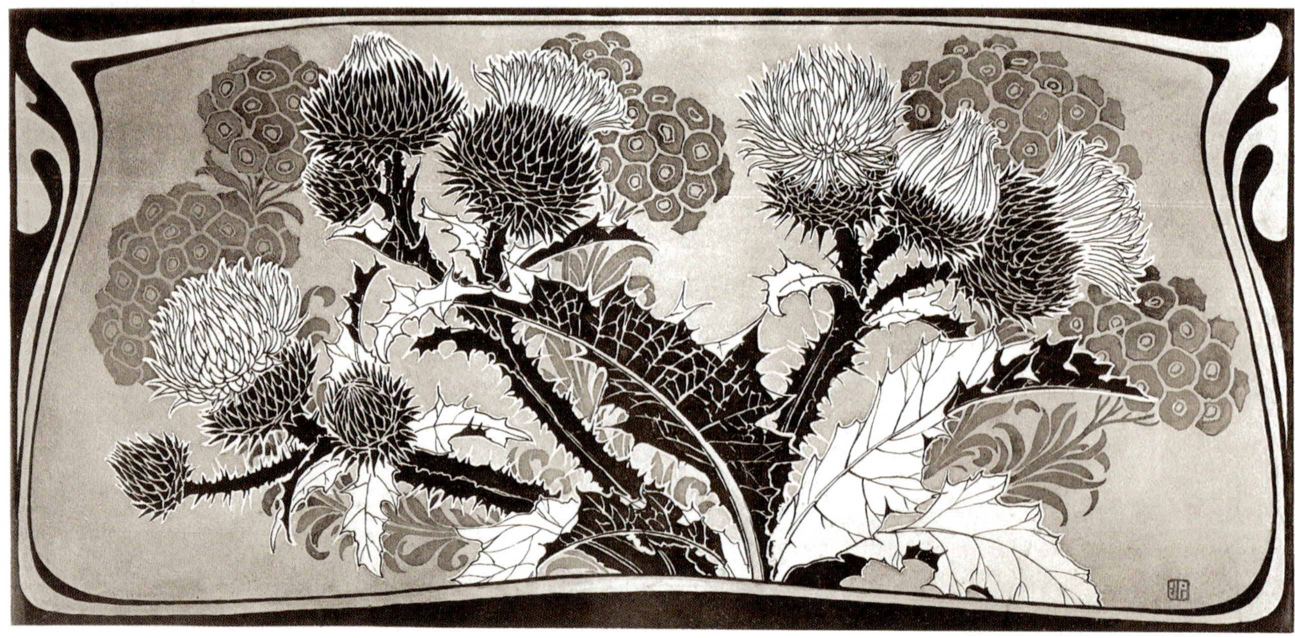

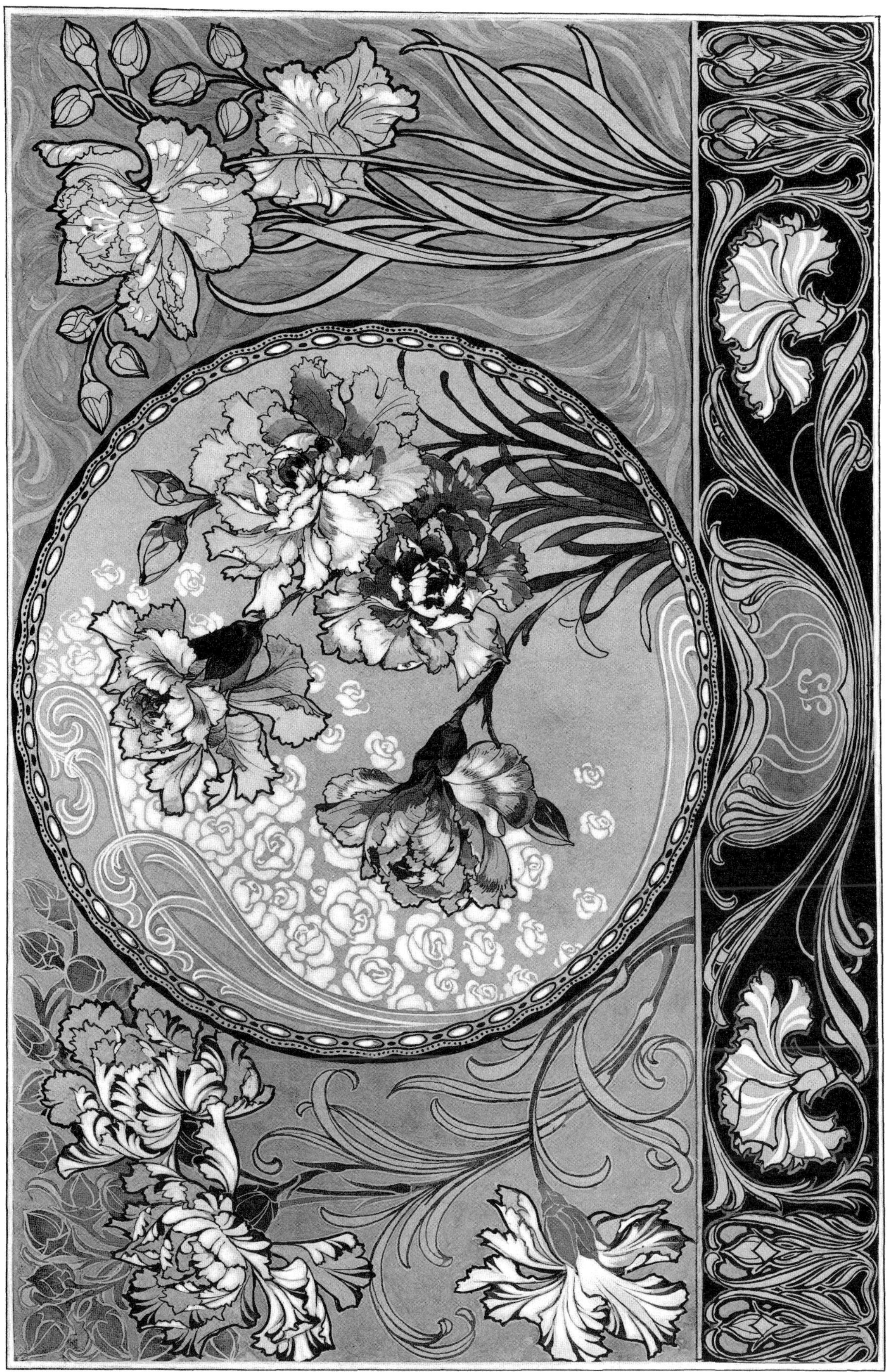

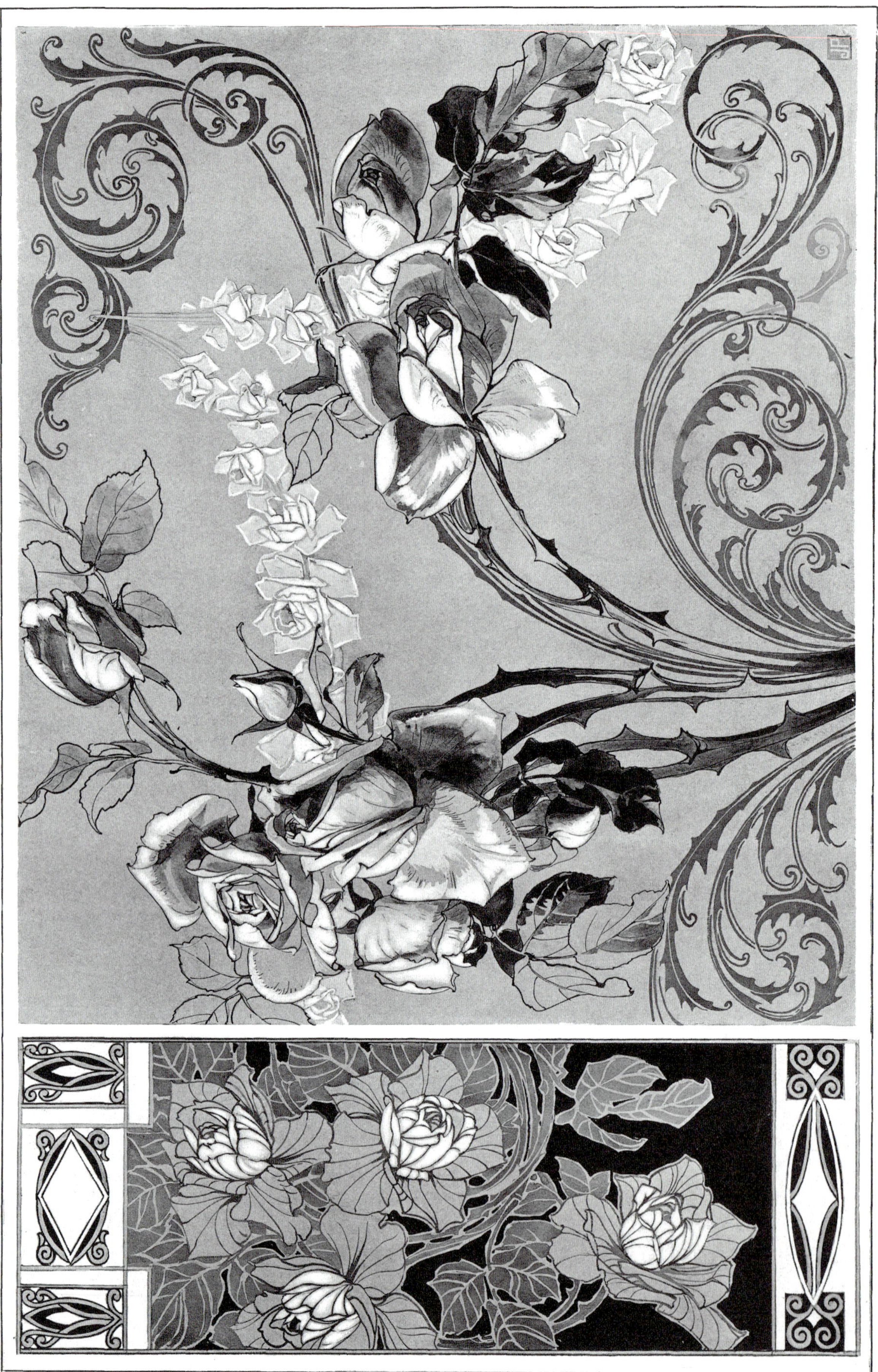

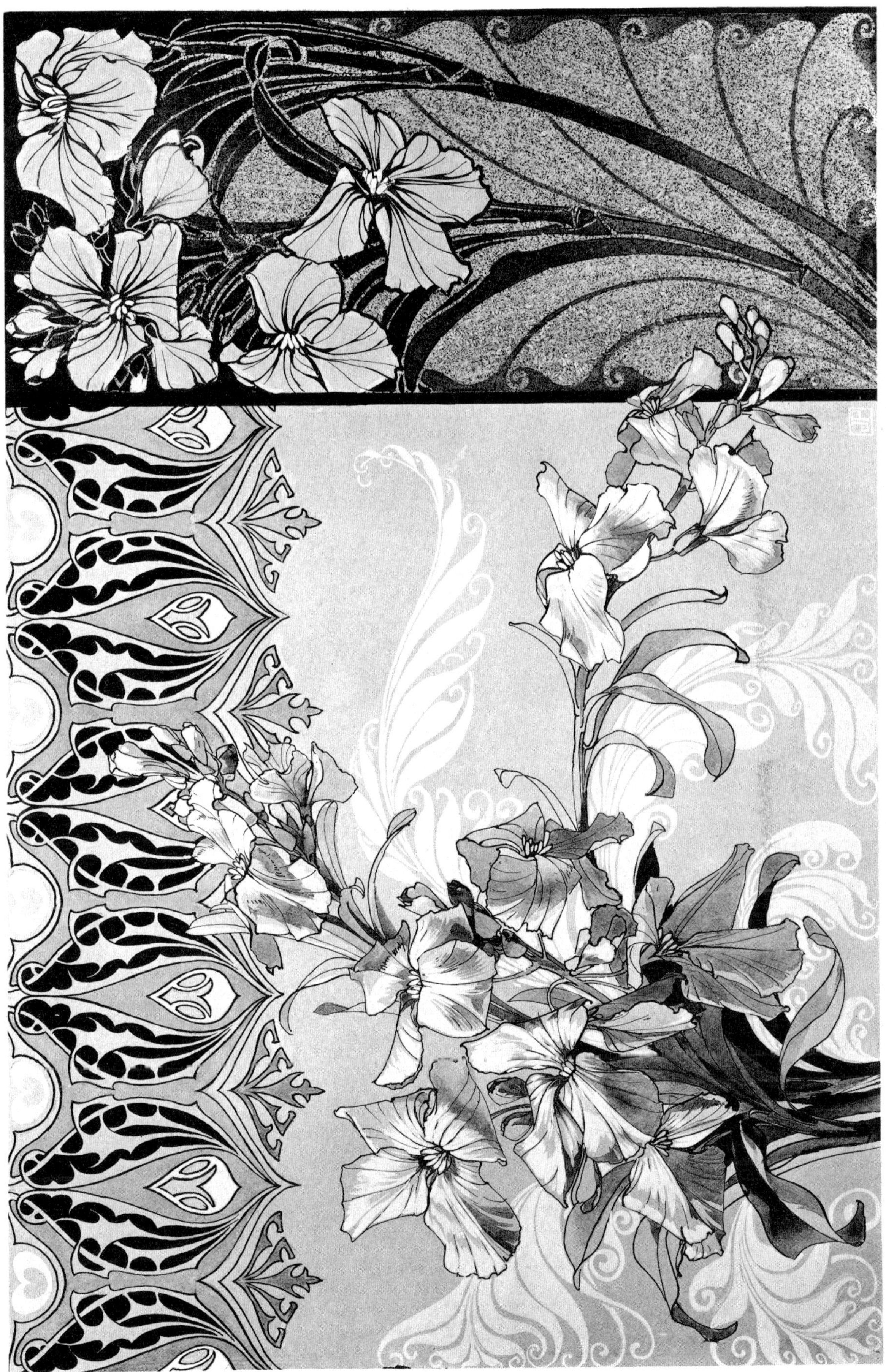

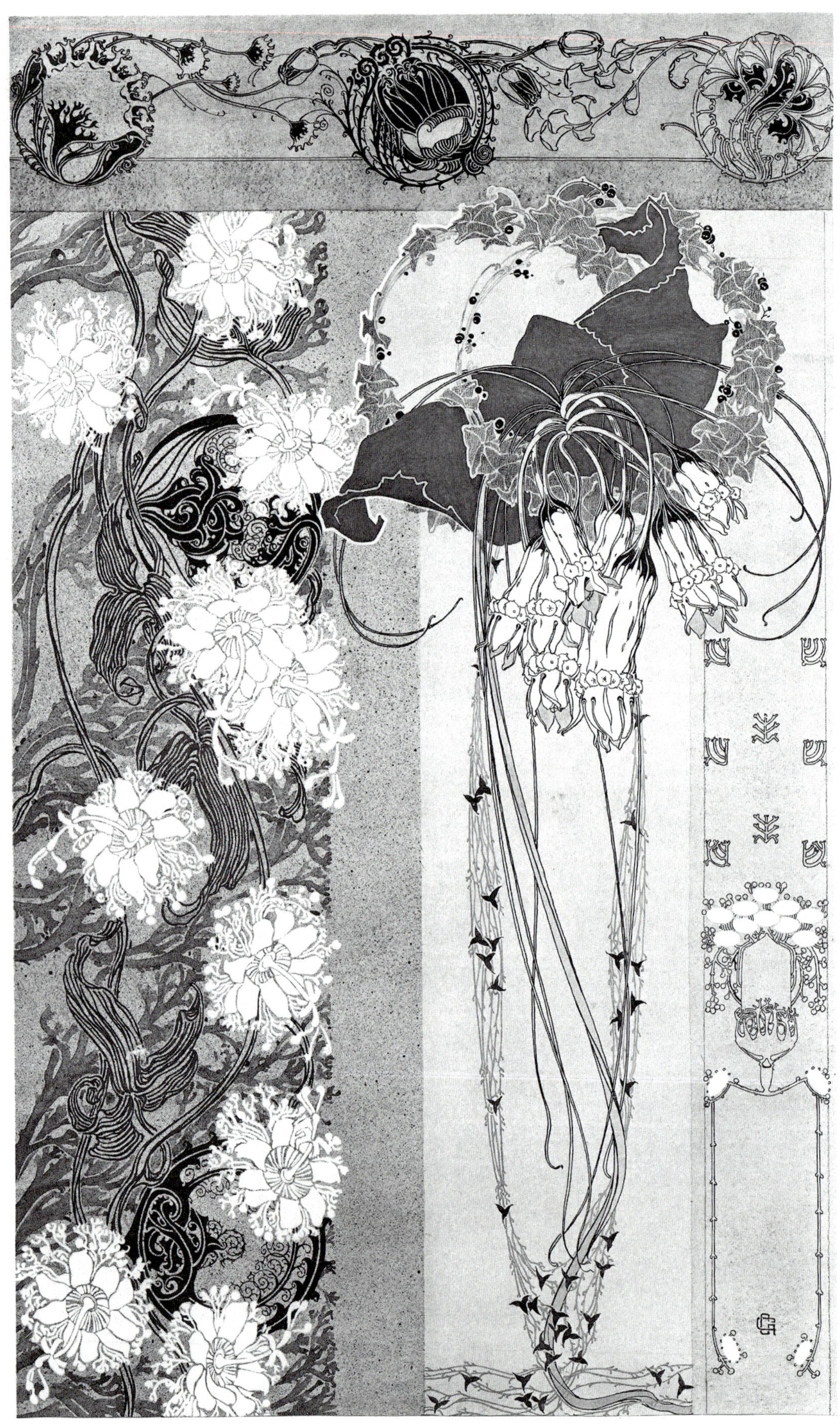

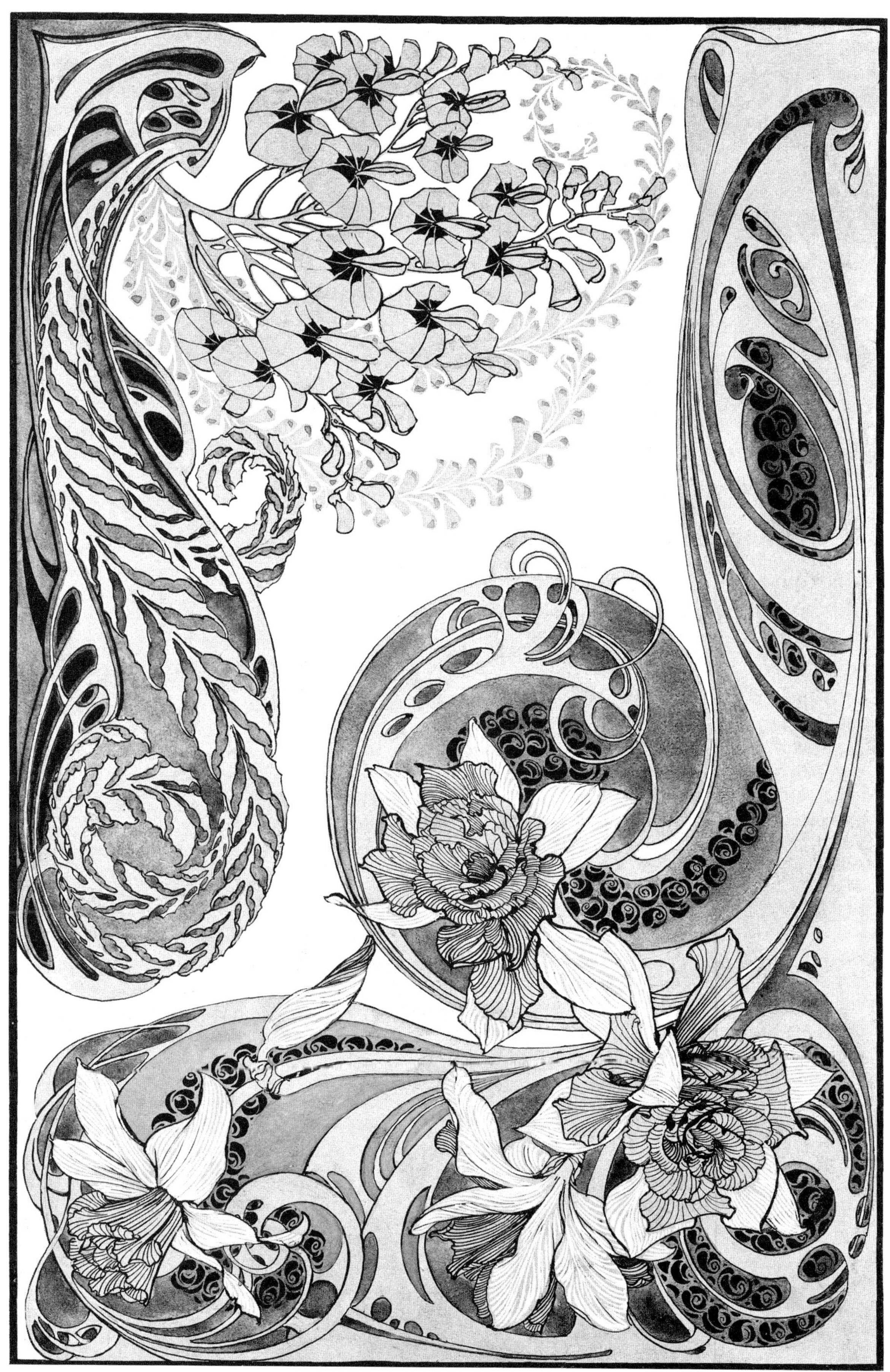

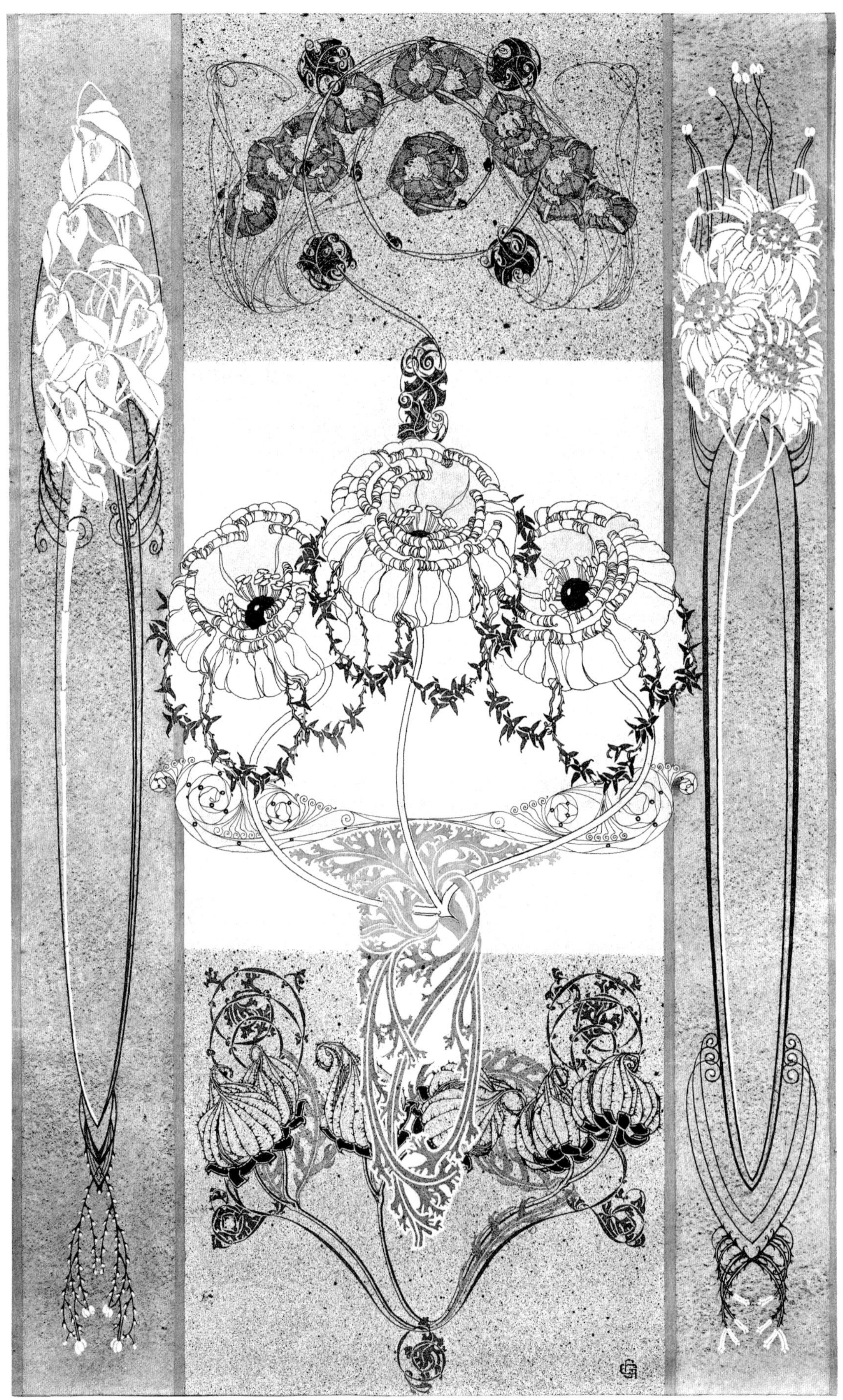

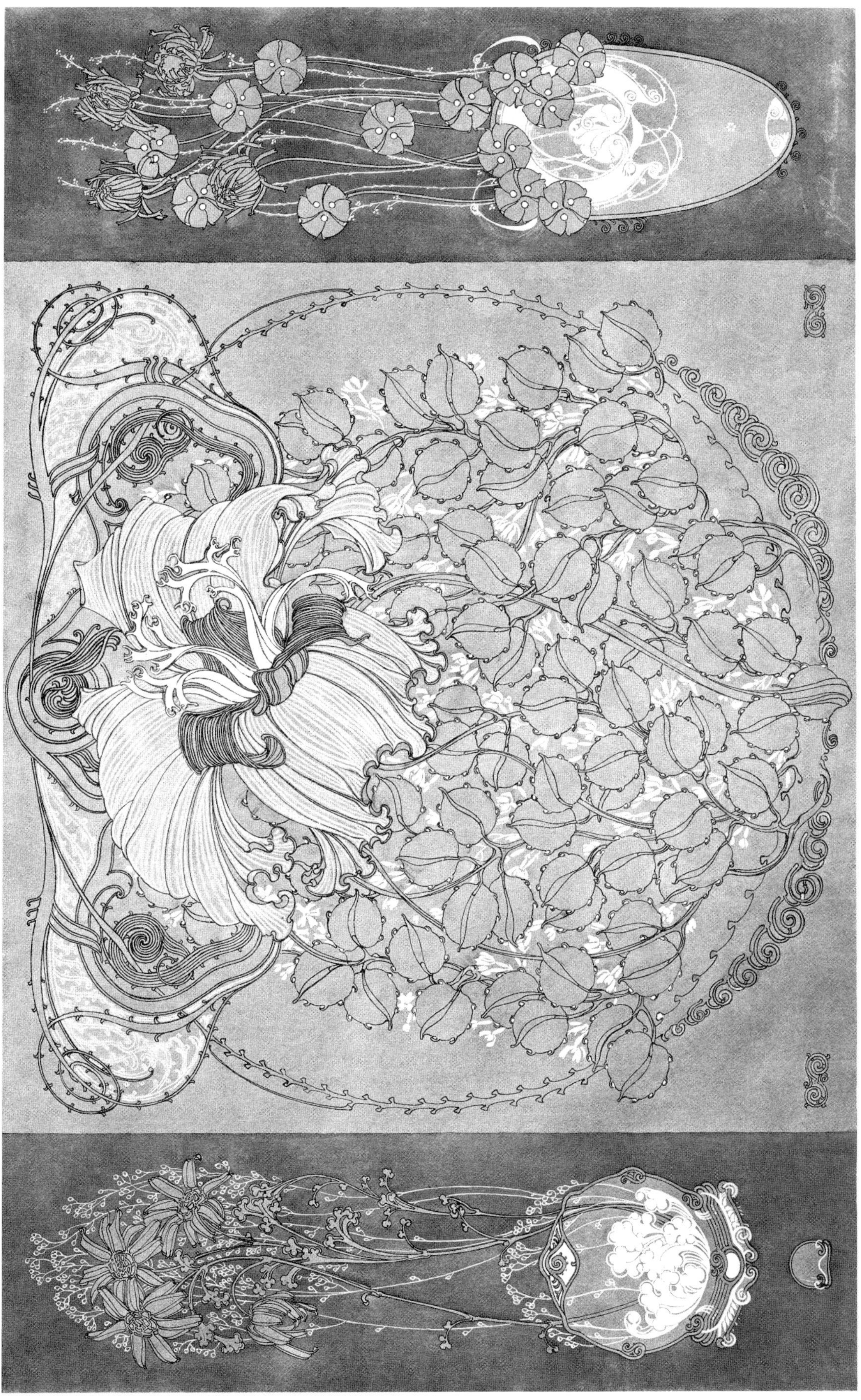

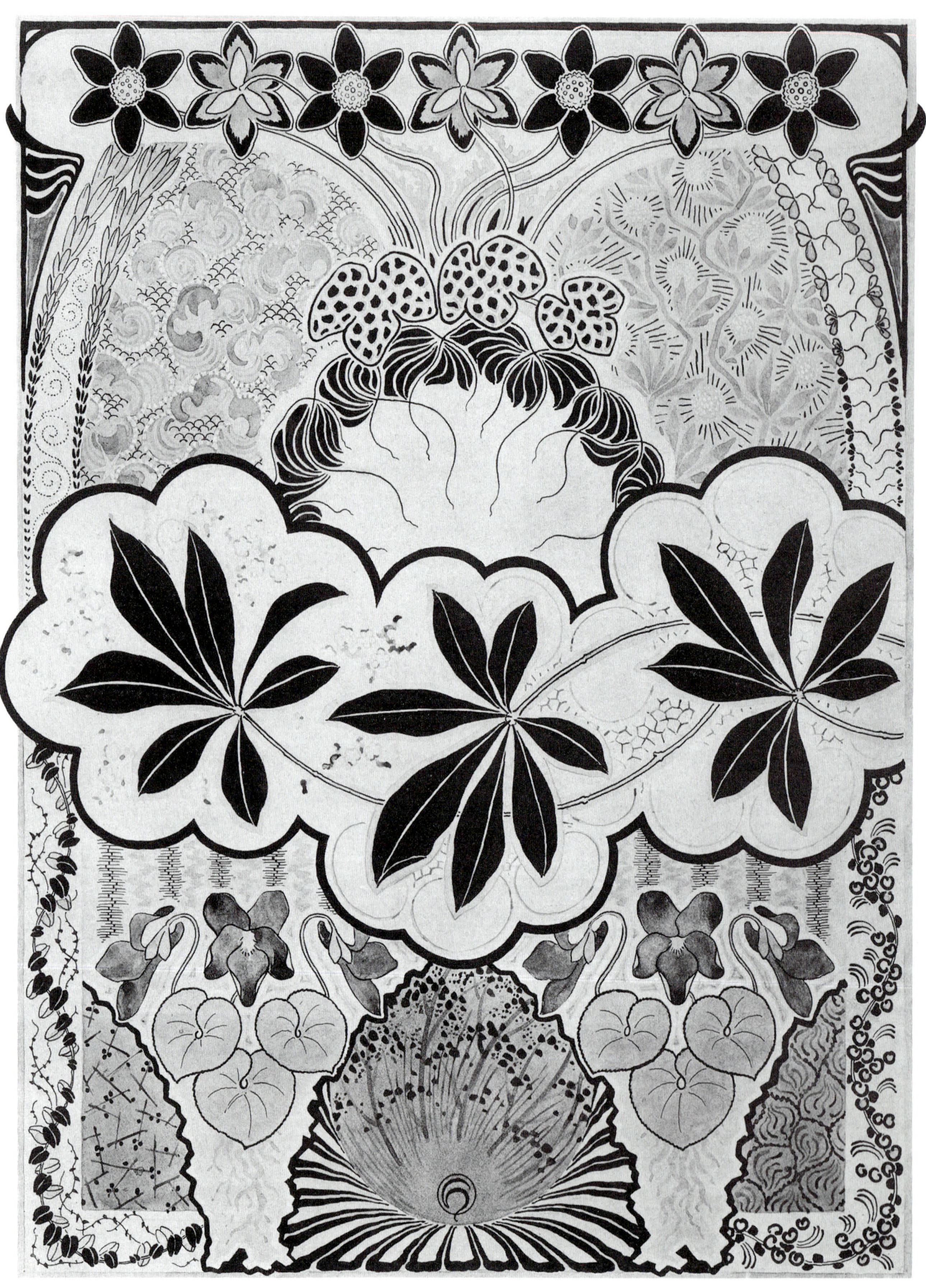

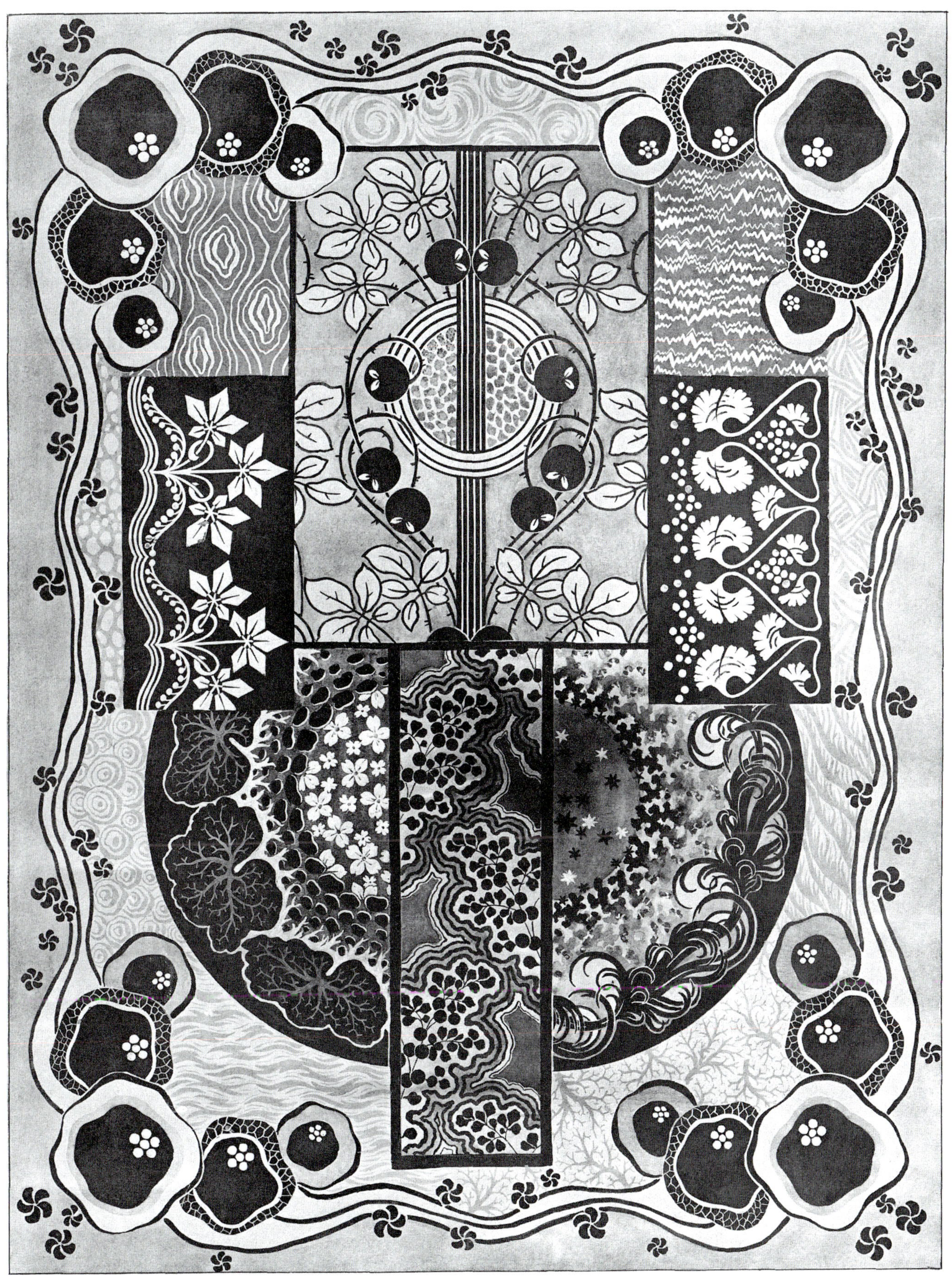

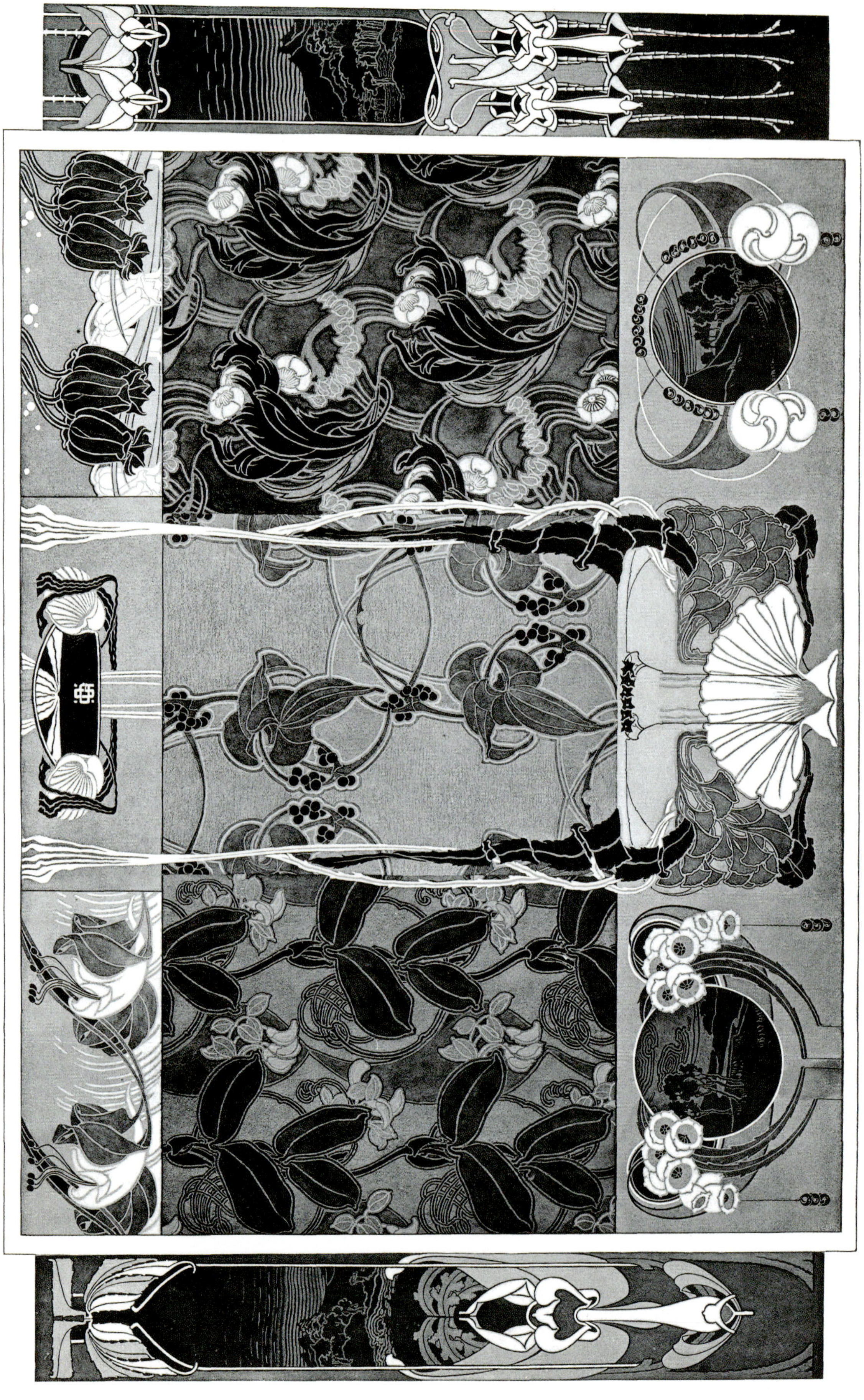

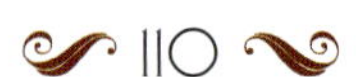

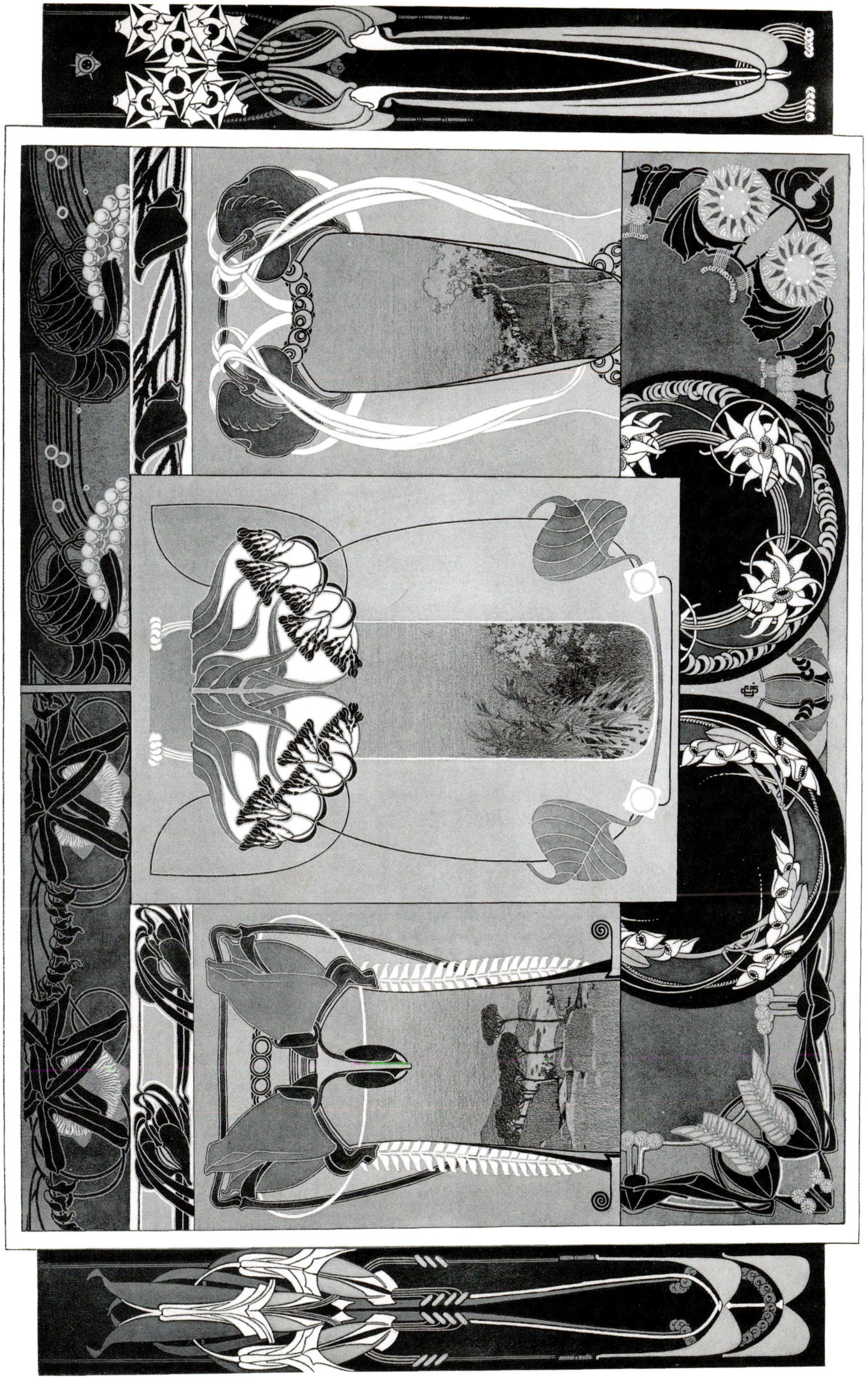

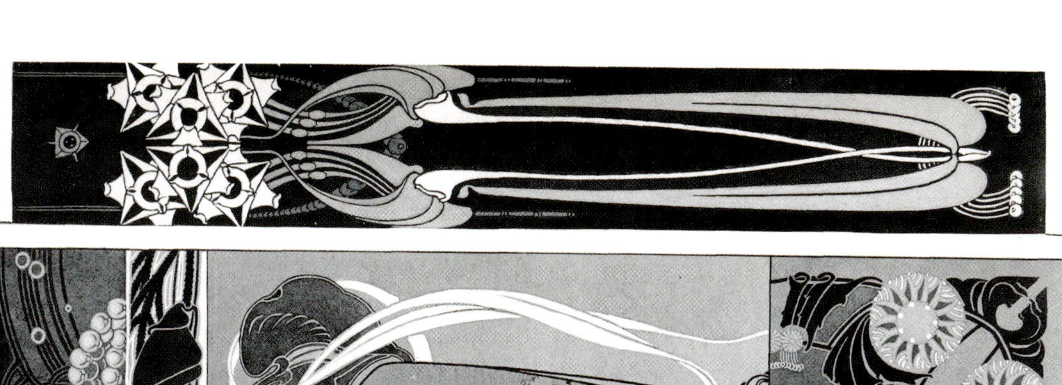

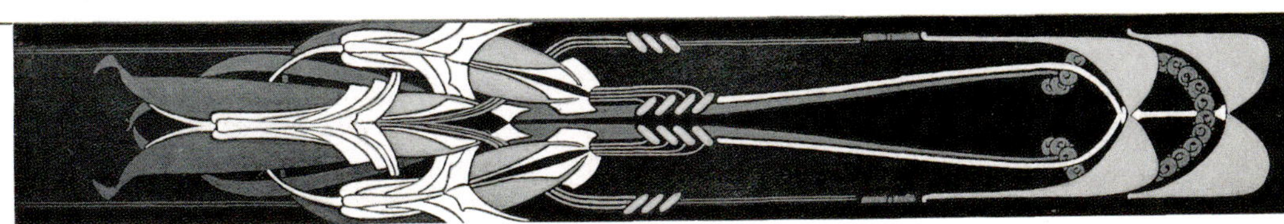

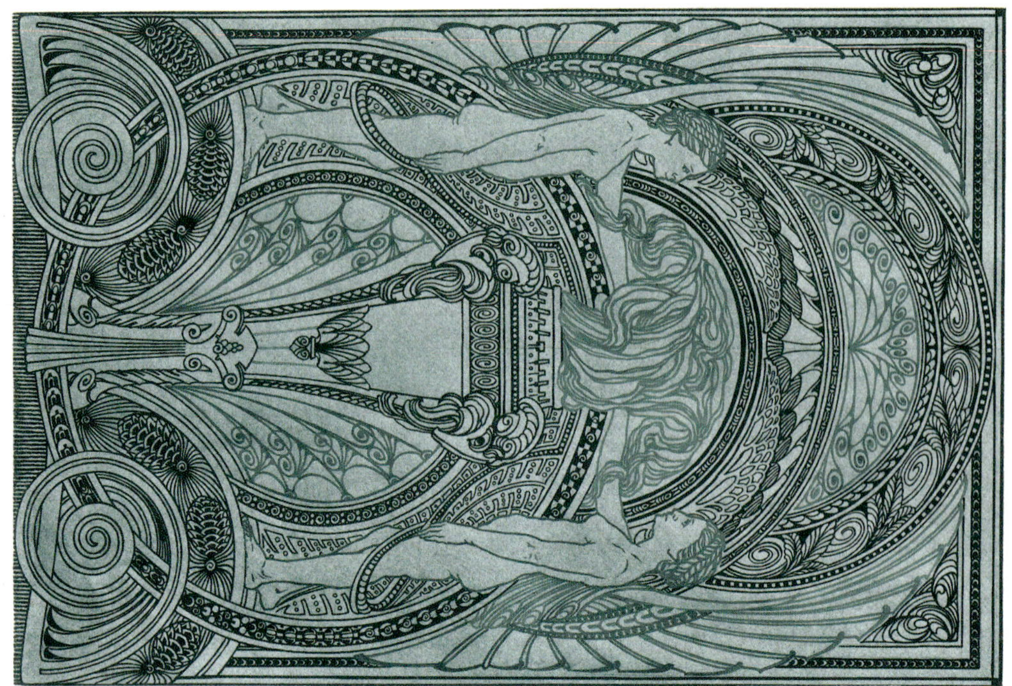

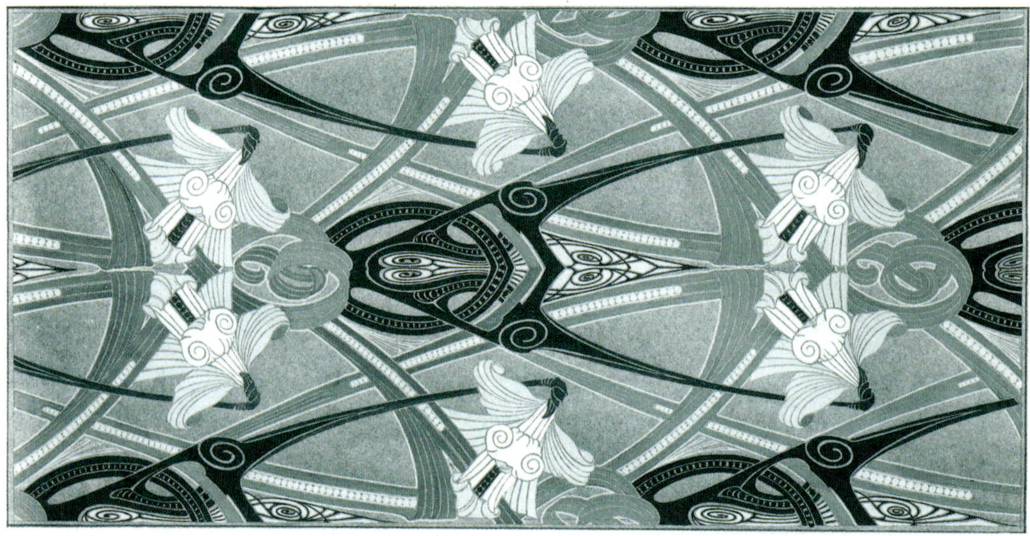

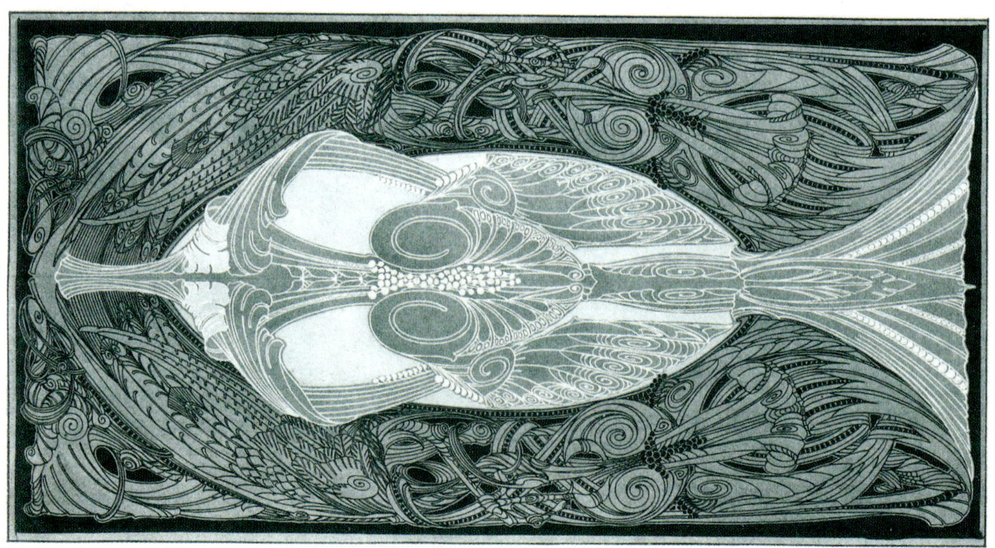

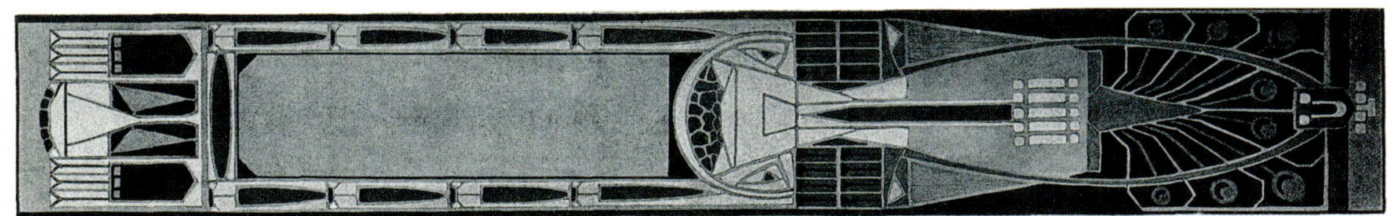

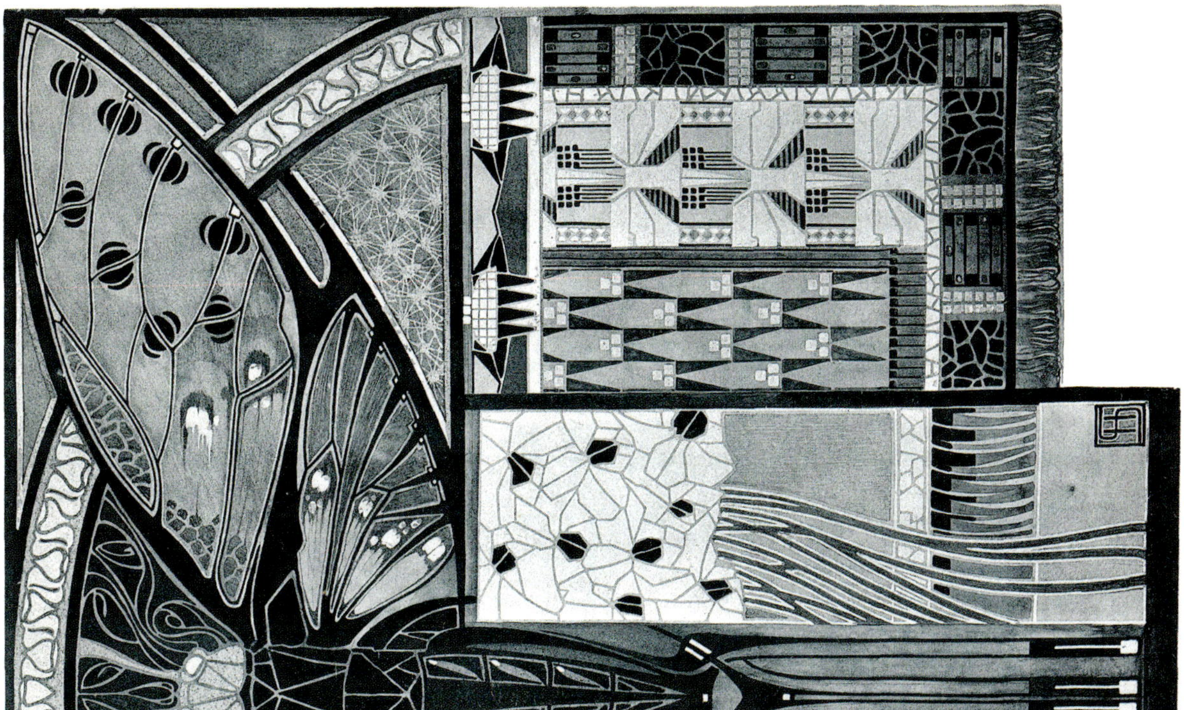

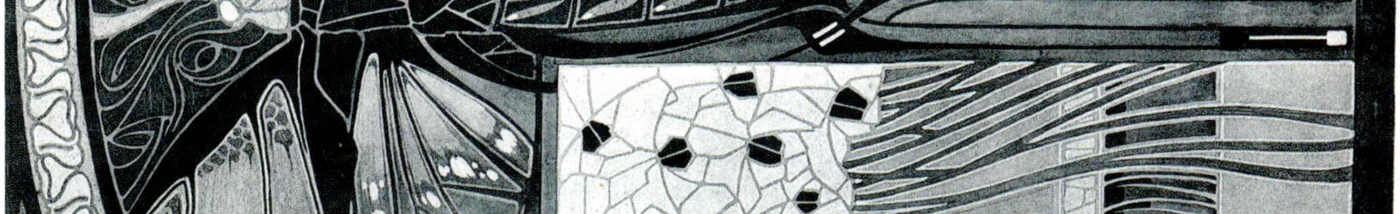

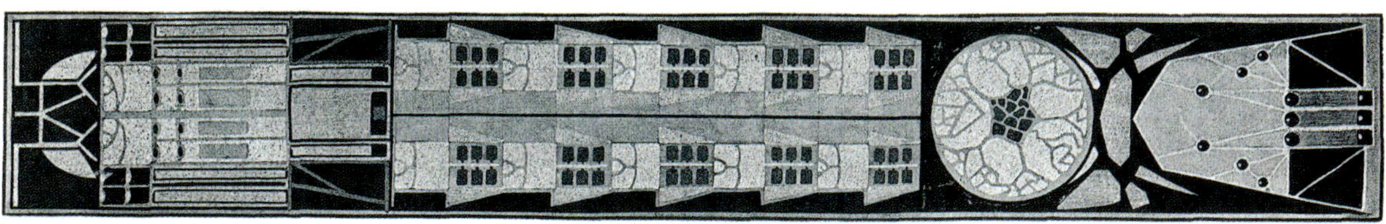

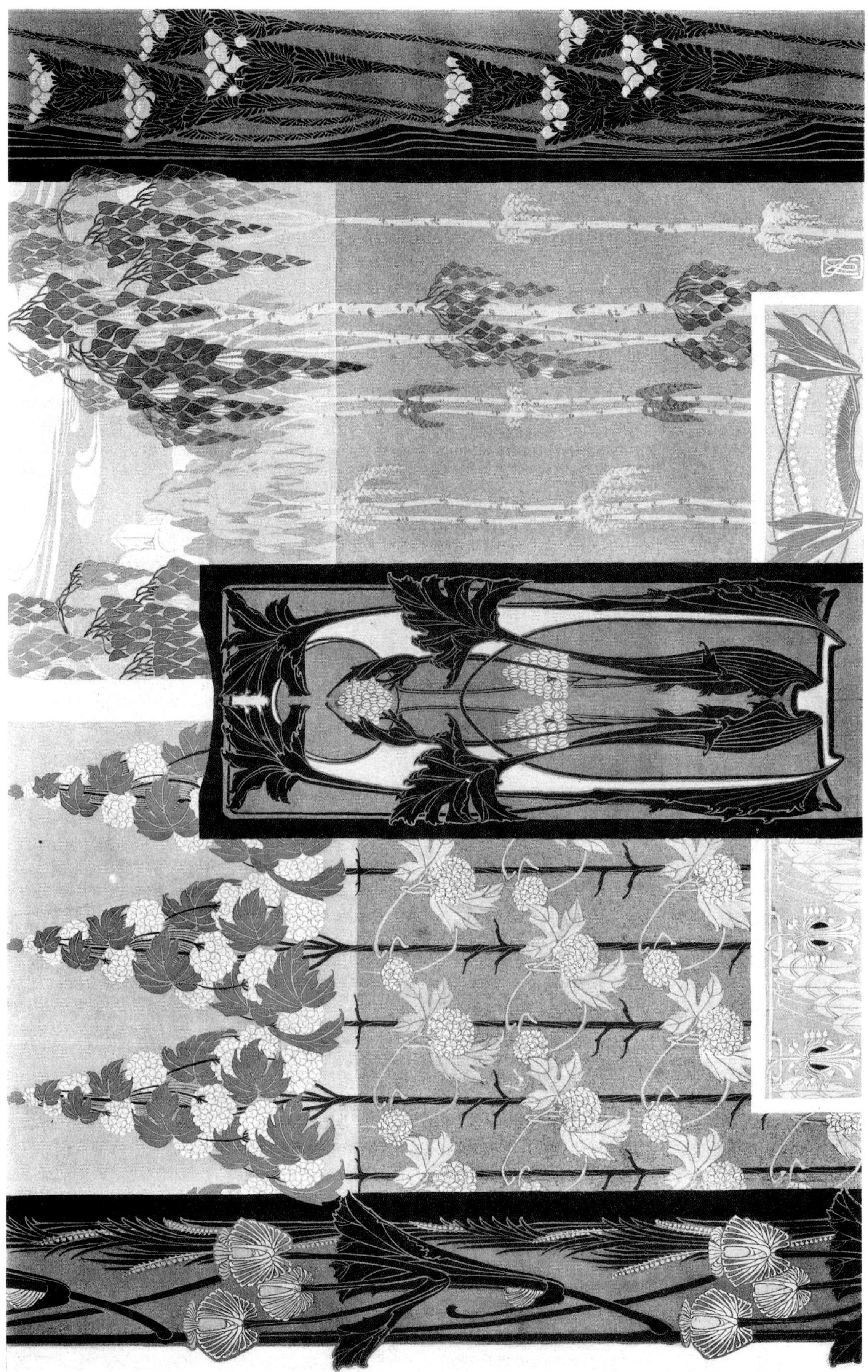

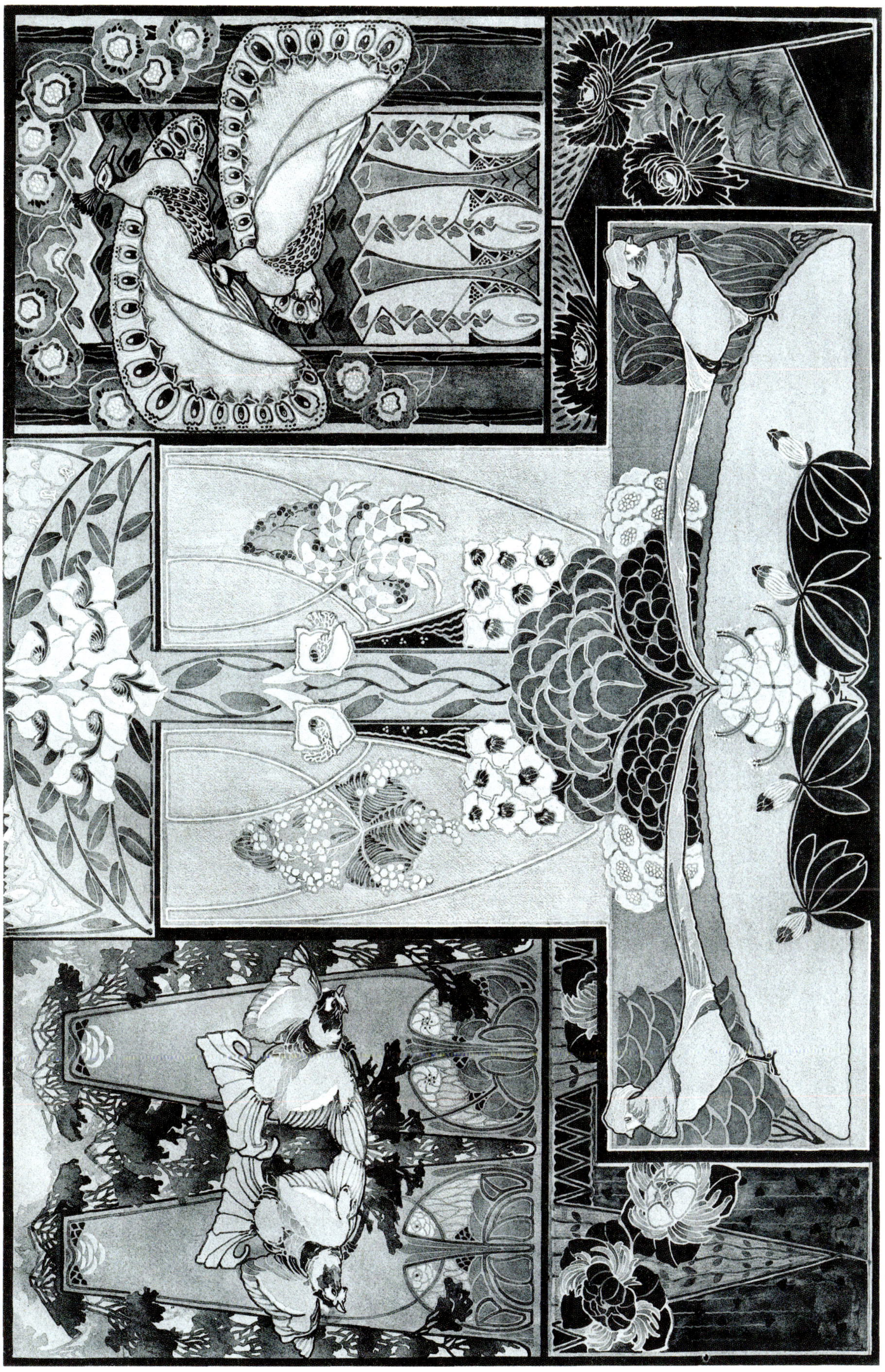

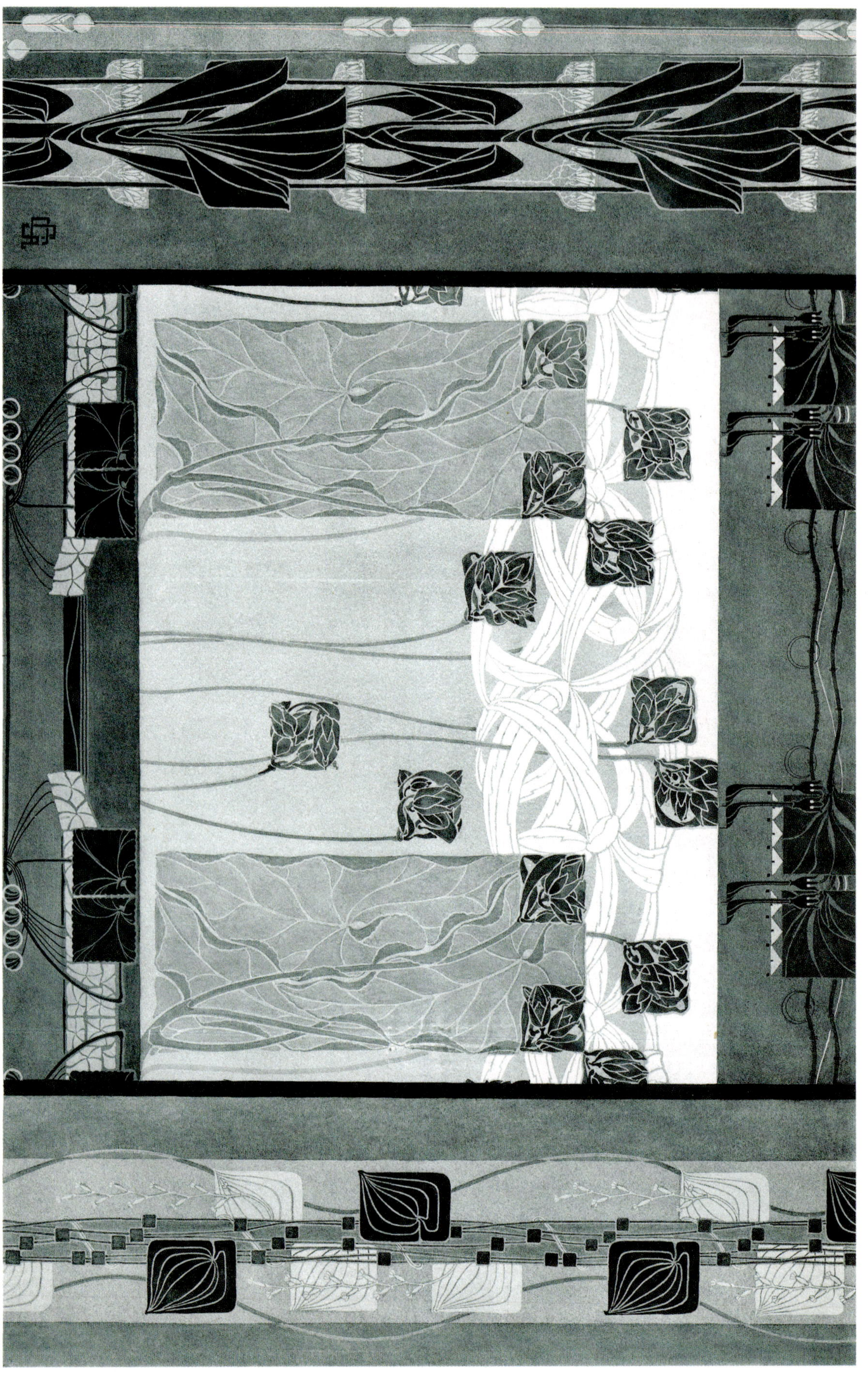

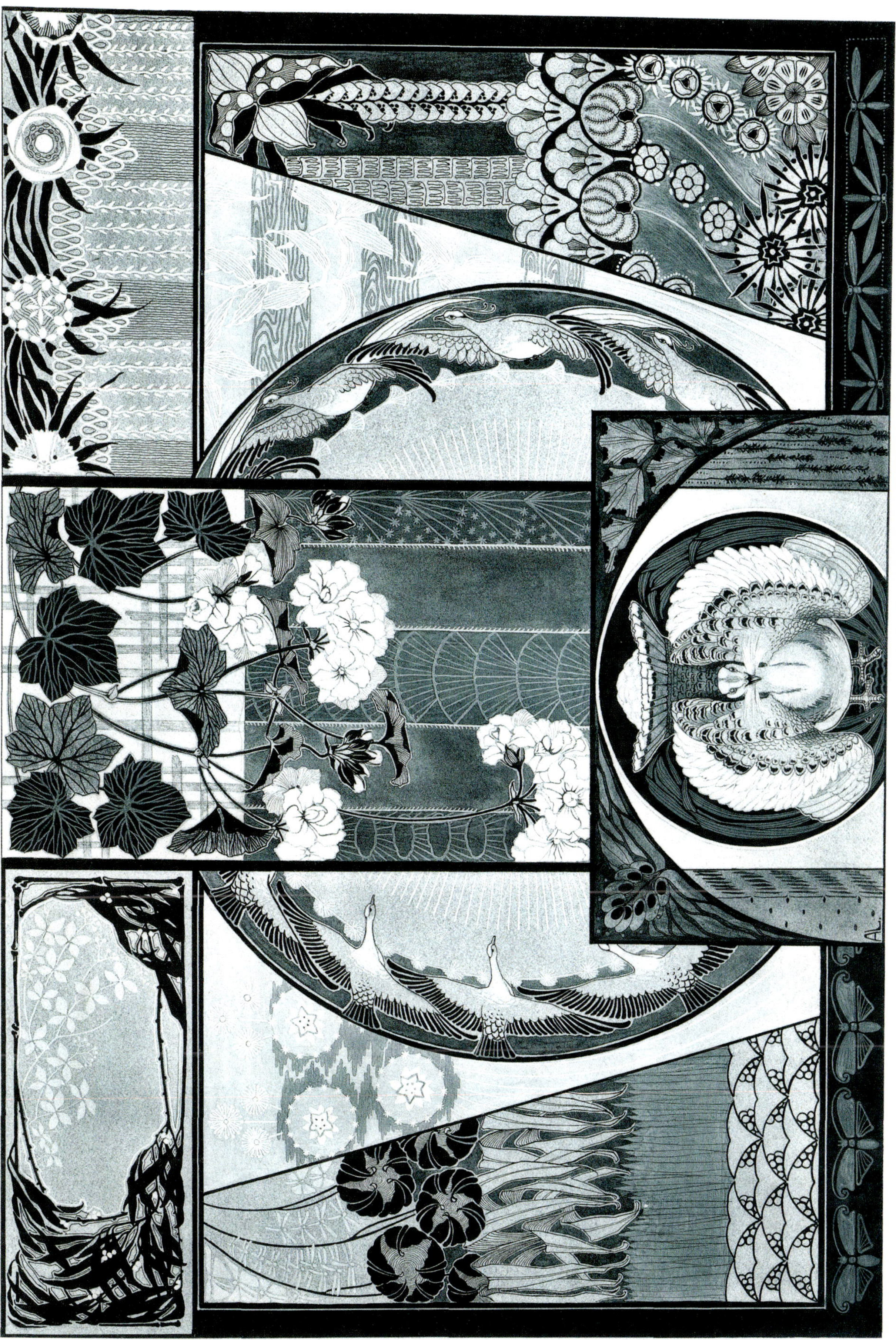

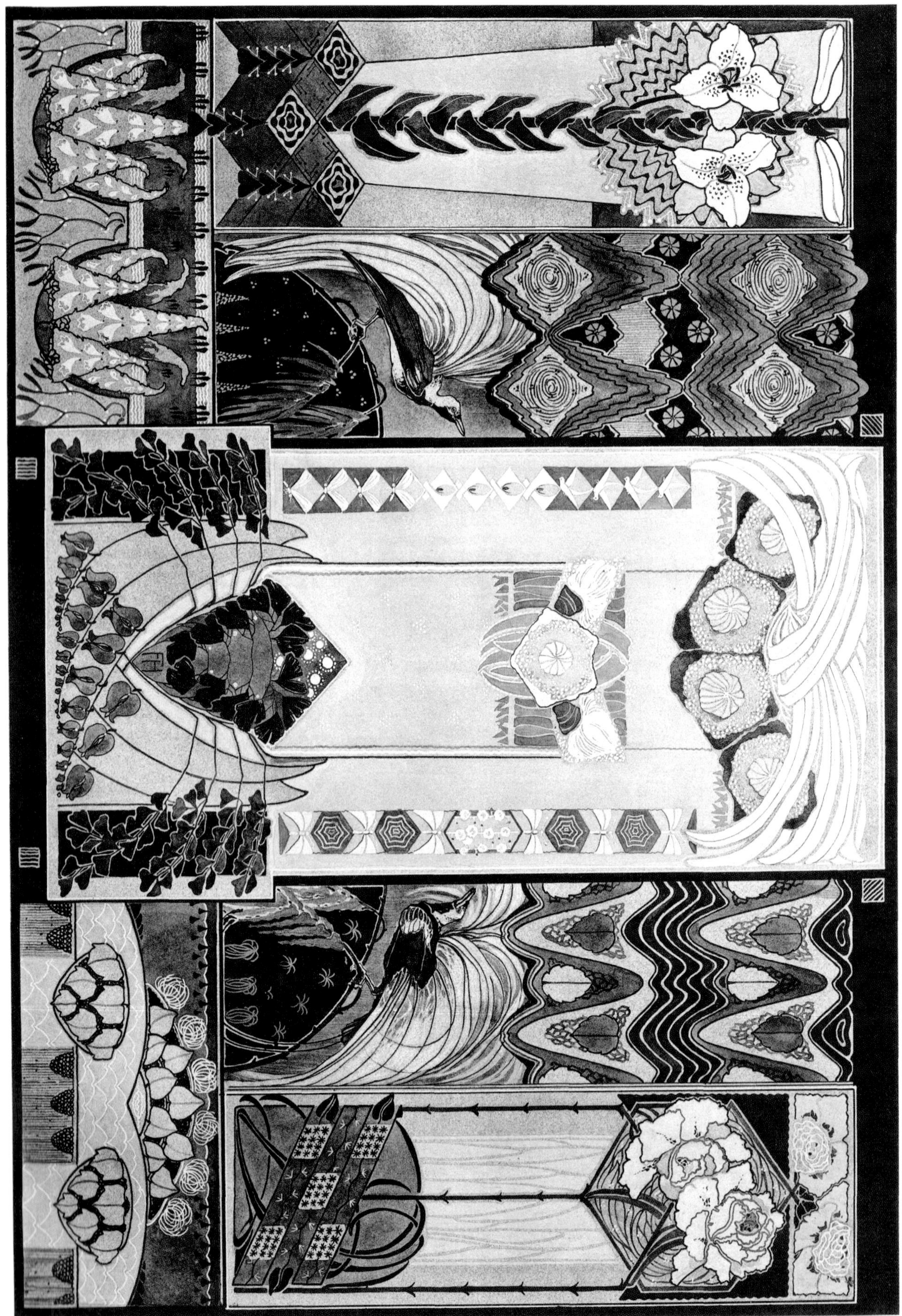